HONOUR, STATUS AND POLITY

HONOUR, STATUS & POLITY

Pratibha Jain

Sangeeta Sharma

RAWAT PUBLICATIONS
Jaipur and New Delhi

ISBN 81-7033-859-X

This book is the first in the series of a major project on "Honour and Status in Indian Political Culture", undertaken by the University of Rajasthan and subsidised by the National Committee on Development Research and Education (NUFU), Norway, under an agreement between the University of Oslo and University of Rajasthan.

Project Coordinator: Prof. Ramakant, Former Director, South Asia Studies Centre, University of Rajasthan, Jaipur.

Published by
Prem Rawat for *Rawat Publications*
Satyam Apts., Sector 3, Jawahar Nagar, Jaipur 302 004 (India)
Phone: 0141 265 1748 / 7006 Fax: 0141 265 1748
E-mail: info@rawatbooks.com
Website: www.rawatbooks.com

Delhi Office
4858/24, Ansari Road, Daryaganj, New Delhi 110 002
Phone: 011-23263290

Typeset by Rawat Computers, Jaipur
Printed at Chaman Enterprises, New Delhi

Dedicated to the revered memory of an educationist and social reformer

Shri Kesarilal Bordia 'Dadabhai'

Contents

III
Transition in Polity and Shift in Paradigm of Honour

Preface

The concepts of honour and status have remained pertinent to human civilization. These have remained central to the lives of the people, history of the region, political behaviour and social hierarchy. In different cultures these concepts are reflected through symbols, rituals, historical narratives, mythology, literary traditions and art forms. They acquire distinctive forms and categories in different regions and cultural traditions. Significantly, status and honour, as exemplified in the region of Rajputana, reveal a specific pattern that is quite apart from that of other regions of India. The code of honour and norms of status differentiation, as they evolved in the region, were linked to a value system that glorified chivalry and hence came to be known as *vir-dharma*, the land was defined as *vir-bhumi* and the goal of human life was *vir-gati*. The projection of the region in literary and historical writings has immortalized heroes, monuments, battlefields and chivalrous exploits commonly associated with the ruling classes of the region – the Rajputs. The romanticization of iconic figures and symbols has made them an intrinsic part of the nation's cultural legacy and historical memory.

The historical construction that has thus emerged and is embedded in popular consciousness however seeks to present a fragmentary and, at times, misleading portrayal of the region's identification with the much-vaunted code of honour. The paean to heroism overlooks certain phases and vital aspects of the region's history, which are contrary to the myth of honour. The political vicissitudes of the region reflect a scenario that contradicts the saga of chivalry. It is seldom realized that several Rajput states had succumbed rather easily to imperialist pressures of the Mughals. The Maratha raids in the 18th century further exposed the military weaknesses of the Rajput states and at the same time were illustrative of the political inadequacies of the Rajput potentates who continued to nurse their sense of clan honour and failed to unite even in the face of political extinction. Ironically, the effortless manner in which the British established their paramountcy over the Rajput states has been seldom questioned.

Honour and status are projected through symbols and rituals, which have formed a significant component of political culture irrespective of the form of polity. The rulers of Mewar and other native states of Rajputana deployed different symbols and rituals in varying political contexts to create legitimacy and to mould people's understanding of the changed political universe. In fact, distribution and conferment of insignia of honour became an arena of conflict amongst jagirdars, as also between them and the Maharana. The preoccupation with symbols that was manifest in the native states in the pre-colonial era literally became an obsession with the establishment of British paramountcy. The British succeeded in engrossing the native rulers in such petty trivialities when they should have paid attention to more serious matters of the decline in virtual authority. Pertinently, this fetish for illustrious symbols amongst the native rulers was perhaps to cover a severe curtailment in their real authority and power. The fact that Rajputs could not envision expansion beyond their region, despite a long tradition of resistance and diehard determination, was partly due to their preoccupation with petty political struggles over the trivialities of clan honour, ritual and spatial symbolism.

The dominant discourse and narratives on the region have not only impacted popular memory and literary works but historical writings too have been influenced by the Rajput centric construction. This has led to the historical neglect of the role and contribution of other communities like Bhils, Charans, Brahmins, Oswals, etc., in the processes of state formation, and later on, its sustenance. The Rajput-oriented biases too have been quite selective. Some rulers of Mewar have been given prominence but the achievements of some of the illustrious ones continue to be on the sidelines of history. While Rana Pratap, Raj Singh and, to some extent, Fateh Singh have been applauded, the valiant saga of Hammir as the real builder of Mewar state, the political, scholarly, architectural and cultural achievements of Maharana Kumbha, and the political vision of Maharana Sanga have been relegated to the background. Similarly, the effort to exalt Mewar as the icon of honour has undermined the stature of other Rajputana states. The perception of gender construction, too, has suffered from generalizations that portray women in the 'victim image'. In this work, certain vital aspects related to honour and status of women and their role in the sustenance of a martial political culture have been examined.

Unfortunately, the whole process of transition from a feudal polity to a democratic way of life has received scant attention. Ironically, narratives on Rajasthan continue to romanticize its royal past rather than applaud its adaptation to a new and progressive political culture. The emergence of nationalism and the manner in which the people of the princely states transcended their regional identities to become a part of the Indian nation needs to be understood. The efforts of the regional and local leadership who were responsible for this remarkable transformation need to be elaborated and analyzed. The achievement of independence and the subsequent integration of the native states in the Indian Union set the stage for a transition from a monarchical rule to a democratic political culture. The process of change was further accelerated by a series of land reform measures that sought to democratize agrarian structure, particularly ownership of land. While people continue to have respect for erstwhile royalty and its symbology, the process of elections to the legislative bodies has unequivocally underscored the emergence of people's sovereignty.

In this work, an attempt has been made to explore the historicity and content of the concepts of honour and status in the erstwhile state of Mewar, which emerged as the epitome of the Rajput ethic of honour. Interestingly, its history since the earliest times underscores the changing dimensions of honour and political status in a range of political contexts. In fact, honour associated with chivalry forms just one aspect of the multifaceted nature of the state's preoccupation with honour. It would be interesting to analyze how the political culture of the erstwhile state of Mewar reflected various dimensions of honour at the levels of individual, caste, community and the state. Very subtle differences in categorization and conceptualization of honour and status can be observed in this context. Some of the distinct types can be defined as projected honour, real honour and ascribed honour. The essays in this volume look afresh at different aspects of political culture in the princely state of Mewar.

The present work is based on historical documents, and to some extent on non-conventional sources. The narratives which have survived in oral traditions have been extensively referred to in the study to portray the vibrant cultural ethos of the region. Folk traditions that are available to us in the form of musical compositions, narratives, songs, tales, religious practices, dances, etc., have been used to understand, reveal and explore the role and contribution of the subaltern groups in the enrichment and sustenance of the distinctive cultural and political ethos of the state. The different forms of theatre like *dangal, gavri, kavad* and *rasdhari* have also enriched our understanding of the distinctive identity of the region. The collective memory of different social groups may not have chronological and factual data to rely upon yet their importance in formulation of the value-structure and code of honour has been immense. The Charans are also known for their seminal contribution towards preservation of historical details. One has to exercise tremendous caution and discretion while using the compositions of the Charans for construction of historical events, the *khyats* (court histories and chronicles) and *vanshavalis* (genealogies) have proved to be of immmense historical worth as there is scarce archival material to rely upon. Moreover, they provide us an understanding of the code of honour and its interrelationship with the political culture of the region. Interesting documents related to the different *thikanas* have been consulted that underscore the peculiarities of the jagirdari system and also the manner in which concepts of honour and status have influenced political behaviour and polity of the region.

Acknowledgements

This book is an outcome of the Project 'Honour and Status in Indian Political Culture: Changing Rajasthani and Tamil Context'. The project was primarily conceived by Dr. Pamela Price of University of Oslo who arranged for providing financial assistance through a grant from NUFU. She initiated the discussions and provided the conceptual approach towards the objective of the project and added to its understanding through her rich experience of working on honour studies in Tamil Nadu.

Professor Ramakant, former Director, South Asian Studies, University of Rajasthan and coordinator of the project provided the logistic support and facilitated the completion of the work by constant guidance and encouragement. There were frequent consultations and interactions with him as well as project directors, late Prof. N.K. Singhi and Shri P.C. Mathur. Prof. Singhi provided intellectual inputs on the subject, which helped in the refinement of the work. Discussions with Shri P.C. Mathur added to better understanding of the subject. Their contribution is gratefully acknowledged.

Discussions with Prof. G.C. Pande enlightened us about the historical perspective of the concept of honour and status in the Indian culture. We are particularly grateful to him. Fruitful discussions with late Prof. G.N. Sharma, Mahamandaleshwar

Mahant Murli Manohar Sharan Shastri, Rani Laxmi Kumari Chundavat and Shri Hukam Singh Bhati helped in formulation of the subject framework. Amongst the people who were involved in the freedom struggle in the native states of Rajasthan, meetings and interviews with veteran leaders like late Shri Balwant Singh Mehta, Ranchoddas Gattani, Rajendra Singh Chaudhari, late Smt. Ratan Devi Shastri, Smt. Shanta Trivedi and Shri B.M. Thanvi were very valuable and enabled us to get an insight into the process of change in political culture. We express our deep gratitude to them.

We are deeply obligated to Shri R.S. Jain who followed the writing of this book with unfailing interest. His extremely valuable comments and constructive criticism have remained indispensable to the finalization of the manuscript. Our special thanks to Mr. Riaz Ahmed Tehsin who was extremely helpful in locating the numerous places and libraries in Udaipur for collection of material. We are thankful to Mr. Ranvir Singh Dundlod for his support and his willingness to share his views with us.

We are indeed grateful to Shriji Arvind Singhji Mewar who kindly permitted reproduction of the photographs and documents from the Palace collection which have enriched the narratives pertaining to the symbols of honour and status in Mewar. We also thank Shri T.C. Sharma, Secretary, Maharana Mewar Charitable Foundation for showing keen interest in the research project and, also for facilitating consultations in the library.

Facilities provided by numerous libraries and research centres that we visited for collection of source material are duly acknowledged. We remember with particular gratitude the invaluable cooperation of the Director and staff of Pratap Shodh Pratishthan, Udaipur; Manikya Lal Verma Tribal Research and Training Institute, Udaipur; Saraswati Library, Udaipur; Rajasthani Shodh Sansthan, Chaupasani, Jodhpur; Charan Sahitya Shodh Sansthan, Ajmer; Nehru Memorial Museum and Library, New Delhi; Rajasthan State Archives,

Bikaner; Centre for Rajasthan Studies, University of Rajasthan, Jaipur; and Central Library, University of Rajasthan, Jaipur.

Mr. Rikhil Shah's assistance in typing the manuscript and also helping in several other ways is highly appreciated. We also mention with particular delight Anushruti's cheerful demeanour and patience throughout the completion of the work. We would also like to thank Mr. Pranit Rawat of Rawat Publications for speedy and attractive publication of the work.

Pratibha Jain
Sangeeta Sharma

Glossary

Aan: honour; taking pledge; commitment

Aant Lena: in common parlance to take a pledge; it was customary to tie a knot signifying determination to take revenge

Abadi: population

Abroo: honour, prestige; opposite of *abroo* is *be-abroo* which means violation of limits of behaviour; discredit; dishonour

Anubhava: influence; fame

Ashram: a place where people live after withdrawing from worldly concerns; Gandhi set up *ashrams* to prepare volunteers to live in disciplined, austere lifestyle and to inculcate sense of commitment for his movement.

Baatposhi: narrator

Badshah: Persian equivalent of king

Begar: forced labour

Benami: ambiguous property deals that seek to conceal ownership of property and land title

Bhajan: devotional songs

Bhakta: devotee

Bhakti: devotion

Chandravanshi: descendants of the moon; clans tracing lineage from the moon

Chanwar: flywhisk

Chanwari: auspicious beginning of wedding ceremonies starts with the placement of pots

Charitra: character; righteousness

Charkha: spinning wheel

Chhand: metre

Chhatri: decorated umbrella; domed building such as cenotaph

Dak-harkara: post messengers

Dan: charity; *Anndan*: charity of foodgrains; *Pashudan*: charity of animals; *Bhoomidan*: land grants; *Jaldan*: provision for water; *Dhandan*: monetary grants

Danvira: a person who has distinguished himself in charity

Dapa: brideprice

Devasthana: widely venerated shrine

Devtas: deities

Dharma: duty; code of conduct, religion

Dharmavira: a distinguished person who is protector of law and is dutiful

Dharati: land

Dhuni: fire-pit

Diwan: couch; the term used in the native states for Prime Minister

Duhas: couplets

Dulhan: bride

Durbar: court; form of address for the Maharana

Durrikhana: Hall of audience

Dushehra: festival to commemorate Lord Rama's victory over the demon king Ravana

Firman: royal order

Gaddi: throne

Gangaur: a very popular and widely celebrated festival by the royalty as well as the common people to venerate Gauri, wife of Lord Shiva

Garhi: fortress

Goon-chor: violator of virtues; abusive term for unfaithful person

Guru-shishya: teacher-taught

Harijan: people of God and was first used by Gandhi for untouchables

Haveli: mansion that belonged to the people who enjoyed high status

Ishtdeva: presiding deity

Izzat: limits of behaviour; respect; prestige: opposite is *be-izzat* which means violation of limits of behaviour; humiliation

Jagir: land assigned as a revenue estate by the ruler

Jagirdar: feudal chief; holder of a jagir

Jati: in common parlance used for caste

Jauhar: when defeat was imminent, to protect honour, wives of the warriors led by the *Maharanis* (queens) often took decision of self-immolation. Women would dress up and collectively jump in the fire, very often within the impregnable walls of the fort

Jhunjhar: the story goes that a *jhunjhar* figure would continue to fight even after his head has been severed; *jhunjharu*: literally means extraordinary bold brave struggler

Kalangi: piece of jewel that adorns the turban; aigrette

Katar: dagger

Kavad: wooden mobile temple; also bamboo balanced on a shoulder for carrying auspicious pots undertaking long journeys

Kesariya bana: saffron robes; symbol of warriors' preparedness for the battle

Khadag: sword

Khadag ki aan: pledge in the name of sword

Khadag Sthapana: ceremonial placement of sword

Khadi: coarse hand-spun cloth; Gandhi propagated and popularized *khadi* during the national movement

Khalsa lands: lands directly under state control; tenancy rights were given by the state

Kharita: official document recognizing the ruler's accession

Khatedar: legally landholders who held lands directly from the government and having transferable and heritable rights

Khudkasht: personally or self cultivated lands

Khyat: clan histories

Khejri: a common desert tree that is worshipped

Khillat: dress of honour presented to the ruler by the paramount power, e.g., the British presented *khillat* to the Rajput rulers

Kirti: glory; name; fame

Kul: clan

Kuldevi: family deity

Kulreeti: traditions and customs associated with a clan

Lag-bag: cesses

Langar: gold ornament worn in the feet

Laj-rekho: to protect honour

Lajana: to bring shame; blushing; *doodh lajana*: to bring shame to mother's milk; *choori lajana*: to bring shame to wife's bangles

Lavazama: royal paraphernalia

Lehenga: long skirt with lots of gathering

Lokachar: popular culture; popular code of conduct

Lokpal: protector of the people

Maang: fiancée

Mahavira: founder of Jainism, the last of the 24 Tirthankars; a spiritual man who has conquered humanly/earthly weaknesses like *kam* (desire), *krodha* (anger), *moh* (attachment) and *maya* (greed)

Malikana haq: ownership rights

Marjad: in colloquial language used for *maryada. Maryada* acquired several meanings – moral law, covenant, law of limits, boundary etc. In the context of honour it is often applied to the *maryada* of the family, caste, clan, royalty and the state

Mela: fair

Mlechha: a derogatory term used especially by Hindus to describe foreign people or outsiders; a person who is not an Indo-Aryan

Moonchha: moustache

Moondkati: *moond*-head; *kati*-slicing off; at times meant compensation for the price of one's life

Navratri: a nine-day festival for worshipping Devi, Goddess who is Shakti

Nazarana: ceremonial offerings

Neg: customary gifts

Niti: policy; expediency

Paat: symbol of superior position, which includes throne

Padshahi: referred to the Mughal emperors

Pagdi / safa: turban; *pagdi* is a type of headgear worn in Mewar; *safa* is also a turban worn in Jaipur and Jodhpur

Pan: betel leaves; leaf is chewed after meals (for further details, see Appendix II)

Pancha: literally means five; elderly respected members of the community

Panchayat: council of five; caste *panchayat*: code of conduct and norms for a particular caste were formulated and implemented by the council. Their injunctions were strictly binding on the members of the caste. In spite of official jurisprudence caste *panchayat* and village *panchayat* wielded great influence in matters of code of conduct and other rules and regulations of the caste

Panchanga: calendar

Pandit: a learned person; Brahmins who performed rituals

Parwana: a royal licence giving certain rights and privileges to individuals, units of administration etc.

Pativrata: loyal devoted wife

Patta: a title deed

Pinda samaroh: bereavement ceremony

Prashasti: adulatory poetic compositions largely in praise of the rulers, available in the form of inscriptions as well as in the form of books

Purohit: priest

Raj chinha: royal insignia

Rajmata: ruler's mother; Queen Mother

Rajyabhishek: coronation ceremony

Ram: popular deity of the Hindu pantheon; he is also the royal hero of the epic-poem *Ramayana*, which is popularly recited, enacted and performed. He is also considered *Maryada Purshottam*, i.e., a supreme ideal human being. He exemplifies ideal conduct and is, therefore, also regarded as an ideal king and ideal son

Ram Rajya: just and righteous state

Ranbankura: *ran*-battle; *bankura*-graceful esteemed warrior

Ranvas: palace of the queen

Rasos: martial epics

Sachcha-jhootha: truthful and untruthful

Sadavrat: good conduct; organization of free kitchens in Mewar

Sadguru: righteous teacher

Sahsun: perpetual grant primarily religious in nature

Sagai: engagement

Saka: when defeat is imminent, still determined to fight the final battle till death

Samskara: pious ceremony; righteous qualities

Sari: long cloth wrapped around by women over a skirt

Satchor: violator of truth

Sati: pious woman; a woman who burns herself alive on the funeral pyre of her deceased husband

Satyagraha: literally means 'to insist on truth'; non-violence protest movement first launched by Gandhi

Satyagrahi: a person who participates in *satyagraha*

Seer: unit of weight, a little over one kilogram

Shatdarshini: entitled to inalienable grants

Shilpshastri: architect

Sihilpshastra: treatise on architecture

Shiva: a prominent deity of the Hindu pantheon

Shreeji: great being; form of address for the Maharana of Udaipur

Shreemukh: pious mouth usually in reference to the Maharana

Sirna or *Sharan*: seeking or offering protection and refuge

Siropav: dress of honour

Suhagin: marital status

Suryapol: portal of the sun

Surya-gokhra: balcony where an imposing symbol of the sun was placed; projected balcony from where one could see the sun

Suryavanshi: descendants of the sun; clans tracing lineage from the sun

Svadharma: one's own duty

Swabhiman: self-esteem

Swami-dharma: fidelity and duty towards the master; code of behaviour towards protector

Teej: festival for veneration of Lord Shiva's wife Parvati

Thath: symbolic of real honour and prestige

Thikana: fief: *Solah Thikana*: sixteen principal chiefs of the state of Mewar

Tika: auspicious mark on the forehead: *Rajtilak: tika* put on the forehead of the king at the time of coronation

Topi: cap

Tuladan: offerings equal to body weight

Tyag: customary offerings to Charans on the occasion of marriage, etc.

Udhari-hanti: partners in loan

Vande Mataram: obeisance to the motherland; During the freedom movement, the term was a popular slogan. The verse was composed by Bankim Chandra Chatterjee and subsequently became a national song

Vanputras: children of the forest; a term often used for the Bhil tribe

Vansha: lineage

Vanshavalis: genealogies

Varta: stories

Vartakars: narrators

Vair: revenge

Vair-bujhana: *vair*-revenge, *bujhana*-to resolve; customarily revenge was resolved by cession of territory or matrimonial alliance

Viranganas: brave chivalrous women

Vir-dharma: code of duty/conduct for brave and chivalrous people

Vir-bhumi: land of the chivalrous

Vir-gati: death in the battlefield, which was considered a befitting and honourable death for a warrior in Rajput polity

Virta: bravery

Vyavhar: behaviour; political and administrative acumen

Yajman: patron

Yatra: journey on foot for religious, social and political purposes; well-known Dandi Yatra was led by Gandhi for salt picketing

Yuvraj: heir-apparent

Zamindar: the holder of the title to a zamindari

Zamindari: a landed domain granted by a ruler

Zenana: female, *zenani dyodhi*: female quarters

List of Illustrations

Plates

Map

Map 1

States of the Rajputana Agency, 1931

RULING HOUSES

CHAUHAN RAJPUTS	- Bundi (Hara clan), Kota (Hara clan), Sirohi (Deora clan)
GEHLOT RAJPUTS	- Banswara, Dungarpur, Mewar, Partabgarh, Shahpura
(Sisodia clan)	
JADON RAJPUTS	- Jaisalmer (Bhatti clan), Karauli
JHALA RAJPUTS	- Jhalawar
KACHHWAHA RAJPUTS	- Alwar (Naruka clan), Jaipur, Lawa Estate
RATHOR RAJPUTS	- Bikaner, Marwar, Kishangarh, Kushalgarh Chiefship
JATS	- Bharatpur, Dholpur
PATHANS	- Tonk

Source: Census of India 1931, Vol. 27 Pl. 1

I

Concepts

1

Defining Honour and Status: Indian Context

The concepts of honour and status have been central to the political culture and social behaviour in all human societies. Status can be broadly defined as a person's social, political or religious position and ranking in relation to others, while honour is acquired by an individual due to his own attainments, excellence and achievements. Although, the two concepts at times operate independently, there are certain situations in which they tend to influence each other. Due to one's status in the political hierarchy and social order, an individual or a group derives certain honour associated with ranking, e.g., member of a specific caste group – Brahmin, Kshatriya or Vaishya – is entitled to varying degrees of honour in accordance with the status and position of the group in the social stratification. However, the concept of honour has an individualistic dimension too. Qualifications and virtues acquired by an individual entitle him/her to a distinctive or personal honour, apart from that of the group to which he/she belongs. Yet, honour is a multifaceted concept which is deeply influenced by the societal relationships, the predominant value structure and cultural ethos of a particular political and social system.

I

In general conversation, honour is intermittently used for a good name, public esteem, high respect, glory, reputation, nobleness of mind, title of rank, illustriousness or distinction. The concept of honour also suggests homage, deference and reverence. Similarly, the antithetical terms which signify loss of honour are dishonour, discredit, disrepute, shame, stigma, humiliation, disgrace, infamy opprobrium etc. Since ancient times, the ethic of honour has inspired human existence to excel, distinguish and aspire for higher objectives and values. Although universal and eternal human values have commonly formed the content of honour, there are numerous examples in history when a particular group, clan, family, caste or nation has evolved and cherished certain distinctive traits of honour which with the course of time even emerged as its primary identifying feature.

Hierarchy is central to the notion of status. Hence, position and ranking are inevitably associated with this concept. In social organizations, there are some groups, which not only enjoy a distinctive status in relation to others, but these status groups have inbuilt honour attached to them. In earlier traditional Indian society, the Brahmins, on account of their superior placement and monopoly over priestly services, knowledge and sagacity, occupied higher status as well as greater honour in relation to other castes. Inversely, some castes like *chandals* (mixed tribe of Sudra father and a Brahmin mother), *chamars* (caste of leather workers) and scavengers, due to their ritual impurity and uncleanliness, carried shame and stigma that has been associated with them ever since the caste system assumed rigidity. Similarly, in modern times, some vocations derive social status and distinction due to their essential humaneness, social recognition and commitment to superior goals, e.g., professions such as teaching, medical practice and military service. Therefore, the notion of honour is derived from status in some situations and are integrated categories while at another level they are distinct and apart from each other. Despite these basic distinctions between status and honour, close interlinkages can be observed between the two categories.

Status can be categorized as ascribed and achieved or personal. While ascriptive status is one that an individual acquires automatically by virtue of his birth in a particular gender, caste, clan, family or kinship network, achieved status refers to an individual's level of achievement or performance. The major determinants of personal status are education, wealth, profession, office, talent, sense of values etc. In modern societies wherein stratification and hierarchy are becoming more flexible and relatively free from the rigidities of traditional social rules, achieved status has superceded the ascribed nature of social status.

In common usage, both these terms have been used intermittently because there exists close interlinkages between the two concepts. At times, the attainment of honour by an individual may not conform to his position in the social hierarchy. An individual occupying lower social status can be conferred honour due to his merits and adherence to superior values. Status therefore has both positive and negative aspects but honour suggests superior virtues, accomplishments and illustriousness of a particular individual or group.

II

In political domain, preoccupation with personal honour and status has remained consistent, although its content and concerns have varied in different periods and systems. In monarchical polities where there is a large gap between the ruler and the ruled, projected honour of the powerholder becomes a powerful source of legitimization of his authority. In monarchical as well as democratic polities, projected honour and all the paraphernalia that goes with it are deliberately and intricately designed. Symbolism and ritualization have remained a pervasive feature in the construction and projection of honour of political actors. In hierarchical political systems authority is glamourized and made visible through various mechanisms. Monarchical polity offers numerous forms of projected honour depending on time, context and place (*desh evam kal*). In this context, claims to respectable ancestry often through divine origin were prevalent among the Rajput rulers. A genealogy and pride in pedigree were cherished not only by the rulers but also by all the social groups and castes, even those who did not occupy a very high standing in both the political and social realms.

In the ancient and pre-colonial monarchical polities in India, honour was commonly associated with virtues like *dharma* and *charitra* (righteousness), *virta* (bravery) and *vyavhar* (political and administrative acumen). Major scriptural texts of the ancient period – the *Ramayana*, *Mahabharata* and *Bhagvad Geeta* – have underscored *kirti* (glory), *pratap* (name, fame) and *anubhav* (charisma) as the essential attributes of a ruler. Kautilya's *Arthashastra* shifted the emphasis of kingship from essentially being a moral enterprise into one that derived its strength and survival from *niti*, i.e., expediency.

However, ever since the inception of the processes of state formation and crystallization of the institution of kingship, basic attribute that endowed the status of a sovereign was his capability to extend a sense of security to civic life. The ethic of protection, patronage and caring has, therefore, remained central to political behaviour in all political cultures. In sum, a model ruler in popular discourse had to be *vira* (courageous), *udara* (magnanimous), *dani* (generous) and *lokpal* (protector of the people).

The concept of Ram Rajya is idealized in Indian political culture from ancient times. It highlights the concept of *maryada* or the law of limits, i.e., not to transcend the *maryada* of one's *kula*, *jati*, *desha* etc. In order to maintain the *maryada* of the Raghukul and his Kshatriya *dharma*, Lord Rama obeyed the order of his father Dashratha to go to forest for 14 years. Therefore, he is generally projected as Maryada Purshottam. The concept can be traced to *Rig Veda* and the *Atharva Veda*. It was further transmitted in the Brahmanic tradition in which it was referred to as the boundary or territorial limits between the kingdoms of Kosala and Videha. However, in later Sanskrit literature, the word *maryada* acquired several meanings – limit, boundary, terminus, shore, bank, mark, moral law, covenant, a goal etc.

In ancient times, King Ashok emerged as the epitome of moral heroism who discarded violence and warfare and yet retained his glory and charisma as a dutiful and courageous ruler. In modern times, the most illustrious example of this alternate paradigm of heroism has been Mahatma Gandhi – the Father of the Nation – who was able to create a model of a hero who epitomized non-violence, truth, fearlessness and selflessness. Gandhi revolutionized and redefined the ethic of honour and glory in political behaviour when he asserted that "sacrifice of self is infinitely superior to sacrifice of others". Gandhian hero derived honour by his capacity to suffer rather than inflict suffering on others.

Gandhi even reinterpreted the meaning of victory in a political struggle. His sense of victory as opposed to its commonplace connotation consisted not in putting the opponent in a position of inconvenience or his apparent defeat, but in the change of mindset consequent on realization of truth. The Gandhian hero aspires for moral victory rather than defeat and humiliation of the enemy, which has historically remained an important element in the construction of honour in the political realm. The illustriousness of Gandhi lay in the fact that his concept of heroism based on moral virtues radically transformed the nature of Indian freedom struggle. He was able to strike a vast psychological revolution not only among those who followed his lead but also among his opponents.

These traditional Indian categories of heroism variously defined as *Mahavira*, *Danvira, Dharmvira*, etc., implying heroism, honour, chivalry and charisma of a distinctive nature forms one of its unique contribution to political movements the world over. Honour associated with such a unique concept of heroism has been a distinctive tradition of Indian history.

2

Honour and Status: Categories and Code

The concepts of honour and status have a defining role for an individual's position in a socio-political milieu; much more so in the Indian context, where the society is by and large hierarchical. These concepts can be examined and understood in different categories and in multiple layers, e.g., an individual's honour and status, at one level, is determined by the group to which he or she belongs. Therefore, the concept of collective honour is extremely important, particularly in the social context. In addition to the status and honour derived at collective level, an individual also attains honour due to his or her personal accomplishments as well as self-perception. Honour and position attained or conferred upon due to personal virtues and achievements are not necessarily derived from his ranking in social and professional organizations.

I

Social status and the place of an individual in traditional Indian society were determined by the caste system. It can be defined as a closed rank status group in which the relative position of the members, their occupations, matrimonial relations and interaction with others are intrinsically linked to their placement in a particular caste. Social status denotes the social identity of an individual and a relative rank in a hierarchy of social order. An individual is entitled to a certain position as a member of a particular caste or profession, e.g., Brahmin, Kshatriya, doctor, administrator etc. Within the group, however, an individual may have distinctive honour due to his personal achievements as well as sense of values.

At an individual level, commitment to values that are upheld as respectable social norms form the basis of his/her honourable position and the ethic of honour defines and shapes an individual's self-respect and self-identity in a particular group or society. Paradoxically, individuals have been conferred honour due to certain attainments that may be very different in nature.[1] For instance, a man who possesses extraordinary acquisitions which are demonstrative of his wealth as compared to one who is ascetic and has renounced worldly possessions. The precedence of knowledge and scholarship over affluence and power is symbolized through the *guru-shishya* relationship wherein even powerful kings and princes paid homage and reverence to their teachers and preceptors. In fact, *varna* system itself is conceptualized in a manner which gives precedence and greater honour to Brahmins, the custodians of knowledge, than the Kshatriyas who had access to power and wealth.

The notion of collective honour has been predominant in the Indian society. Honour associated with and derived by virtue of his/her membership of a particular family, caste, community and region has underscored social and political behaviour in India. The essential collectivity and cohesiveness of the Indian families has naturally led them to nurture a collective sense of honour and dishonour. The behavioural patterns and norms for different members of the family are, therefore, regulated and controlled by a code of conduct prevalent in the society for centuries. A demeaning activity of any member of the family tarnishes the name of the entire family. Preservation of the *izzat,* i.e., honour of the entire family is the collective endeavour of all it members.

Caste that emerged as the basic organizing principle of the determinant of social order and hierarchy in India involved meticulous and inbuilt mechanisms of power and honour, as well as dishonour or humiliation. An individual's identification with his caste has been so pervasive that humiliation and dishonour of an individual meant discredit to the entire group. Caste conflicts often led to rape of women of the rival caste and have emerged as a persistent and pervasive mode of inflicting shame on the entire castes. Similarly, acts of impropriety or violation of caste rules by an individual bring ignominy and social opprobrium to the entire caste members. The practice of ostracization was a mechanism that was adopted to keep erring individuals outside the group and keep its honour and purity intact. Caste continues to be a highly volatile issue, especially in the rural areas, as far as operation of the notion of honour at group level is concerned. Another distinctive form of collective honour in Indian society has been clan or *vansh* consciousness and a sense of glorious past that they cherished as members of a particular clan. Projection of clan's superiority and its glorious traditions has remained central to the code of honour amongst the Rajputs.

II

The concepts of honour and status have remained pertinent to political culture as well. In political domain, preoccupation with personal honour and status has remained consistent. Nevertheless, its content, requirements and concerns have varied in different periods and contexts. In monarchical polities, where there is a large gap between the rulers and the ruled, projected honour of the powerholder becomes an effective source of legitimation of authority. In such hierarchical political systems, authority is glamourized and made visible through various mechanisms.

In addition to projected honour, there are certain indicators and qualities of a king's status in monarchical polities. At the same time, there are some values that have defined the honour of the monarchy and the commoners alike, e.g., *dharati-prem* (love for the land), *swami-dharma* (fidelity and duty towards the master, code of behaviour towards protector), etc. Laying down one's life in the course of living upto these ideals was considered as the highest virtue in the life of an individual.

Political symbolism is crucial for affirming and communicating the legitimacy of powerholders in all kinds of polities, whether monarchical or democratic. However, the rites, rituals and terminology employed in the democratic polity digress sharply from those used in the monarchical political set-up. In monarchies, the bond between the ruler and his subjects is based on his largely unquestioned authority, glamour and his divinely ordained status, whereas in a democracy sovereignty is vested in the people. In monarchical form of government, the kingship derives status, aura and honour through rites and symbols of exaltation, which distinguishes and distances the ruler from the commoners. Contrary to this, the political actors in democratic societies seek legitimacy and acceptance by rites of egalitarianism and identification with the masses. They seek to project a lifestyle that is austere and humble and, at least visibly, intends to bridge the gap between the powerholders and the masses. In India, the construction of this public image is most visible, elaborate and competitive during the election campaigns wherein the contestants belonging to rival parties, in a bid to outdo each other, resort to rituals which signify their identification with the people. Mixing with the tribals, participating in their dances, adorning themselves with their head dress and ornaments, visiting the villages, sharing food with them, lifting their babies are some of the symbolic gestures that Indian politicians resort to.[2]

III

In the medieval times, the erstwhile princely states of Rajputana had become associated with a distinctive and, to some extent, exaggerated notions of honour, pride and self-esteem. In fact, political behaviour had become synonymous with the popular dictum "death rather than dishonour". The notion of honour cherished in the political culture of these states has been deeply embedded in popular imagination, historical narratives and national memory of the country.

In the erstwhile states, in common parlance, varied terms, proverbs and narratives signified honour and also loss of honour. Some of the words used for honour included *laj, aan, izzat* and *pratishtha*. *Maryada* or more popularly *mer-marjad* was one of the colloquial terms for honour. It means limits of freedom or bounds of etiquette. It also denoted the behavioural norms that defined an individual's relationship with other individuals placed at various hierarchical levels within the family and the larger community as also his respect for institutions like caste, royalty, marriage and the state. Yet another widely used term for honour was *laj*, which actually means shame and is frequently used in lieu of honour. *Laj rekho* meant "preserve my honour from shame". The term *lajana* means to bring shame; *doodh lajana* (bring shame to mother's milk) and *choori lajana* (bring disgrace to wife's bangles) were proverbs that were often employed to cast aspersions and ridicule on a person who failed to live up to the Rajput code of honour.

Aan was another widely used term for unusual reverence for divinities, individuals and even inanimate objects. *Aan* was also a pledge which was widely observed in the honour of deities, individuals and weapons. Such pledges were considered inviolable. *Aan* also implied unquestioned allegiance to the ruler and the chief. In the context of public honour of an individual *be-abroo* meant inflicting indignities on an individual and was quite prevalent in the medieval Rajput culture. The simple epithet of *sachcha* (truthful) implied a comprehensive measure of praise and respect for an individual who adheres to a superior set of values. *Sachcha* literally means opposite of untrue; in common parlance, it stood for loyal, upright and just. Conversely, the affix of *jhootha* (untruthful) was held to be the most contemptible mode of address. The state of Mewar was addressed by the honourable title of *sachcha durbar* due to its heroic historical past.

IV

While certain symbols, rituals and objects were widely deployed to project the public aura, authority and placement of an individual in a given hierarchy, achievement of real honour was linked to a code of conduct which had been evolved over a period of time in the Rajputana states. The paradigm of honour associated with these erstwhile princely states was best exemplified in a set of values that set the ideal standard of conduct and also defined Rajput identity. These values were not linked to religious faith but were basically chivalric norms and humanitarian practices indicating a rather high standard of ethics and moral behaviour. These behavioural norms came to be defined as *vir-dharma* and Rajput *kulreeti.* The term *vir-dharma* signifies the predominance of chivalric ideal. It was not a constrictive concept implying mastery over weapons, reckless courage and glory on the battlefield. It, instead, referred to a comprehensive set of ethics involving adherence to a code of conduct that focussed on four principles: war, *vair* (revenge), *swami-dharma* (fidelity and loyalty towards one's senior and protector) and charity. The individual's honour in the erstwhile state of Mewar was linked to his capacity to sacrifice and suffer. There are numerous examples wherein individuals were endowed with an illustrious standing because of their exemplary courage, spirit of sacrifice and utmost generosity. In Mewar, Choondavats were held in high esteem because their illustrious predecessor Choonda, in fulfilment of vow given to his father Maharana Lakha, had relinquished his rightful claim over the throne in favour of his younger brother,

Mokal. Henceforward, the Maharana was said to possess only *paat* (throne, symbolic of highest status) as opposed to *thaath* (symbolic of real honour and prestige) which remained the preserve of the Choondavats.

These norms were evolved in accordance with their political and military requirements. Significantly, as is often misunderstood, the so-called Rajput *dharma* or *vir-dharma* was not confined to the warrior or ruling classes but permeated even the lower levels of social stratification as also the classes and communities other than Rajputs – Brahmins, Oswals, Kayasths, Vishnois, Jats, etc. The tribal population comprising Bhils, Mairs, Banjaras, Kalbelias, etc., too adhered to certain principles that formed code of honour for them.

Heroism was the supreme virtue for the Rajputs and the groups closely associated with them. Their education and anticipatory socialization sought to inculcate rather deeply the notion that warrior can go to heaven only if he died in a battlefield or emerged victorious. Similarly, it was asserted that a Rajput's food was not digested without war. War in itself was upheld as a value. The Rajputs literally worshipped heroism. Not only heroes but inanimate objects associated with battle were equally venerable. There were specific rituals and festivals for worshipping the arms, especially the sword and the shield. The pledges in the name of sword (*khadag ki aan*) and weapons (*ya sila ki aan*) were held to be inviolable. The shield was considered the most exalted vessel for offering gifts. It was widely believed that the sword of a hero possessed healing and curing powers.

A warrior who died fighting in a battlefield was deified and worshipped. There was a deified *putra* (son) in every family. In Mewar, Raghudeva, Choonda's younger brother, acquired divine honours and a place among the *Pitri Deva* (deified patrimony) of Mewar after his martyrdom. His image was to be found on every hearth and is daily worshipped. Twice in the year, he received homage from the entire clan – from the Rana to the lowest member in the hierarchy.[3] Significantly, enshrinement of such heroes took place, irrespective of their caste status. An image of a Meghwal who died in a battle is worshipped in the temple of Karnimata.[4] In fact, during the early stages of state formation, the primary consideration for the conferment of honour on clansmen was the exemplary courage shown by them in the battlefield. An elaborate code of conduct was evolved which a true warrior was expected to conform to.[5] For instance, retreat from the battlefield was the biggest disgrace for a warrior.

The *langar* (gold worn in the feet) worn by a warrior was not a decorative ornament but it was emblematic of his resolve to remain undettered in the battlefield or return victorious. It was popularly known as *laj ka langar* (symbol of honour). Similarly, it was unheroic to strike at the enemy's back. Even on the arena of warfare, the ethical values were adhered to the hilt. It implied courteous and hospitable behaviour towards the adversary, which even involved offering the initial strike to him. The highest form of heroism displayed on the battlefield is that of a *jhumjhar*, literally meaning struggler.[6]

Jhumjhars figure amongst the most illustrious of heroes because they continue to fight even after their heads had been severed. Many Rajput families deeply cherish and revere their *jhumjhar* myths. They are revered as quintessence of heroism. *Jhumjhars* are worshipped in the form of a stone image of a warrior on horseback placed outdoors on the village boundary or near the village well. In fact, the warriors before embarking on a military expedition used to utter the name of a *jhumjhar* hero while girding their sword so that they could unleash similar havoc on the enemy. In Mewar, the urge to make supreme sacrifice was so strong that rival Sisodiya *khamps* (septs) tried to be in the *harawal* (vanguard) of the army so that they could either receive or make the first assault.[7] It is this ideology of combat that continues to define the image of the Rajputs and their distinctive sense of honour in popular perception.

An essential component in the Rajput notion of honour and heroism was the ethic of protection. The primary basis of deference for members of nobility and royalty as also for individuals is their ability to extend protection to the commoners. Rajput rulers looked upon protection and welfare of the people as their primary goal.[8] Deification of folk heroes has been the result of their ability to extend protection to the commonfolk and their cattle. Among the major folk Gods are Pabuji, Tejaji, Devnarayan, Gogaji and Harbhuji. Shrines in their honour are found in almost all the villages and towns. These are largely pastoral heroes who fought for the welfare of the village communities, often dying in the process. The aforesaid folk heroes are able to protect the faithful against cattle disease, snakebite, poverty and sickness. These deified heroes were not necessarily Rajputs, yet they received reverence from both – Rajputs and non-Rajputs, especially the cattle breeding castes.[9]

Another prevalent practice valued in Rajputana states was *vair* (vendetta) or *aant lena* (customarily tie a knot signifying determination to take revenge). In popular sayings, a son is deemed to be a *kaput* (a worthless son) if he fails to retaliate or is unable to seek revenge. Each individual, especially so the Rajput, is born with a debt to die (*marne ka rin*) in vindication of his personal and family honour and for upholding the glory of his clan. These blood feuds are over possessions such as land, water and women or result from incidents of humiliation. These blood feuds were not peculiar to Rajputs but were to be found among men of every community including the lower classes. Thus, the principle of revenge was universal and not caste- or class-specific. Failure of an individual to prosecute a feud is tantamount to an acknowledgement of self-disgrace. The *vair* was transmitted from generation to generation since it was largely believed that to sheath a sword till the feud is balanced would be a blot that could never be effaced. It is an accepted fact that more people lost their lives in the pursuit of *vair* rather than in battles. The basic principle of a *vair* was blood for blood, better known in common parlance as *moondkati* (slicing of the head). Later, the term came to be known as compensation for the price of blood. If the king or the jagirdar was powerful enough, he could compel acceptance of *moondkati* or compensation to close the feud and thus avoid bloodshed and destruction. In medieval Rajasthan no money compensation was acceptable for termination of the feud. Only *dharati* (land) and *dulhan* (bride) from the guilty clan or family carried enough worth for the pacification of the adversary. There are numerous instances when *vairs* were quenched (*vair bujhana*) by cession of territory or by matrimonial alliance, at times of wholesale character between boys and girls of opposite party either voluntary or forced by the stronger party.

Gratification of revenge despite being a noble sentiment and integral to the Rajput notion of a man of honour brought doom and darkness for people in Rajputana. In their frenzy for revenge Rajputs and non-Rajputs courted ruin and loss of everything a man ought to hold dearest and nearest, namely, his country's liberty and his ancestral religion. As Qanungo has rightly observed: "It is all the more regrettable because the Rajputs did not learn to sink petty enmities, unite for a common cause and thus divert the lava of a retaliatory spirit of *vair* from individual and the class to a national channel which would have transmuted it into territorial patriotism as in European countries."[10]

The ethic of honour was also the ethic of fidelity and gratitude to one's lord, i.e., *swami-dharma* or *syam-dharma*. According to Tod, "Gratitude, honour and fidelity...were the fountain of all virtues of Rajputs. Ask a Rajput which is the greatest of all crimes. He will reply 'forgetfulness of favour'. It is a rare thing for a Rajput to betray his *Thacoor*, while instances of self-devotion to him are innumerable. Fidelity to the chief, *swami-dharm* is the climax of all virtues."[11] Basic to the Rajput system of value was his duty to preserve and strengthen the *kul* (lineage). However, despite the centrality of *kul* as the foremost source of honour and prestige, the primary political allegiance of the Rajputs was to their ruler or the chief whom he served. According to Lindsay Harlan, "Although Rajputs understand *kul* or *shakh* blood as the source of their prestige, they also understand that glory gained by their ancestors, the glory that proved and strengthened their *kul* blood is derived from service, that is not necessarily direct service of the *kul*."[12] The ethic of fidelity, in fact, prevented many intrigues and challenges from within the states and the ruling lineage. The spirit of total commitment to the ruler remained crucial to the sustenance and strength of the polity of the erstwhile states of Rajputana.

In the states of Rajputana the sentiment of gratitude was not confined to the political realm but permeated the common cultural ethos. A person found wanting in *swami-dharma* was not deemed fit to live and was doomed to eternal pain. The *goonchar* (ungrateful, literally means people who abandon virtue) and *satchor* (violator of truth) were consigned by the authority of the bard to 60,000 years suffering in hell.

Hospitality and charity, motivated by a sense of social good and free from any sense of self-gratification, have been considered integral to construction of honour. Exalted individuals, famous visitors, well-known scholars, writers or artists are very well received in all countries. However, in Rajputana states, due to an acute sense of honour, hospitality and charity were not influenced by hierarchies of wealth, power or learning. Piety was shown to a visitor or guest just because he has entrusted himself to a man and his dwelling. These sentiments formed a part of the *vir-dharma* as it evolved in Rajputana states. Not only the Rajputs but other castes and communities as well viewed granting *sharan* or *sirna* (protection, refuge) even to the strangers as a privilege. Charan enjoyed the prerogative of offering *sirna* to endangered lives as his roof was considered inviolable even by his rivals. Religious shrines and their head priests were also endowed with the privilege of *sirna*. Giving refuge was not confined to the ruling classes but the ethic of protection was a part of the *lokachar* (popular culture) wherein a person was granted shelter and treated most hospitably, irrespective of his status in the class hierarchy, his religion or his political affiliations.

In different cultural traditions giving has been perceived not only as a higher ideal but also a greater pleasure than receiving. In Rajputana states, in addition to reckless courage, his generosity and his capacity to sacrifice for others defined an ideal hero. Among the people of Rajputana, some of the common charities were *anndan* (giving of foodgrains), *pashudan* (giving of animals), *bhoomidan* (land grants), *jaldan* (provision for water) and *dhan dan* (monetary grants).

Sadavrat (perpetual charity) was one of the most popular hospitable rites in which free kitchens were organized for travellers and the needy in perpetuity. Rulers, jagirdars, wealthy mahajans and the religious shrines commonly organized *sadavrats*. Nevertheless, there are numerous examples when members of a particular caste group subscribed to the establishment of a *sadavrat*. Such community participation for the cause of social service testifies to the prevalence of high values and commitment to the deprived sections, even amongst the commoners.

Truthfulness to one's word formed yet another cherished value in the medieval Rajput culture. Observance of *aan* (pledge) even at the cost of one's life or by incurring losses was a common practice in Mewar. In common parlance, people took pledge in the name of Eklingji known as Eklingji *ki aan* as well *gaddi* (throne) *ki aan* and Maharana *ki aan*. The fact that such promises remained binding despite the fact that they did not carry any official acknowledgement show on the one hand the revered status of the Maharana and on the other it emerges as an example of Mewaris adherence to their word. As soon as a chief or jagirdar was appointed, his *aan* was declared in the area within his jurisdiction. Significantly, even tribals like Bhils, Mairs etc. had rituals that signified total adherence to their word.

The code of honour had deep impact on people's psyche. It determined values and affected socialization process. It also invoked a sense of commitment in public life. It is true that some of the concepts proved disastrous and led to their decline. In this context, a reference must be made to the pervasive practice of *vair* which engaged rulers, jagirdars and the common populace in endless internal feuds. In summation, one can say that code of honour provides useful insights into Rajput policy, interrelationships of social groups and formulation of social values.

V

The concepts of honour and status have remained crucial to the determination of political behaviour in a variety of political contexts. Claims to respectable ancestry were prevalent amongst Rajputs rulers. A distinguished genealogy and pride of pedigree were cherished not only by the rulers but also by all the groups and castes, even those who did not occupy a very high standing, both in the political and social realms. The context of honour in political culture is multifaceted and multi-dimensional in nature. It is interesting and also necessary to understand very subtle differences at the level of categorization and conceptualization of honour and status in the political arena of the erstwhile Rajputana states, particularly the state of Mewar. Some of the distinct categories can be identified as projected honour, real honour and ascribed honour.

One of the earliest methods through which they sought to reinforce the legitimacy of the ruling house was through divination of the king. Sisodiyas, the ruling clan of Mewar, acquired sacral status by claiming divine ancestry which linked them to Lord Rama, a mythical prince-hero and popular deity of the Hindu pantheon. To further enhance their larger than life image they proclaimed themselves as divine appointee of Lord Siva, who was considered as the real crowned king of Mewar. Such an ideology was propagated by embellishing it with a diffuse system of symbols and powerful rituals through which the Maharana's all-powerful status was made visible to the population. The well scripted and detailed genealogies of the ruling clans, while seeking to endow them with an impressive lineage, also tended to camouflage the reality that political ascendancy of the numerous Rajput lineages had been the result of a political struggle and of gradual ascent from a feudatory subordinate status to an independent one.

Symbolism and ritualization have remained pervasive features in the construction and projection of honour of political actors in all political systems. In the graded polity of the erstwhile state of Mewar, symbols, ceremonies and rituals were a powerful means to project and dramatize the supreme status of the Maharana amongst his subjects as well as the jagirdars. Within the Rajput state system the members of the clan considered themselves along with the ruler as descendants of the same ancestor, enjoying their patrimony by the same right as the ruler himself. The state, in fact, did not belong to the ruler but to the clan as a whole. The ruler's status was first among equals. To establish his primacy, the ruler needed to distinguish himself from his kinsmen and other potential rivals. His exclusivity as a ruler was bolstered by embellishing his person with an arsenal of traditional emblems associated with power and rule. In addition to this, symbols and rituals were effectively used to calibrate degrees of power and status amongst the jagirdars.

The different members of the clan were entitled to jagirs (landed estates) and gradations of royal honour depending on their service and status within the clan. The members of the nobility and other high officials battled incessantly over a prestigious ritual placement in the *durbar* (court), as it was pertinent to one's hierarchy and status in the political set-up. In fact, distribution and conferment of insignia of honour became an arena of conflict amongst jagirdars, as also between them and the Maharana. The fact that Rajputs could not envision expansion beyond their region, despite a long tradition of resistance and diehard determination was partly due to their preoccupation with petty political struggles over the trivialities of ritual geography and spatial symbolism.

In addition to *durbars* and formal ceremonies, which confirmed the primacy of the ruler's position by a virtual display of the hierarchies, a popular mode by which the rulers in Rajputana sought to consolidate their identity and distinctness as the supreme authority among his people and the nobility were through celebrations of major religious festivals patronized by the state. The palace celebrations of *Gangaur* (festival to venerate Gauri, wife of Lord Siva, by married women) in Mewar, *Teej* (festival for veneration of Lord Siva's wife, Parvati) in Jaipur and *Dushehra* (festival to commemorate Lord Rama's victory over Ravana, the demon king) in Kota assumed widespread popularity, even outside their own states, among the masses who looked forward to participation in these splendid festivals.[13] Palace celebrations not only reinforced the supremacy and glamour of the royalty but also formed a means of communication between the ruler and his subjects. These were rare occasions when ruler appeared in person before them.

The ritualization tended to become more extravagant, after the Rajputana states entered into treaties with the British and accepted their paramountcy. The net effect of these treaties was to divest the ruler of his key function as heroic protector of his subjects, ready to die a passionate death in the battlefield. Stripped of his primary source of power and claim to honour, the clamour for symbols and ritualized displays assumed inordinate importance, a trend encouraged by the British. 'Pampered and petty favourites' as the British referred to these rulers, became more and more ineffective in governance, while the latter acquired greater political control. The Rajputana rulers now sought to establish their relative importance through symbols conferred on them by the British. For varied reasons, these ceremonial trappings, symbols and rituals remained equally pertinent to the sustenance and diffusion of the idea of British imperialism in the native states.

Another dimension of the projected honour were the various objects, animate and inanimate that became intrinsic to the image construction of the Rajputs as powerholders. The following couplet brings out some of the features that were considered to be essential ingredients of a distinctive status:

> "*Ghodo, jodo, pagdi, mooncha, kug, Marwar,*
> *e panchu rakhe atal Rajputi Rathore.*"[14]
>
> (Horse, dress, turban, moustache and sword of Marwar,
> these five things are inseparable from a Rajput Rathore.)

The symbolic importance of turban worn by the elite as well as the commoners far exceeded its utility as a protective covering for the head. The colour and shape of *pagri/safa* (turban)[15], as the Rajasthani headgear was known, was indicative of the caste, clan and region of the individual. It was believed that "in a man's turban rests his honour and to snatch your enemy's turban was the ultimate victory". Exchange of *pagri* (turban) was seen as the highest mark of confidence and as a symbol of friendship. While wearing of saffron turban signified final confrontation with the enemy, taking off or lowering one's turban was perceived as sign of subservience and disgrace. Another cherished possession in the region was horse. Horses have played an important role in Rajput history, both in warfare and in the feudal set-up. Their possession and use in military campaigns remained integral to the rise and prominence of different clans. In the course of time, horses emerged as a veritable symbol of high status and the ruling aristocracy viewed possession of horses as their privilege. The predominance of equestrian images of Rajput rulers is a clear indication of the pride of place occupied by the horse. Lower classes were debarred from riding horses. In fact, in most parts of Rajasthan, especially so in rural areas, horses are still an index of a person's status in the village hierarchy. The lower castes still do not have social sanction to ride a horse, which is viewed as the privilege of the upper castes. There are numerous instances, when individuals belonging to the lower castes are humiliated and punished by the rural elite when they try to appropriate the privilege. In a recent incident, a bridegroom could ride a horse only in the presence of the police official.[16] The caste *panchayat* (council) of the higher castes still exercise the power to punish, humiliate or ostracize those who indulge in the infringement of this customary practice. In some areas, even an elephant ride was seen as a prerogative of the upper castes and elite groups.[17] Conversely, ride on donkey signified lower status in the social and political hierarchy, at times even disgrace. A person indulging in an act deemed immoral or unethical by caste or community norms was made to feel a sense of shame and stigma for his misdeed by a ride on donkey.

The projected honour of the erstwhile Mewar state is also accompanied by equally honourable actions and commitment to cherished ideals. Numerous incidents and accounts related to heroism, struggle, sacrifice, resistance and pride in independence of the Mewar princes, princesses and people form some of the most glorious chapters of Indian history. This achieved honour of Mewaris was best exemplified through their persistent armed resistance to expansionist designs of the Mughals, when other states like Amber, Bikaner and Dholpur had capitulated to the demands and rewards of the Mughal emperors and princes. The latter states derived honour through titles, insignia and enormous wealth, Mughal emperors conferred on them, e.g., the rulers of Jaipur took great pride in their title of *Sawai* (one and a quarter) conferred by the Mughal emperor. Similarly, Amber rulers felt exalted by the construction of Tripoliya (structure with three gateways), a special privilege granted by the Mughal emperors. Their positions at the Mughal court, too, placed them in a distinctive position amongst the Rajputana states. Mewar rulers, however, considered this capitulation to Mughal demands as shameful and disgraceful and despite excessive hardships that they had to undergo for their refusal to bow before the Mughal emperors, they did not compromise with their ideals.

History of Mewar is replete with heroic figures who risked adversities, repression, suffering and sacrifice for upholding the code of ethics which was integral to their sense of self-respect as well as glory of their king, clan and land. Choonda's abdication of the throne is a shining example of truthfulness to one's word. Oswal Pradhan Bhama Shah has become legendary for his generosity and spirit of *swami-dharma* towards the Maharana. Tribals like Bhils have been hailed for their strict adherence to virtues like commitment to Bhil solidarity and autonomy, resistance to external intrusion and sanctity of a given word. Perhaps, the most amazing example of commitment to one's vow is the nomadic life led by the tribe Gaduliya Lohars (blacksmiths) who refused to lead a settled life till Chittor was liberated from the clutches of foreign invaders.

Though sad but the most important example of lived in honour is the practice of *jauhar* or collective immolation by women to protect their chastity and their husband's, clan's and state's honour, when defeat at the hands of the enemy became imminent. Mewar history is replete with examples of *jauhar*, especially during the Turkish and Mughal invasions.

These examples of achieved honour by Mewaris distinguish their paradigm of honour. Their chivalric deeds revealed in honour which was not necessarily associated with conquest, expansion and victory but was derived through persistent struggle, resistance, hardship, sacrifice and suffering. 'Valour without regard to consequences' and death in the battlefield (*virgati*) defined their notion of self-respect. The honour derived through the spirit of sacrifice and suffering was also reflected in their way of living that was marked by simplicity and austerity. They lived in simple dwellings, free from show and splendour. Although in grandeur and glamour, their courts and lifestyle were not comparable with the other rulers, yet it did not adversely affect their distinguished status among the Rajputana states.

Even after the Sisodiyas lost their heroic status under British paramountcy and the termination of their dynastic rule after achievement of Indian's independence, the Mewar ethic of honour continues to hold a cherished place in the Indian cultural tradition and national memory. The explanation for the phenomenon lies in the high level of ascribed honour received by the erstwhile state of Mewar. The military and chivalrous abilities of the stalwarts of Mewar were repeatedly projected in historical and literary writings of various genres, especially during the period of renaissance and the freedom struggle.

The challenge posed by the west in the cultural and political realms sought to be counteracted at two levels. In the initial stages, the western critique of Indian culture was sought to be counteracted by a reinterpretation of India's past with a view to project the Vedic period as the golden age. The emphasis was on high civilizational standards of the ancient times as opposed to the degeneration that had set in during the later period. The historical reconstruction thus undertaken was pertinent to the inculcation of a heightened sense of a cultural identity and self-respect among Indians. With the passage of time, the imperatives of the struggle against imperialism led to a subtle shift in the historiographical trends. The emphasis on Vedic classicism was substituted by writings that gave extensive coverage to heroic communities, most notably the Rajputs and the Marathas.

The negative qualities of effete, unmanly, timid, slothful and slack people imputed by a section of European writers on Indians was sought to be dismissed by projecting a tradition of resistance. The high ideals and valour of the Rajputs inspired historical novels during renaissance in the 19th century. Telugu and Bengali novels often used Rajput rulers like Rana Pratap, Raj Singh, etc., as their heroes and Mewar as the locale, their main interest was to highlight the tradition of struggle in Indian history with view to generating self-confidence. Similarly, during the freedom movement, the heroes of Mewar provided a statement of independence and courage for Indians who suffered from subjugation and loss of honour. Even in the present times, a selective use of heroic images from Mewar is quite noticeable. Portraits of Maharana Pratap, Panna Dhai, Maharana Sanga, Maharana Fateh Singh, etc., are displayed in tourist literature, palaces of erstwhile Mewar state and in public places like airports, railway stations, etc. In fact, prominence ascribed to these images is an integral part of our heroic tradition.

However, such ascriptions of honour have tended to eclipse the fact that there were phases and individuals in Mewar history who did not live up to these high ideals, e.g., the period, which followed the death of Rana Sanga, was marked by weak rulers. Similarly, after Raj Singh's death, there was degeneration in the fighting class of Mewar, which ultimately could not offer desired opposition to the Marathas and encouraged feudal lords to assert their authority and independence. Finally, as the Mewar rulers accepted British paramountcy, they were stripped off the attributes and authority of sovereign power and if one reviews the actual operation of the treaties, it is clearly evident that English officials were interfering in the minutest affairs of the Mewar state, thus leaving the royalty largely with a theoretical or a decorative recognition of honour. Moreover, such ascription of honour in historical writings has led to projection of certain heroes, while others continue to be neglected. The extraordinary romanticization of the Rajputs initiated by Tod and perpetuated by later historians has pushed other groups and communities who played significant role in the sustenance of Rajput polity into historical oblivion. Quite pertinently, the effort to exalt Mewar has resulted in historical marginalization of other Rajputana states, most notably the premier states of Jaipur and Jodhpur, who had made outstanding contribution in the realms of art, architecture and literature but have received scant attention. Selective projection produced certain gaps in historical writings and also led to the formulation of a notion of honour that is quite exaggerated. Nevertheless, the legacy of Mewar, as enshrined in its symbols, heroes and value structure, continues to have immense inspirational value and seminal place in the national psyche of the Indians.

An elucidation of the concept, code and categories of honour provides insights into the nature of Rajput polity. It is evident that some ideals that were deeply cherished in the region were codified and conceptualized over a period of time. An understanding of these ideals and values helps us to grasp the centrality of the concept of honour in the political culture of the native states of Rajputana. At the same time, the subtle differentiation in the categories of honour enables us to understand certain aspects of Mewar polity along with its complexities and sophistication. At times, they also suggest and project historical reality. The evolution of elaborate symbols and rituals perpetuated ideals, shaped values and determined code of conduct. It is true that, at times, the concept of honour associated with these states was exaggerated and glamourized in literary tradition and popular memory. In totality, however, the numerous dimensions of honour reveal the characteristic features of the identity of the region.

Notes

1. For understanding certain dimensions of the concept of honour refer, Gabriel Marcel, 'The Reintegration of Honor', in Whit Burnett (ed.), *The Human Spirit*; pp.303-306.
2. One can illustrate this tendency in certain gestures and behaviour patterns exhibited by the candidates. For exemplification in political rituals, it would be appropriate to look at the Nehru-Gandhi family that has dominated Indian democracy since independence. They perfected the art of symbolic gestures through which they reached out to the masses and in the process emerged as charismatic figures in the post-independence democratic polity. The latest entrant of the family to politics, Sonia Gandhi (daughter-in-law of the former Prime Minister Indira Gandhi) instantly struck a chord with the masses and reminded the public of her illustrious predecessor when she picked up some of the typical rituals and gestures. For more interesting examples regarding the nature of symbols and rituals in different types of polities in other countries, refer, Koertzer, *Ritual, Politics and Power*.

3. James Tod, *Annals and Antiquities of Rajasthan*, (henceforth, *Annals*), p.225.
4. Rajendra Joshi, 'Charan: The Contextual Dynamics of Caste in the Rajput System' in N.K.Singhi and Rajendra Joshi, *Religion, Ritual and Royalty*, p.308.
5. For a detailed exposition of the value-structure of the Rajputs refer, Raghavendra Singh, *Rajasthan ke Rajgharanon ka Sanskritik Adhyayan.*
6. Lindsey Harlan, *Religion and Rajput Women: The Ethic of Protection in Contemporary Narratives*, pp. 197-199.
7. *Harawal* was the traditional privilege of the Choondavats whose chief was the commander-in-chief of the Maharana and they led the Mewar army in all the expeditions.
8. According to genealogists, in earlier times, instead of *Singh* (lion) the rulers in the native state of Mewar used the affix *Pal* that means protector.
9. Tejaji was a Jat. Devnarayan's father was a Chauhan Rajput. However, he brought disgrace upon himself when he violated caste rules to marry 24 wives from different castes. Henceforward, he and his descendents were given the stigmatised caste name of Bagdavat. Devnarayan was widely revered by the cattle-breeding castes like Gujars.. Even Rana Sanga, to secure the support of the Gujars, had started wearing Devnarayan's sacred flowers around his neck and erected a shrine commemorating the hero near Daulatgarh. For further details, refer, Dinesh Chandra Shukla, *Rajasthan ke Pramukh Sant evam Lok Devta*; Mahendra Bhanavat, *Lokdevta Tejaji*; Mahendra Bhanavat, *Devnarayan Ro Bharat.*
10. Qanungo has devoted a full-length chapter to the practice of *vair*. K.R. Qanungo, *Studies in Rajput History,* pp.68-79.
11. *Annals,* pp.156, 139. This value had permeated the other classes also who revered the concept of *swami dharma* as much as the Rajputs. Like *vair*, this ideal was also transmitted from generation to generation. As Tod has observed, "Allegiance is as hereditary as the land."
12. Lindsey Harlan, *op.cit.*, p.33.
13. These festivals are publicly celebrated till present times and continue to attract large crowds.
14. Although, at times, the word *jodo* is translated as shoes, the more appropriate meaning would be dress or robes. *Annals*, pp.596-597; Rani Laxmikumari Choondavat, *Sanskritik Rajasthan*, p.100.
15. *Pagri* is worn in Mewar; *safa* is worn in Jaipur and Jodhpur.
16. *Dainik Bhaskar*, 9 May 2002. In another recent incident on March 7, 2003, in village Barthala in Tonk two dalit bridegrooms were physically assaulted by the Rajputs of the village and forced to dismount from the horses. The issue rocked the session of the State Assembly in Rajasthan. *Dainik Bhaskar*, 8 March 2003.

17. In Sikar in 1934, a Jat agitation broke out against the social disabilities imposed by the ruling clan. The immediate cause of the agitation was refusal on the part of jagirdars to allow a Jat cultivator to ride an elephant in a procession. Similarly, three persons lost their lives in a village Khoori in an encounter with Bhomias for not allowing a Jat to ride a horse. Dool Singh, *A Study of Land Reforms in Rajasthan*, p.35.

3

Regional Identity and Historical Construction

The state of Rajasthan, situated in northwestern India, with an area of 3,42,239 sq. kms., is the largest state in India. The most conspicuous physiographic feature of the state is the Aravalli range – one of the oldest mountain systems in the world. It divides the state diagonally into two natural but unequal regions. The west and the northwest region, which is about three-fifths of the state's area, is of varying physiographic features.

Historically, the region has been known by such names like Rajputana (land of the Rajputs), Rajwara, Raethana (land of the kings), Marusthali, Marwar (region of death), Virbhumi (land of the chivalrous), etc. The expression 'Rajasthan' (land of the royals) was first used as far back as 625 AD in the Basantgarh stone inscription and later, in Muhnot Nainsi's *Khyat* and Veerbhan's *Rajroopak* in the 18th century. However, it was Col. Tod's pioneering reconstruction of the state's history that popularized the nomenclature of Rajasthan that he defined as "that part of the country where Rajputs reside" or as "regal dwelling".

The Mughals first drew a boundary approximating the modern state of Rajasthan. In 1594, during Akbar's reign, the newly subdued Rajput states were grouped together to form the Subah of Ajmer.[1] This was the first formal delineation of Rajasthan as political space, which was later affirmed by the British after they had established their hegemony over the princely states of Rajputana in the aftermath of the destructive Rajput-Maratha wars in the 19th century. They were grouped together under Rajputana Agency later named as Rajputana province with headquarters at Ajmer.[2] The modern state of Rajasthan came into existence in 1949 as a unit of the Sovereign Democratic Republic of India. The process of integrating the various heterogeneous princely states (19 states and 2 chiefships) of the region began in 1948 with the formation of the Matsya Union (Alwar, Bharatpur, Dholpur and Karauli) and finally completed in 1956 when Sirohi and Ajmer were merged into Rajasthan.

To an outsider Rajasthan instantly conjures up images of sweeping desert vistas, rugged hills dotted with fortresses and crumbling battlements, rows of camels, robust men attired in vibrant tie and dye turbans, women in colourful sarees and other traditional outfits, its rich heritage of folk music, dance and songs. Above all, the region is known for its warrior culture symbolized by a Rajput, a chivalrous hero defending land, religion and honour from the Muslim invaders. Perhaps, no other state is so vitally linked to the stirring and the nostalgic memories of the past as Rajasthan. Due to this romanticization of the state's history and culture and its association with the most evocative legends of chivalry, sacrifice and martyrdom, Rajasthan is often referred to as India's showcase state attracting large number of tourists.

The distinctive traits and unique contribution of numerous communities have enriched the socio-cultural and political ethos of the state. The tribes like Bhil, Kalbeliya, Girasia, Sahariya and Meena were not only able to live in comparatively large numbers in the Rajputana states but have been able to retain a considerable part of their social, cultural and religious institutions in spite of radical changes in their economic and political relationships with others. The distinctive and vibrant cultural life of the numerous tribes contributed to the enrichment and preservation of various traditions and folk theatre. They evolved various dance forms like *gavri*, *dhol*, *teratali*, *kachchi ghodi*, *rasmandal*, etc. Dances performed by Kalbeliya women have earned international acclaim for their breathtaking body movements. They imitate the appearance and mind of a snake charmer when he hypnotizes them by his muse. Another well-known tribe of Rajasthan based in the state of Mewar was Gaduliya Lohar – the blacksmiths and armourers of Chittor. They left the citadel when Mughals had conquered it, swearing to return only after its recapture by the Sisodiyas. They have lived up to the vow of their ancestors and generations of them have spent their lives as nomadic blacksmiths travelling in carts through Rajasthan tending to the needs of villages and towns they pass by.[3]

Banjaras were yet another nomadic tribe who were roving traders and transported the goods of other merchants. They too were endowed by peculiar traits. It is said that if a Banjara was plundered and killed by wild animals or bandits while transporting merchandise of other traders, his family compensated the losses. The Banjaras derive a sense of pride not only from their exalted character but also from the Rajput lineage that they claim for themselves. It is a common belief amongst them that when Rajputs gave their daughters in marriage to the Mughals, they came to live in the forests and hence their name Banjara, *ban* means forest and *jara* means wanderer. Similarly, Jats have been known for their struggle against the tyranny of the Rajput jagirdars and who later carved out a powerful kingdom of Bharatpur under Surajmal in 1751 which held out against the Rajputs, Mughals and Marathas. The Jat community is known for gutsy, robust and hardworking peasants and diehard warriors. Yet another distinctive group is Bishnoi community which was founded by Jamboji in 1485 AD. While claiming to be a sect of Hinduism, the group evolved distinctive social, cultural and religious practices. The word 'Bishnoi' refers to twenty (*bis*) proscriptions (*noi*) laid down by the founder. These included sacred prohibitions regarding cutting of wood, taking life of an animal, the gelding of bulls and the drinking of unfiltered water.[4] Jamboji was deeply concerned about the preservation of green trees and humane treatment towards animals. He has been rightly described as the harbinger of the environmental movement in an age when nobody in the world had even thought of it.[5] The followers of Jamboji have upheld these principles even at the cost of their lives and until date are known as ardent conservationists. According to another version, the tribe derived its nomenclature 'Vishnois' from its devotion to Lord Vishnu.

Bishnois have special reverence for Khejri tree due to its tremendous utility in desert areas and they conserve these trees even if it involves sacrifice of lives. About 150 years ago, in 1730, Jodhpur Maharajas ordered that a number of Khejri trees be cut for his furnace. The Bishnois resisted the move and in a bid to stop the felling down of the trees, they clung to them. The Maharaja's men went ahead and cut down the trees and with them perished 363 men and women. This unparalleled sacrifice of the early conservationists is commemorated annually through a special ceremony.[6] It is indeed commendable that Bishnois until today cherish an undying fervour for and fierce faith in conservation of nature and any violation of their norms by an outsider leads to uproarious rather violent protests.

Another important community was the Marwaris of Shekhawati region who have earned international renown for their skills and acumen in trade and entrepreneurship. It is indeed incredible that the development of industries and native capitalism in India owes a great deal to the initiative of these merchants and traders from Marwar who spread to far-flung areas of the country. The Marwaris had set up the major industrial houses in the nascent stages of industrialization.

However, in public consciousness, the state's primary claim to identity as a region is the historic dominance of the Rajputs in the area, who rose to power and prominence in the early medieval period. The rhetorical dominance of the Rajput ethic, which stressed honour and valour without regard to consequences, has survived in public memory till today. Symbols, rituals, proverbs, behavioural gestures and norms implying Rajput notion of honour are rampant in the colloquial culture of the state. Eulogized as the *vir-bhumi* (land of the chivalrous) soaked by the blood of the chivalrous warriors, variously defined as *jhumjhar*s and *ranbankura*s, the martial and heroic deeds of the Rajputs have remained the hallmark of the state's regional character.

The distinctive political and military system of the Rajputs was based on clan system. In every state monarchy was the exclusive preserve of the exclusive clan. The major landholding kinsmen (jagirdars) of the clan participated in the management, sustenance and expansion of the territories. To define the gradations amongst jagirdars, an elaborate arsenal of symbols and emblems of power and honour were devised which became intrinsic to the sustenance of the Rajput polity.

The clan loyalties of the Rajputs surpassed the tremendous sense of loyalty and sharedness that they derived from a distinctive polity, marital ties based on clan exogamy and common social customs. They failed to develop any sense of consistent political cohesiveness in case of a potential external threat from the Muslims and the Marathas and later on, the British. Apart from clan-based polity and concept of brotherhood that formed the basis of clan system, another feature that sought to suggest a pattern among the different states of Rajputana was the extremely elaborate and distinctive approach towards construction of genealogies. Ancestry and lineage have held a deep fascination not only at the individual level for seeking recognition and glamour from the past, but even at group level, nations, castes and particularly clans have sought to reconstruct and trace their lineage from glamorous legends in order to seek glory, grandeur and legitimacy. In the context of Rajputs, this clamour for a divine origin had become a pains-taking obsession. In Tod's words, "Some plume themselves on a celestial origin, whilst others are content to be demi-celestial. Reduced in power, circumscribed in territory, compelled to yield much of their splendour and indignities of birth, they have not abandoned an iota of pride and high bearing arising from a knowledge of their illustrious and regal descent."[7] The major clans which traced their origin from Lord Rama called *Suryavanshis* (descendants of the sun) were of Mewar, Jaipur, Bikaner and Marwar. While ruling clans of the states like Jaisalmer and Kutch traced their descent from the lunar line of Lord Krishna and hence were known as *Chandravanshis*.

During the Mughal period, in the native states of Rajputana, two conflicting political trends emerged distinctly during Akbar's period. For instance, the heroic resistance of the rulers of Mewar against the hegemonic designs of the Mughals which has shaped the popular perceptions of Rajput chivalry, honour and fierce sense of independence. The other trend was symbolized by the matrimonial alliances between the Mughals and the Rajput states of Amber, Bikaner, Marwar and Dholpur. These marriage ties proved to be mutually beneficial. They brought prominence, power and affluence to Rajput states, particularly Jaipur, which had held the status of feudatories and dependent allies. According to Taft, by the end of Akbar's reign, Raja Man Singh of Amber had emerged as the single most powerful figure in the empire after the Emperor himself.[8]

Similarly, the Mughal emperors derived tremendous advantages from the military abilities of their Rajput allies. In fact, the role of Rajput rulers in ensuring the stability, success and expansion of Mughal empire has received widespread recognition. They served with distinction as provincial governors, military commanders and advisors. Man Singh occupied important positions as those of governor of Kabul and Bihar and led consequential military expeditions, especially in the Deccan and Kabul, with success. He is accredited with the expansion of Mughal empire in western India.

Paradoxically, the Rajputs who carried the Mughal flag to northwest, northeast and the south could not expand their territories beyond hills and deserts of the region of Rajputana. An exaggerated sense of clan upmanship and superiority resulted in irresponsible political behaviour and petty sense of honour. They indulged in continuous warfare amongst themselves at the slightest pretext, even at the cost of their own political survival. Occasionally, they cooperated with the Mughals and Marathas to strengthen their own political position in inter-state wars.

Significantly, Rajput states did not resist British intervention, evidently to buy peace from the repeated plundering activities of the Marathas and with a view to bring the assertive and hostile jagirdars under control. The British political alliances in the Rajputana states led to changes in the structure of political institutions and a shift in the centre of authority. The establishment of British paramountcy sought to preserve the visibility of the independence and honour cherished by the Rajputs. However, real freedom was considerably restricted as the British made considerable inroads in their status as sovereign rulers by depriving them of the various essential attributes of sovereignty leading to virtual collapse of the Rajput chivalric ideal.

II

The state of Mewar has held a deeply admired status in living upto the chivalric ideal that constituted the dominant ethic of the Rajput sense of honour. The kings of Mewar, styled as '*Maharanas*', occupied a supreme position among the princely states of Rajputana. They were bestowed with the coveted title of '*Hindua Sooraj*' (Sun of the Hindus) not only as a mark of respect for their antiquity and ancestry but also for their persistent struggle against the Mughals for preservation of *dharma*, independence, honour and prestige. This heroic resistance of Mewar not only shaped the timeless image of the Rajput as a chivalrous warrior fighting until the end but also defined the paradigm of honour for a Rajput.

The nomenclature of Mewar is an adaptation of the word '*Medapat*' meaning the land that led to the destruction of the '*Mlechchas*'. According to G.N. Sharma, "the word 'Medapat' appears sound enough as it bears the distinguishing mark of a peculiar period of history." According to G.H. Ojha, this region is known as Mewar because Medas or Meras inhabited it. He contends that the north-eastern part of Mewar is still known as Mewal and Merwara – the land of the Mers and Mevs. Yet another evidence points to Mewar being the land of the Sibis and hence known as Sibijanpada.[9]

The boundaries of Mewar varied from time to time, primarily due to Mughal conquest. During the 14th and 15th centuries, it extended until Bayana in northeast, Rewakanta and Mahikanta in the south, Palanpur in the west, and Malwa in the southeast. The repeated incursions of the Turks, Mughals and Marathas led to the constriction of the wide expanse of the Mewar state. The erstwhile state of Mewar was bound on the north by Ajmer-Merwara and Shahpura; on the west by Jodhpur and Sirohi; on the southwest by Idar; on the south by Dungarpur, Banswara and Pratapgarh; on the east by Nimach, Nimbahera, Bundi and Kota; and on the northwest by Deoli and Jaipur.

The peculiar physical features of the state have played a prominent part in shaping the history of the state. The state is divided into two well-marked natural divisions. The northern and the eastern portions consist of an elevated plateau of fine indulating country watered by Banas. This region is called 'Uparmal'. It stretches from Chittor to Begun, Bijoliyan and Mandalgarh. Rocks, hills and dense forests cover the most part of southern and western portions. The widest ridges of Aravallis, which is the oldest range in India, extending along the entire western part, form the western border of the state. This part formed the natural bulwark of Mewar, providing shelter and protection against enemies.[10] The long lines of mountains and wide dense forests leading to the inevitable isolation of Mewar, fostered among people a spirit of independence, simplicity, discipline and hardships. Culturally, this induced a sense of exclusion amongst them and fostered a sense of glory and allegiance towards their ancestors. The numerous artificial lakes that dot Mewar have contributed in a large measure to the geographical identity and beauty of the region and a source of pride for the Mewaris. Some of the finest lakes are Pichola, Fateh Sagar, Raj Samudra, Jai Samudra and Udai Sagar. These lakes constructed by different kings alleviated the sufferings of the people in the dry regions.

The Ranas of Mewar sought legitimacy and distinction not merely by seeking descent from the mythical hero and popular God Rama but they even bestowed divinity and divine grace on their kingdom by regarding it as the dominion of Lord Shiva. The Ranas sought to advertise and popularize the religious symbolism in their official correspondence and even when they visited the shrine of Eklingji, they superseded the priests and performed the ceremonies themselves. The rulers considered it highly honourable to donate to the shrine of Eklingji and conferring and distributing holy emblems and insignia of religious authority to the priests of Eklingji. It has been a ritual with the Maharanas to seek permission of the Eklingji before leaving the confines of the city. The present scion of the Sisodiyas adheres to this tradition. Due to their status as divine representatives, the words Maharana uttered were taken to have descended from *Shree Mukh*, the pious mouth and their persons were dignified as *Shreeji*, a great being.[11]

The preoccupation of Rajput political elite with sacred and divine kingship reveals that personal/clan honour and status in political domain was a major concern even in the preliminary stages. It is indeed true that divinity did elevate them, placed them above their subjects, and helped them to secure their position and status as rulers. It gave the people greater sense of security if the rulers have a larger than life image and superhuman qualities. Rajput claims of origin of their *vansh* from supernatural sources should be interpreted not merely in terms of legitimization of newly acquired political status and formation of identity as a distinct clan but the real agenda in these genealogical claims was the construction and formulation of the Rajput notion of honour. These distinctive and elaborate tables formed an integral element in shaping their honourable status.

III

In recent times, Tod has been largely responsible for perpetuating a historical construction in which the erstwhile state of Mewar has continued to occupy a honourable status as compared to other states of Rajputana. Pertinently, identification of Mewar, its rulers and people with heroism, valour and protection of honour has its origin in the bardic histories and genealogies which began to arise in the 16th century from bards popularly known as Charans and Bhats and also from Brahmin courtiers. These genealogies tried to link the Rajputs with the ancient Kshatriya dynasties of Rama and Krishna. The extremely elaborate and distinctive genealogical construction undertaken by these scholars was a conscious effort patronized by the Mewar rulers who sought to legitimize their status as genuine Kshatriyas. Even Mughal emperors Babur and Jehangir have been eloquent in their praise of the state and its rulers – the Guhilots.[12] Dirk Kloff asserts that by the mid-19th century a genealogical orthodoxy defining the 'Rajput Great Tradition' developed and took its firmest root in the court of Mewar.[13] Before Tod, Malcolm had stressed the antiquity and durability of Rajput rule and institutions and to Mewar he paid a special tribute. In his words, "Sisodiya princes enjoyed the highest rank amongst the rulers of Rajasthan and an alliance with them was the greatest honour to which a Rajput prince could aspire."[14]

However, its Tod's *Annals and Antiquities of Rajasthan*, which even after 170 years of publication, remains one of the most popular, exhaustive and referred works on the erstwhile Rajputana states. Lieutenant Colonel James Tod is considered by many to be the originator of Rajasthan historiography.[15] He has been conferred upon with such honorific like the 'Herodotus of the history of Rajasthan', 'the founder of modern historiography on Rajasthan' and 'Rajasthan ke Itihas ke Pita' (the father of the history of Rajasthan).[16]

James Tod was the son of an indigo planter of Mirzapur (U.P.). He started his career in the East India Company's army as a cadet. From 1800 to 1822, he served in a variety of official positions in India, culminating in the position of Political Agent for the western Rajputana states. As he became familiar with the Rajputs, Tod was totally overwhelmed by their traditional chivalry, generosity and cultural values. Their sufferings at the hands of the Pindaris and Marathas moved him, as also the Company's policy to subvert the independence of these states.

Tod's fascination with the Rajput character stimulated within him a strong desire to introduce the chivalric race to the western readers. Before taking up his pen, from 1812 to 1822, Tod devoted himself to the arduous task of collection of data through investigation, personal observation and consultation of literary and archaeological sources with the assistance of local scholars. To undertake this exhaustive work, he travelled extensively, and hence A.C. Banerjee observed, "To travel in mountains and deserts of Rajasthan was no pleasant or easy task in those days. Tod covered a wide ground at the cost of much personal discomfort."

After returning to England on his retirement, Tod arranged the historical materials collected by him. He produced the *Annals and Antiquities of Rajasthan* in two volumes in 1829 and 1832. The *Annals* comprises a series of chapters which cover the histories of Rajput states of Mewar, Marwar, Bikaner, Jaisalmer, Amber and the Shekhawati federation, Harouti and Kotah. However, Tod's voluminous work is not pure political history but gives a clear and exhaustive picture of Rajput society, polity and culture along with geographical details of the region. It has been rightly described as an "encyclopedia on Rajasthan and Rajputs". In addition, his less well-known *Travels in Western India* provides further accounts of the history, religious life and customs of the central and western India. A distinctive feature of the *Annals* is Tod's excessive admiration for the Guhilots of Mewar and a decided prejudice against the Kachchawas of Jaipur which has led him to devote a major portion of the book to the dynastic and cultural history of Mewar. He uses epithets like *Sachcha Darbar* (the truthful court), a honourable connotation and the *Jhootha Darbar* (untruthful court), a derogatory connotation to define the political culture in the states of Mewar and Jaipur respectively.[17] Tod sees Mewar as the seat of oldest and purest forms of Rajput society. He notes, "with the exception of Jaisalmar, Mewar is the only dynasty of these races which has outlived eight centuries of foreign domination, in the same lands where conquest placed them... we can carry (the line of the princes of Mewar) into the region of antiquity more remote than the Persians, and which would satisfy the most fastidious in respect to ancestry."[18]

The administrator-cum-scholar's preferential treatment to Mewar has been questioned by serious historians. According to A.C. Banerjee, during Tod's days, Mewar had ceased to be a leading state of Rajasthan and no political observer in the early 19th century would have overlooked the patent fact that politically speaking Marwar and Jaipur were premier states of Rajasthan and entitled to historians attention in a greater measure than Mewar.[19] Susanne and Lloyd Rudolph have expressed their anguish over the perpetuation of a historical reconstruction wherein Jaipur, which produced a series of capable rulers who excelled in war, politics, administration, science and literature, has received scant credit.[20]

Conversely, extensive coverage to Mewar in the *Annals* has been justified by various scholars.[21] Rudolphs have sought to explain Tod's attachment to Mewar against the background of European Romanticism. Like its other protagonists, Keats, Wordsworth, Lord Byron and Shelly, Tod opposed French Revolution's 'enlightened rationalism', the Industrial Revolution's 'commercialism' and utilitarianism's 'self-interested individualism'. In addition, Tod was influenced by Henry Hallam's trend setting work, *View of the State of Europe during the Middle Ages,* published in 1819. For Hallam, feudal Europe, far from being the dark ages, was an era when honour, heroism and devotion inspired great deeds by great men.[22] Tod applied the same understanding to the feudal system of Mewar. He characterizes Mewar's resistance against the Mughals as a struggle of brave rulers who sacrificed even the basic comforts of life in defense of their independence, religion and culture.

Tod's vehement defence of Rajput institutions and character could also be motivated by the idea of orientalism. Earlier, the term 'orientalism' implied an empathetic and romantic understanding of oriental civilization, history and institutions. However, Edward Said in his famous work, *Orientalism* endowed the term with much broader connotation when he described it as a 'strategy of subordination'.[23] Said defined the concept "as a way of coming to terms with the orient that is based on the orient's special place in European Western experience as its 'cultural contestant' or the other and the persistent schemes and tropes by which orient is contained and represented by dominating frameworks."[24] Orientalism thus became a deep-rooted, deliberate and systematic effort to arouse people's love for their own kind of heroism, art forms, cultural practices and religious ideas. This trend captivated people's imagination and investigation into the past became a very significant preoccupation with the people as a venture of knowledge. While there may be lack of clarity regarding the factors, which led Tod to place Mewar in the history's proverbial 'hall of fame', there is not a single voice of dissent regarding the immensity and intensity of the impact of his work. The legendary historian has, indeed, cast a long shadow as far as popular consciousness and historiographical trends are concerned.

Tod's historical construction went a long way in crystallizing the views of the colonial administrators towards the Rajputs. Lynn Zastoupil clearly spells out the influence of this romantic point of view within the ranks of British administrators in the 19th century. Zastoupil states: "Mill took up the common view of British administrators that the Rajputs were the ruling class of India. This romanticized notion is usually credited to James Tod. Tod compared the rajas and thakurs to the kings and barons of medieval Europe and this became the dominant view amongst the British administrators."[25] Tod's exaltation of Mewar influenced British decision to accord precedence and supreme position to the state amongst the chiefs in Rajputana. In 1832, when Governor General Lord William Bentinck visited Rajasthan, he stated: "His Highness, the Maharana being lineally descended from one of the greatest families in the country, his rank and dignity have been the highest among the Rajas of Hindustan and will continue to do so."[26] Further, the British had made it clear to the Rajput Maharajas that Udaipur was their titular doyen. In 1870, when the Maharaja of Jodhpur had declined to attend the Viceroy's Durbar, in case he had to concede precedence to the Maharana of Udaipur, he was asked to leave the viceregal camp pre-emptorily, without being accorded any salute or ceremonial honours.[27]

Incidentally, the publication of *Annals* coincided with a tumultuous period of Indian history. The Indians, due to a long spell of political subjugation, were suffering from loss of esteem and self-confidence. Their cultural identity and pride were being eroded by imperialist assertions of cultural superiority of the west. At such a critical juncture, the portrayal of Rajput heroes as diehard defenders of land and faith directly appealed to popular consciousness. The heroes of Mewar and their struggle against a powerful empire provided to the Indians iconic and inspirational figures from their own past. The whole range of political symbolism created and venerated by Tod's *Annals* had appealed to creative writers in regions which lay faraway from the erstwhile states of Rajputana, e.g. Bengal, Maharashtra, Andhra, Kanada and Utkal.[28] The entire genre of regional literature plays, novels, poems and short stories echoed Tod's choicest symbols - Haldighati, the fort of Chittor, *Jauhar, Saka,* Pratap, Padmini, Chetak and so on. K.K. Ganguli notes this extensive influence on Bengali writers of 19th and 20th centuries: "Many of the leading figures in Bengal appear to have gone back repeatedly to the fountain of Tod's exposition of Rajput traditions in order to regain sustenance in the age old culture of their own. Notable literary figures in Bengal as Bankim Chandra, Dvijendralal, Rabindranath Tagore and Abindranath Tagore – all make reference to Tod while building the patriotic ethos in their work."[29]

Significantly, the *Annals* laid down the parameters for future historical writings on Rajasthan. Subsequent historians, while refuting certain factual errors of Tod's historical construction, have not been able to subvert or challenge his basic theme. The patriotic school of historians that emerged during the nationalist period further endorsed Tod's narrative. Even British historians accepted the hierarchy of Rajput states as laid down in *Annals* wherein "sovereigns of Mewar are highest in rank and dignity". Prinsep, Malcolm, Grant Duff, Elphinstone and J.C. Brookes have been unanimous as far as Mewar's supreme and honourable position is concerned.

Tod's romantic, poetic and exhaustive account of the Rajputana states, however, lacks historical vision and he failed to analyze certain key questions: Why the state of Mewar, despite a strong tradition of resistance and reckless courage, succumbed so easily to British domination? Why, unlike the Marathas, they failed to cherish an imperial vision? Even from point of view of honour, the Maharanas were not able to preserve the same when confronted with the Marathas and later, the English. Apart from this, the transition from medieval to modern trends has not been visible in Mewar while it was making inroads in other states like Jaipur. Moreover, even while focusing on Mewar, he has highlighted only the contribution and exploits of its ruling elite, i.e., the Rajputs. He has not analyzed the crucial role of other communities, castes and tribes in sustaining, enriching and strengthening the polity of the erstwhile Rajputana states. In the entire narrative the references to these communities are scattered and incidental and they are projected as groups totally dependent on the Rajputs for their survival and protection, which was not entirely true. In fact, Tod gave credence to a historical construction wherein history of Rajasthan became synonymous with Rajputs, although they formed just 7-8 percent of the population of the state. Objective perusal of the state's history would reveal that there were groups other than Rajputs and institutions other than royalty which deserve a fair share of glory and acclaim that has, hitherto, been the preserve of the Rajputs.

Notwithstanding these gaps in Tod's *magnum opus, Annals and Antiquities of Rajasthan*, his historical legacy continues to haunt and dominate not just historical writings on Rajasthan, but has impacted literary tradition all over India. In fact, the legendary historian became crucial to the whole process of evolution and creation of a nationalist historiography in India. Seen from this perspective, Tod occupies a significant place in the development of Indian historiography and political consciousness.

Another major historical work on Mewar is *Vir Vinod: Mewar ka Itihas* in two exhaustive volumes, written by Shyamaldas, official historian of the erstwhile state of Mewar during the reign of Maharana Sajjan Singh. He was a Dadhvadiya Charan whose family originally belonged to the Rann of Kutch where they were the *Pol-pat* (Lord of the Gate, i.e., the premier Charans who received *neg* or ritual offerings from the bridegroom at the gate) of the Sankhla Parmars. They were *sasun* (perpetual grant, primarily religious in nature) holders of village Dadhivada and hence called Dadhvadiya

Charans. In the mid-15th century, when Ranmal and Jodha occupied Rann of Kutch, Sankhla Parmars migrated to Mewar along with Dadhvadiya family. Maharana Kumbha conferred upon Jait Singh, the head of the Dadhivada family, two villages of Dharta and Gopita. Eventually, the family rose to eminence in the Mewar court. Shyamaldas, one of the four sons of Kayam Singh, was born in 1837, received good education and became a renowned scholar of Sanskrit poetics. Maharana Shambhu Singh who entrusted him with the task of writing a comprehensive history of Mewar along with Pandit Padmanath in 1871. During the reign of Maharana Sajjan Singh, he became an important figure in Mewar polity. He was appointed as the librarian of the palace library and the confidential advisor of the Maharana. He was conferred upon with the title of 'Kaviraja' in 1879 by the Udaipur Maharana.

For the purpose of compiling an exhaustive history of the state a sum of one lakh rupees was sanctioned and a department called *Itihas Karyalaya* was established with a team of competent scholars. The team collected a veritable collection of inscriptions, copper plates, coins, historical works in Sanskrit, Persian, Arabic and English, besides old *pattas*, *parvanas*, *firmans*, *nishans* and official correspondence. Though the work was first published in 1886, the copies of the book were sealed on the orders of the then Maharana Fateh Singh. There is controversy surrounding the ban imposed on the monumental work of history, which was the product of enormous hard work and painstaking research. It is a well-known fact that in his later years his influence in the court had declined considerably. It is contended that perhaps the authorities did not approve of his reflections on the private lives of the Maharanas. Noted historian G.N. Sharma has suggested that Shyamaldas' detractors in the court of Maharana Fateh Singh had instigated the latter against the historian. They insinuated that the historical work has portrayed the achievements of the nobles in a manner that confirms their special privileges and rights. Maharana Fateh Singh feared that such a glorious projection of the jagirdars might embolden them and endanger his policy of resumption of *jagirs*.[30] The text was made available in 1945 when Maharana Bhupal Singh released it.

Vir Vinod covers the period until 1884, i.e., until the reign of Maharana Sajjan Singh. The work is largely based on the method of scientific investigation and research of historical materials. The historian admitted that he had been free from personal prejudices and needless praise. He has also not hesitated to highlight the weaknesses and licentious habits of some of the Maharanas. As Qanungo has aptly noted, "the modern method of research on a comprehensive scale dawned upon Rajputana with Shyamaldasji."[31]

Nevertheless, certain factors did influence his objectivity as a historian. Firstly, as a court historian, he certainly must have experienced constraints. Moreover, as mentioned earlier, his ancestors were deeply ingratiated to the patronage of the Sisodiya Maharanas for their rehabilitation and rise in Mewar. Secondly, Tod' writings, perhaps, influenced Shyamaldas' historical writings. Shyamaldas has not been able to reject or modify Tod's exaltation of Mewar. He does highlight the personal failings and licentious habits of some of the Maharanas but he is possessed with a similar adulation for Mewar's antiquity and supreme status among the Rajputana states. He has prefaced his voluminous work by innumerable references and quotations wherein historians, writers, administrators, both Mughal and the British, have endorsed the honourable position of Mewar. He has observed: "There will be hardly any ancient or modern literature in Persian, Arabic, Urdu and Hindi that deals with the history of Hindustan and does not mention the supreme position of the Maharana of Mewar. Even if a gist of these books is compiled then a booklet can be formed."[32] He attributes the glory and greatness of Mewar to its divine ancestry which can be traced to Lord Rama; its antiquity; to its relentless struggle against the Muslim rulers and Mughal Emperors of Delhi; and above all, the tolerant and magnanimous attitude of the Maharanas, who despite their primary devotion to Saivism, provided shelter, freedom and respect to followers of other sects and religions. Kaviraja grew up in an atmosphere of bardic lore that had been a family tradition for generations. Familiarity with bardic writing and extraordinary narrative capabilities qualified him to recapitulate vivid descriptions of the events of martial action but at the same time he could not escape the eulogistic tone of a bard for reconstruction of events and achievements of his patrons – the Sisodiyas.

Notwithstanding these limitations, his work, as a whole, is commendable and trendsetting in many ways. Firstly, like the *Annals*, it is not merely a narration of political events but it portrays the cultural ethos and social life of the erstwhile state of Mewar. It also sketches the manners and habits of different castes and tribes like Brahmins, Charans, Rajputs, Vaishyas, Bhils, Gaduliya Luhars, Meenas, Sansis, etc. There is also a description of numerous festivals that were celebrated by the people of Mewar along with an account of the religious shrines or *Devsthanas* of the state. In addition, Shyamaldas has enriched the historical account by interspersing the Mewar saga with brief accounts of geographical description of Europe, Africa, Asia and India along with dynastic histories of other states of Rajputana. He has also narrated the history and achievements of the rulers of Mandu, Gujarat, Bhavnagar, Patiala, etc., and has made repeated references to the Mughals and the British as and when the narrative demanded. Noted historian G.N. Sharma has observed that, "these dynastic histories definitely interrupt the unity of the historical narrative of Mewar, yet these digressions are the most interesting portions of his work for those who are curious to make a comparative study of the history of Rajpuana."[33] Undoubtedly, until date, *Vir Vinod* continues to be one of the most monumental histories of Mewar and has been recognized by contemporary historians as an exhaustive and detailed work. Despite being a court historian, his accounts show accuracy and painstaking details. It forms an obligatory reading and a major source material for any historical research on Mewar. Along with Tod's *Annals*, *Vir Vinod* has crystallized and shaped historical construction and popular perception regarding Mewar and its rulers.

Gaurishankar Hirachand Ojha was another historian who made seminal contribution to the writing of history of Rajputana. He had started his career as a historian under Kaviraj Shyamaldas as his assistant secretary. Later, after he met Lord Curzon, the latter was duly impressed by his scholarship and set up a museum at Ajmer with Ojha as the curator. In 1914, he was awarded the title of Raibahadur and in 1928, the British conferred upon him the title of Mahamukhopadhyaya.[34]

Ojha's most important works are the various volumes on the erstwhile native states of Rajputana, viz., Udaipur, Banswara, Dungarpur, Jodhpur, Bikaner and Sirohi. Ojha has adopted an identical format and plan in these works. The political history of every state is preceded by the description and meaning of the nomenclature of the state, area, flora and fauna, forts, routes, population, religions, etc. The subsequent section focused on the political vicissitudes of the state since the establishment of dynasty. In the last section, he threw light on the *thikanas*, important families, social classification, art, literature and other cultural aspects.

In his *Rajputana ka Itihas*, Ojha has discussed the various theories regarding the origin of the Rajputs and has further enhanced the glory of the Rajputs by endorsing the view that Rajputs are the direct descendants of the Kshatriyas of the Aryan stock. Ojha published the history of Mewar in two volumes entitled *Udaipur Rajya ka Itihas*. Amongst the numerous Rajputana states, his works portray a special preference for the state of Mewar and there is an attempt to denigrate the ruler of Jodhpur. He has himself explained the reasons for admiration for Mewar. Firstly, the Mewar ruling clan was the oldest one. Secondly, the history of the state was replete with glorious instances of struggle for independence. Some scholars have considered Ojha's adulation for the native state of Mewar partisan. According to G.N. Sharma, Ojha has completely overlooked the fact that from Guhil to Hammir, Sisodiya dynasty did not become a fully sovereign power ruling over Mewar. Moreover, he has not paid sufficient attention to the forts and palaces built by Pratihars, Panwars and Solankis in the Mewar region and thereby has presented a fragmentary historical account of the state. A critical evaluation of the contribution of the Rathores during the reign of Maharana Kumbha is also lacking. While delineating the destructive nature of the Maratha raids in detail, Ojha has failed to discuss the weaknesses of the Rajput rulers that resulted in this precarious situation. In addition, the historical narrative focuses mainly on the contribution of the elite, i.e., the governing classes. The role and contribution of other communities like Bhils and Charans, who had played an important role in the sustenance and continuation of Sisodiya rule goes largely unnoticed, in the absence of comprehensive account of their contribution.

Significantly, his account of the British period too lacks objectivity and fails to give the complete picture. He has largely used the works of British officials to describe the process of change during this significant political phase, thereby leading to a narrative which has been written from a colonial perspective. It is unfortunate that his historical writings overlooked the social and religious reform movements of the 19th century. According to H.S. Bhati, "It was due to Lord Curzon's benevolence that Ojha became the curator of Ajmer Museum and this explains his partisan attitude towards the British."[35] While he conceded sizeable space to the activities and achievements of the British officials, he has completely ignored the rise of political awareness and protest movements. Despite these limitations, G.H. Ojha's systematic approach in his numerous volumes on the history of Rajputana states has imparted coherence and consistency to his narrative. In fact, as compared to other monumental histories of Mewar, Ojha's volumes appear to be more methodical and also a more serious attempt at history-writing. Hence, his comprehensive work on

Rajasthan remains a significant source-material for scholars who undertake studies in Rajput history.

Subsequently, there have been historiographical trends, which seek to digress from the dominant narrative constructed by Tod and perpetuated by later historians of Mewar. The dissent has been effectively voiced by another prominent historian of Mewar, G.N. Sharma. His major works include *Social Life in Medieval Rajasthan, Mewar and Mughal Emperors* and *Glories of Mewar*. In his trendsetting work *Mewar and Mughal Emperors*, he has commented on the futility of the paradigm of honour popularized by earlier historians. Tod's eloquent appreciation of "undaunted heroism, inflexible fortitude that which keeps honour bright, perseverance and the determination that this country should not be abandoned to the Toork", has been set aside by G.N. Sharma in favour of more practical norms of conduct: "Great as he (Pratap) was, one might speculate whether the struggle tended to contribute to the welfare of the country as a whole or produced adverse effect on the future of the land. It is to be admitted that Akbar was a great and benevolent sovereign who pursued the grand policy of unifying the country, both politically and culturally. Pratap's remaining aloof from the union was a great impediment in that noble task. To that extent, it was injurious to the interests of his country. If at this stage, Pratap would have joined the Mughal order he could have saved his country from disaster and ruin. Even his long resistance could not avert the days when during his own son's time Mewar became a subordinate state of the Mughal empire. Had this opportunity been given to Mewar earlier much of this backwardness could have been mended."[36]

G.N. Sharma's plea for a more practical political perspective has been endorsed by various other historians like A.C. Banerjee and Susanne and Lloyd Rudolph. According to Banerjee, "Speaking from purely political and military points of view, Rana Pratap's policy must be condemned as unrealistic. Marwar and Amber – the latter an upstart favourite of the

Padshahi court – became the leading states of Rajputana and Bappa's kingdom paid for its resistance to Mughal imperialism by quietly sinking down to the status of second rate principality. Never again did Mewar recover the place which it had held in the Rajput state system before the advent of the Mughals."[37] Rudolphs have tried to support this alternative historiographical trend by applauding the pragmatic policy of Amber and Jodhpur, "one that ignored the Rajput ethic in order to achieve results and be creative, to succeed in the domains of war, statesmanship and commerce and to innovate in the realms of science and art". According to them, "the glories of Chittor, the romanticisation of the battle of Haldighati and admiration for the long and imprudent resistance of Udaipur to Mughal power may not survive a revisionist history less concerned with valour than with the human and economic costs of its pursuit."[38]

The second perspective as regards historical writings on Rajputana states challenges and subverts the historical construction created and popularized by Tod, Shyamaldas and Ojha and perpetuated by subsequent literary and historical works. They seek to reject the recklessness and suicidal idealism reflected in Mewar's resistance to the Mugals. However, this alternative trend has not been able to diminish either the historical significance of Tod's sentimental eulogy or the distinctive, honourable and heroic status of Mewar. The determination of Pratap, supreme sacrifice of Panna Dhai, gallantry of Hammir, loyalty of Chetak, exploits of Rana Sanga, scholarship, diplomacy, love for art and heroism of Rana Kumbha, Meera's *bhakti* and piety and pride of Fateh Singh have become an integral part of our cultural and national identity. Spanning various historical epochs from renaissance to the freedom movement and upto the present times, the heroic images from Mewar enjoy widespread visibility in tourist literature, public places like airports, railway stations, etc., which testify not only to their immense inspirational value but their fascination and glamour for foreigners as well.

In summation, one needs to appreciate the remarkable contribution of the early historians of Mewar. It is true that their work suffered from certain drawbacks as regards perspective, approach and methodology but it is amazing that they took upon themselves the task of writing such an exhaustive history of the state. These historians had to traverse the harsh terrain of the region to collect source material, mostly at their own expense and at considerable personal risk. They should be credited with the initiative of applying the method of historical writing and systematic methodology that was not applied earlier by scholars in recording the political events and annals of the native states. It is creditable that they undertook the arduous task of compiling and narrating such comprehensive history that required a lifetime of dedication, commitment and devotion.

Notes

1. Deryck Lodrick, 'Identity as Process', in Scohmer, Rudolph & others (eds.), *Idea of Rajasthan: Explorations in Regional Identity*, Vol. I, p.1.
2. *Ibid.*, pp. 6-12.
3. Royina Grewal, *In Rajasthan*, pp. 123-124.
4. *Ibid.*, pp. 192-196.
5. Pahariya and Panagariya, *Political, Socio-Economic and Cultural History of Rajasthan (Earliest Times to 1947)*, pp. 157-158.
6. Royina Grewal, *op.cit.*, pp. 192-196.
7. James Tod, *Annals and Antiquities of Rajasthan* (henceforth *Annals*), p.174.
8. For details refer, Francis H. Taft, 'Honour and Alliances: Reconsidering Mughal Rajput Marriages', in Schomer, Rudolph & others (eds.), *op.cit.*, pp. 217-241.
9. Gaurishankar Hirachand Ojha, *Udaipur Rajya ka Itihas*, vol. I, pp.1-2.
10. G.N.Sharma, *Glories of Mewar*, p.1.
11. *Ibid.*, p.107.
12. Shyamal Das. *Vir Vinod*, Vol. I (henceforth, *Vir Vinod*), p.230.

13. Dirk H.A. Kloff, 'Naukar, Rajput and Sepoy: The Ethnohistory of the Military Labour Market in Hindustan, 1450-1850', in Schomer, Rudolph & others (eds.), *op.cit.*, vol. II, pp. 72-73.
14. *Vir Vinod*, Vol I, pp. 225-226.
15. For details regarding Tod's life and impact, refer G.N.Sharma & V.S. Bhatnagar (eds.), *The Historians and Sources of the History of Rajasthan*, Hukam Singh Bhati (ed.), *Itihaskar James Tod: Vyaktitva aur Krititva*; A.C. Banerjee, *The Rajput States and British Paramountcy*, pp.226-238.
16. K.R.Qanungo, *Studies in Rajput History*, p.103; Sukumar Bhattacharya, 'James Tod' in S.P. Sen (ed.), *Historians and Historiography in Modern India*, pp. 416-24; G.H.Ojha has referred to Tod as father of the history of Rajasthan, Swaroop Singh Choondawat, 'Kaljayi Amar Itihaskar Tod', in Hukam Singh Bhati (ed.), *op.cit.*, p.200.
17. Lloyd and Sussane Rudolph, *Essays on Rajputana: Reflections on History, Culture and Administration*, p.43.
18. *Annals*, pp. 173-174.
19. A.C. Banerjee, *op.cit.*, p.233.
20. Lloyd & Susanne Rudolph, *op.cit.*, pp.42-43.
21. According to Vashishtha, wider spaces occupied by Mewar in the *Annals* was due to the fact that source material on the princely state was easily and profusely available. Moreover, Mewar was a more ancient state as compared to the other Rajputana states. V.K. Vashishtha, 'James Tod as a Historian', in G.N.Sharma & V.S. Bhatnagar (eds.), *op.cit.*, p.160.
22. Kesri Singh, *The Hero of Haldighati*, p.3.
23. For a discussion on orientalism as a strategy of subordination, refer, Edward Said, *Orientalism*.
24. Susie Tharu & K. Lalitha, *Women Writings in India*, p.43.The editors have discussed the concept of orientalism and the broader connotation that the term assumed particularly in the wake of Edward Said's well-known work on Orientalism.
25. Lynn Zastoupil, *John Stuart Mill and India*, pp.122-123.
26. K.R.N. Swamy, *Mughals, Maharajas and the Mahatma*, p.155.
27. D.L. Paliwal, *Mewar and the British (1857-1921)*, pp.110-111; K.R.N. Swamy, *op.cit.*, p.155.
28. Narayan Singh Chundavat, 'Tod ka Vyaktitva aur Krititva' in Hukam Singh Bhati (ed.), *Rajasthan ke Itihaskar*, pp.58-59.
29. K.K. Ganguli, *Cultural History of Rajasthan*, pp.24, 254-260.
30. G.N. Sharma, *op.cit.*, p.34. G.N. Sharma has deeply regretted the fact that Gaurishankar Hirachand Ojha had borrowed many facts and details about the history of Mewar from *Vir Vinod* without acknowledging the veteran historian's work. Sharma has suggested the later historian

perhaps took advantage of the fact that Maharana Fateh Singh had imposed a ban on the circulation of Shyamaldas' work.

31. K.R.Qanungo, *op.cit.*, p.105.
32. *Vir Vinod*, p.230.
33. G.N.Sharma, 'Kaviraja Shyamaldas', in G.N.Sharma & V.S.Bhatnaghar (eds.), *op.cit.*, p.66.
34. K.S. Gupta, 'Dr. G.H.Ojha as a Historian', in G.N.Sharma & V.S.Bhatnaghar (eds.), *op.cit.*, pp.72-74.
35. Hukam Singh Bhati, 'Dr. Gaurishankar Hirachand Ojha', in Hukam Singh Bhati (ed.), *op.cit.*, p.130.
36. G.N. Sharma, *Mewar and the Mughal Emperors*, p. 121.
37. *Ibid.*
38. Lloyd & Susanne Rudolph, *op.cit.*, pp.42-44.

4

Symbols and Political Legitimacy in Mewar: From Khadag* to Khadi

The relationship between culture and nature was expressed through symbolism even in the early stages of human history. In each culture, a set of powerful symbols has evolved over centuries that not only have a high inspirational value but also provide specificity to a particular group. Every nation-state and society communicates its identity through a set of symbols. A social group conveys its aspirations, way of live, behavioural code, familial relationships, fantasies and taboos through symbols. Symbology, coupled with ritualism, has been popularly associated with religious sphere. Anthropologists have defined rituals as culturally standardized repetitive actions, primarily symbolic in character, involving the supernatural and the religious realm. This is, however, a restrictive definition for there is hardly a realm, even in modern times, which does not transmit its system of beliefs and values through rituals, often projecting certain symbols. In different social organizations performance of specific rituals has contributed towards preservation of separate identity for each of the groups. Rituals are used for socialization of new entrants to a social group and to familiarize them with the distinctive

---

* Sword

Sword

Emblem of the Mewar State

Courtesy: Maharana Mewar Foundation and Maharana Mewar Historical Publication Trust.

Gangaur

Offering of *Nazar*

Courtesy: Maharana Mewar Foundation and Maharana Mewar Historical Publication Trust.

features of that particular group. The total worldview of the Hindu religion can be grasped through its in-depth symbology and an elaborate system of rituals. The *samskaras* or the lifecycle rites not only controlled and provided entry to various roles in the Hindu society, but no one could take on a new status or role without performing the prescribed *samskaras* as these rites were 'effective symbols' which determined placement of an individual in the social organization. These could be compared to the sacraments in the Roman Catholic Church.[1]

An important realm, which has a strong symbolic dimension, is the political universe. As the states grew larger in size and the powerholder became distanced from the ruled, the political environment became dependent on symbolism and rituals. Authority is an abstraction that can be communicated through symbols and rituals. It would be interesting to note as to how people had associated themselves with the vast Roman Empire with which they did not have direct contacts. People living in distant areas were not familiar with either the military or civil officials who rarely visited them. It was perhaps the grand monuments of the Roman Empire that served as symbolic expression and reminder of the might of the empire. Occasionally, people also participated in rituals and rites that ensured their allegiance to the empire.

Symbolic apparatus has remained crucial in a range of political systems and movements upto the present times. Commonly, rituals and symbolic devices that communicate authority have been associated with monarchical polities in which rulers were considered divine and distant who radiated supernatural power. Nevertheless, in modern political systems too, whether democratic or communist, which are based on rational principles, symbolism and rituals have remained an essential ingredient for image construction of the political actors, legitimization of authority and garnering public support. In a political culture, performance of rituals has special significance for legitimization of authority. It has been aptly observed that "ritual is used to constitute power, not just reflect power that already exists."[2] In a monarchical system coronation ceremony adds to the legitimization and continuation of authority. In a democratic polity oath-taking ceremony ensures and legitimizes the position of the powerholder. From tribal to monarchical and democratic polity, change and continuity, enthronement and legitimization are intrinsically linked with performance of specific rituals.

Significantly, monarchical and democratic polities require different kinds of political rites for legitimizing authority and seeking recognition of status. In monarchical polities, the symbols of the divine and royal that were clustered around the *raja* were motivated by the need to place more distance between the ruler and his subjects. The rituals of a monarchical system reinforce exaltation, segregation and distinction. Contrary to that, the major thrust of democratic polities is on bridging the gap between the rulers and the ruled. The rituals, dress and behaviour of the political leaders in a democracy tend to accelerate a process of equalization and identification with the masses and the commoners. Significantly, democratic polities witness a reversal of monarchical system and emphasize desegregation and parity.

Although the idiom in a democratic political culture differs, the schedule of many modern leaders is replete with ceremonial gestures, rites and visits which express the importance of their office, charisma of their personality and project their authority in the public eyes. International relations, in the present times, are heavily burdened with ritual observances. The reception of a foreign dignitary and his subsequent visit is marked by precise formalities and protocol prescribed for him.

Symbolic icons and rituals have been crucial to all political systems for bolstering the authority of the powerholders. However, at the same time, they have a more important role to play in political conflict and political change. Just as there are symbols of stability and maintenance of an order, there are symbols of struggle and revolution. The periods of struggle are those historical moments when the established network of symbols and rituals undergo change. The leaders of a political struggle either generate new symbols and ritual forms to delegitimize the existing regimes or they transform the existing and potent classical symbols by infusing them with new meanings and adapt them for their own political purposes.

I

In the context of symbols, it would be apt to examine the elaborate system associated with different native states of Rajasthan. In the warrior culture of the state, *pagri* or *pag* (turban), *moonchha* (moustache), *khadag* (sword), horse, etc., assumed inordinate importance as symbols of honour and heroism. The donning of *kesariya bana*[3] (wearing saffron robes) and the scenario of Rajput princesses in their complete adornment marching to commit *jauhar* (collective immolation) persist as poignant yet ultimate examples of Rajput chivalry, sacrifice and courage. Pertinently, both honour and dishonour are significant in political culture. While sharing *thali* (platter), food, opium, *pan* (betel leaves) and *pag badalna* (exchanging turbans) were considered as a highest mark of confidence and friendship, refusal to do so was perceived as dishonourable to the other person.

Amongst the Rajputana states, the erstwhile state of Mewar occupies an illustrious place in the history's proverbial 'hall of fame' not only as mark of respect for its ancestry and antiquity but also for its persistent armed struggle against the Muslim invaders for preservation of freedom and honour. Political symbolism associated with its chivalrous saga not only occupies a place of pride in the historical and creative writings but has also captivated the imagination of a people belonging to diverse regions, communities and political contexts over a period of centuries. Mewar, itself, has survived in public memory as a symbol of fierce pride in one's independence and self-respect as well as resistance and suffering.

Founded towards the close of the 5th century, the erstwhile state of Mewar was ruled by the illustrious clan of the Guhilots, also known as the Sisodiyas, till independence. Forced by circumstances, Maharana Bhim Singh had to recognize the sovereignty of the English over Mewar in 1818. British paramountcy over Mewar led to clear and undeniable restrictions on effective sovereignty of the Maharana and despite treaty stipulations and pledges to the contrary, intervention in internal affairs led to the dilution of the internal sovereignty as well. It was a subtle move on the part of the British Raj to preserve and sustain the monarchical rule, its outward symbols of authority and the inviolability of the ruler's person in his state. Meanwhile, the third decade of the 20th century gave rise to popular agitation in Mewar, against the British imperialism, aristocratic rulers and the reactionary feudal chiefs. In 1948, the state of Mewar with its capital at Udaipur, became a part of the Indian Union. Consequently, the state underwent a transition from a monarchical to a democratic polity. From being the exclusive preserve of the monarchs of a single clan, the state of Mewar adapted to democratic institutions, norms and way of life. Significantly, different symbols and rituals were employed in all these varying political contexts to create legitimacy and to mould people's understanding of the changed political universe.

Hierarchical political systems, especially the monarchical polities, often use potent icons or myths of legitimacy, in most cases revolving round the divine origin. One of the earliest symbols that Mewar rulers carefully evolved, as their legitimizing and identifying feature, was the myth of ancestry that bestowed divinity on the ruler. They sought to establish their supernatural antecedents not only by claiming ancestry from Lord Rama, a popular and predominant deity of the Hindu pantheon, but they regarded Lord Shiva, another powerful divinity of the Hindus as the real crowned king of Mewar. These myths were perpetuated in public memory by rituals that were performed by the kings to reinforce their divine nature, e.g., the ruler superseded the Brahmin priest as officiant of the ceremonies at the shrine of Eklingji; he reserved the right to distribute symbols of religious authority to the priests of Eklingji; assumption of the title of *Diwan* of Eklingji; exhibition of this divine connection on official correspondence. In all the royal processions on important occasions, the deity of Lord Shiva preceded Maharana. The shrine of Eklingji, a small stone emblem, evolved as a symbol that implied the continuity of Guhilot rule over Mewar.[4] The name of Eklingji was invoked in common parlance as well as by the ruling elite, while greeting each other. Swearing in the name of Eklingji ensured a commitment to a promise.

The Ranas regularly relegitimated their link with Lord Rama through various symbols and rituals. The banner or flag of the Sisodiyas with a gold sun on a crimson field was a symbol that proclaimed their relationship with the *Suryavansh* (race of the sun). In fact, sun, as a symbol of their divine descent, was given universal precedence in Mewar. The chief entrance to the city is called *Suryapol* (portal of the sun), chief apartment or hall of the palace was called *Surya Mahal* (hall of the sun) and to the *Surya Gokhra* (balcony where an imposing symbol of the sun was placed) the Maharanas paid their obeisance which formed a daily ritual performed before every meal.[5] These served as constant reminders of the Maharana's status as the sun's representative.

In addition to this, rituals, forms of worship and art forms were also devised that sought to reinforce the illustrious and divine descent. A popular mode by which the Maharana sought to consolidate his identity and distinctness as the supreme and divine authority among his people and nobility was through patronization of religious festivals organized by the state. Religion became a potent political instrument for perpetuation and enhancement of the ruler's legitimacy and status. *Dushehra* was the most prominent as a state festival in almost all Rajput states where rulers claimed descent from Lord Rama since the festival was celebrated as *Vijayadasmi* (victory festival) in commemoration of the victory of Lord Rama over Ravana – the demon king. It sought to refurbish their divine link with the deity. The Maharana worshipped the *khejri* tree on *Dushehra* since Lord Rama had performed the same ritual while leaving for a life in the forest. The Maharana even held his *durbar* in a canopy fixed on the platform near the tree, known as *Khejri ka Durrikhana*.[6]

Another festival celebrated with great splendour was *Gangaur*, celebrated in honour of *Gauri* – the Goddess of creation and abundance, consort of Lord Shiva, and the presiding deity of Mewar. The state sponsored spectacular celebrations on these two festivals. Processions were organized in which the Maharana and the nobles participated in full *lavazma* (royal paraphernalia) which added to the grandeur and glamour of the occasion. At the head of the dazzling cavalcade was the Maharana, resplendently dressed and surrounded by regalia, radiating divine power and behind him came the jagirdars in order of precedence. The royal retinue led by Maharana and followed by jagirdars symbolically represented his supreme position in the hierarchy of authority and power. Moreover, these festivals formed those rare occasions when people had the *darshan* (glimpse) of the *Durbar* (Maharana) who was not commonly accessible for public viewing. Hence, they eagerly looked forward to these splendid festivals and participated with great zest and enthusiasm. More significantly, by staging large-scale rites people were able to identify with the power and supremacy of the ruler and the jagirdars subservience to the central authority.

Apart from festivals, some interesting forms of folk art were also used for communicating to the rural masses the glory of the *Suryavanshis*. A significant mode of communicating the king's sacral antecedents was a wooden mobile temple known as *kavad*.[7] Kavadia Bhats (people of Bhat community) carried the *kavad* to far-off parts of the state. The main deity residing in these *kavads* was that of Lord Rama, his consort Sita and brother Laxman. The *kavad* has multiple doors folded together.

On each door, there are pictures that signify the important events of *Ramcharitmanas*. While in some *kavads*, the pictures on some of the doors may be derived from the life of other mythological heroes but the sanctum sanctorum of the *kavads* was invariably presided by Lord Rama. On the top of the *kavad* was the image of the *Suryavanshi* Maharana that demonstrated the ruler's origin from Lord Rama. People belonging to all castes assembled to hear the rendition of Rama's heroic and moral enterprise by the Bhats. It was a great art of storytelling which had very interesting prose narrative and a typical style mastered by the Bhats. This was an effective indigenous communication skill in oral tradition for disseminating the *kirti* (glory) of the *Suryavanshis* and the legitimacy of the Maharanas' authority. Another popular form of folk art was the *Rasdhari*. It was a form of dance drama based on the *Raslilas* of Brij that portrayed and dramatized the life of Shri Krishna.[8] *Rasdharis* were mobile theatre troupes that toured the villages but the *Rasdharis* of Mewar changed the theme and content to suit their local needs and adopted Lord Rama as their hero instead of Lord Krishna. Amongst the Rajput states, this peculiar form of dance drama was popular only in Mewar. Like *kavad*, their narrative style and visual presentation had mass appeal and were extremely popular in the villages.

Amongst other symbols popular in Mewar include the sword of Bappa Rawal. As the popular legend goes, the sword was given to him by Bhagwati Charbhuja and was said to be specially crafted by Vishwakarma. The Sisodiyas, as a veritable symbol of legitimacy, jealously treasured it.[9] Bappa Rawal, the founder of Guhila line, was himself embellished with symbols and legends that transformed him from a feudatory into a superhuman hero who not only became a symbol of the Guhilas but more than anything else he became a symbol of their long association with the defence of Chittor. The rulers and people of Mewar regarded the throne as a divine seat and, hence an object of veneration. Rana Sanga refused to sit on the throne after he lost an eye in the battle as he felt that one who occupies this sacred seat should be free from defects. This diffuse system of symbols and their transmission through ceaseless ritualization vitally linked the ruler to supernatural forces and were able to arouse popular emotions in support of their legitimacy.

The *raj chinhas*, which constituted insignia of royal power, were indispensable in a political system that depended on the unity of clan, hierarchical system and ranking. The ruler to distinguish himself from his kinsmen and assert his status and power to potential rivals embraced the traditional emblems associated with power and rule. The commonplace arsenal of these rulers comprised the *durbar*, *gaddi* or throne (symbolic of a higher seat), *chanwar* (flywhisks), *chhatri* (decorative umbrella), *kalangi* (a decorative piece of jewel that adorns the turban), the honorifics and the titles etc. The *garhi* (fortress) and horse had also emerged as status symbols for Rajput chieftains.

Durbar, court of the rulers, formed the centre-stage of their symbolic apparatus and main theatre where hierarchical relationships were symbolically and ritually defined and acted out. The word '*durbar*' is of Persian origin introduced in Indian political set-up by the Mughals. "It could be used to describe a ruler's court, and even the ruler himself, who might be referred to as *Durbar Saheb.*"[10] The ceremonials and grandeur of the *durbar* served as an open and visual confirmation of the primacy of the ruler and also an opportunity to define the hierarchy of the jagirdars. A prestigious ritual placement in formal *durbar* was pertinent to an individual's status and honour. In comparison to other states, the seating arrangement in Mewar *durbar* was symbolic of their parity with the Maharana. In *durbar,* they ranked above the crown prince, who occupied a lower/inferior seat, "a custom unprecedented in India" and granted in consequence of the stigma that came to be attached to the heir-apparent after he attended the Mughal emperor's court.[11]

Ceremonial protocol for each chief comprised of a well-choreographed and intricate process that had to be scrupulously observed by the Maharana. The Maharana honoured his chiefs by issuing royal insignia and marks of honour and through transactions of specified gifts which were considered symbols of honour on important occasions throughout the year, e.g., horses, *siropav* (dress of honour), *pag* (head dress), *langar* (wearing gold in the feet), jewels and the privilege of having meals with the Maharana. These symbols and ritual performances were in the sense 'barometers' or 'visual statement' of variable honour and status. The transgression or unauthorized appropriation of royal insignia by any chief invited punishment from the Maharana, e.g., Rawat Padam Singh of Salumber was fined Rs.1,100 because he had worn pearls in his *kalangi* (decoration adorning the *pag*) a royal symbol to which only the Maharana was entitled.[12] In fact, distribution and conferment of regalia itself became an arena of conflict and struggle amongst the jagirdars and also between the Maharanas and the jagirdars. Originally, the criteria for awarding royal insignia to the chiefs were their unusual valour in the battlefield and loyalty to the Maharana but later these privileges were largely hereditary and based on precedent.

Symbolic gestures, rituals and regal ensigns were also bestowed to extend legitimacy and express gratitude to groups other than the Rajputs for their past deeds and sacrifices for the state. Such groups included even the tribes like Bhils. At the level of actual participation in the affairs of governance, the Bhils were not so conspicuous but their enduring contribution in the emergence and survival of the state of Mewar was acknowledged by the key position accorded to them in the primary ritual of *rajyabhishek* (coronation ceremony) of the Maharana. The descendants of two Bhil aboriginals, who helped Bappa Rawal found the state of Mewar, played lead role in anointing of each successive ruler. After the application of *tika* (auspicious mark on the forehead) on the Maharana's forehead by slitting the thumb, the Bhils held him by the arm and made him sit on the throne.[13] Such rites administered by the Bhils ritually demonstrated the dependence of the Maharanas on the tribe who, through the performance of this ritual, conferred legitimacy on every new incumbent.

Significantly, certain historical developments have influenced the status of the jagirdars in the court hierarchy and their position *vis-à-vis* the ruler. Choonda's supreme sacrifice, when he renounced his throne in favour of his younger brother Mokal in fulfilment of a vow given to his father Maharana Lakha, was rewarded by his superior ritual placement that at times superseded even the Maharana. It became a well-known political tradition that *pat* (throne) belonged to the children of Mokal, whereas *thath*, i.e., power and prestige, were to be with Choonda's progeny. As a recompense for his renunciation, Choonda and his successors, represented by the house of Salumber, were conferred upon the premier's position in the councils of the kingdom and in all grants made to the vassals of the crown, his symbol, the lance, was superadded to the autograph of the prince. Similar distinctive symbols were bestowed on the Jhala chief Manah who had seized Maharana Pratap's royal vestments including the umbrella and the gold sun and bore the brunt of the attack himself on the battlefield of Haldighati. He saved his sovereign by making the supreme sacrifice of his own life. The descendants of Manah were honoured with the privilege of decorating their person with the exclusive insignia of the Maharana and have since enjoyed the right side of the Maharana in the *durbar*.[14]

Another symbolic dimension of public recognition about which the princes were deeply sensitive was the titles and the styles of address. The titular designations of the rulers were based on a variety of criteria. Some were hereditary, self-awarded by ancestors to bolster their prestige or at times bestowed by an external power, e.g., the Mughals and later on, the British. The Mewar potentates adorned themselves with numerous titles that not replenished their legitimacy within their dominion but also reinforced the dominance of their clan Sisodiya over other ruling clans in the native states of Rajputana. The title of '*Hindua Sooraj*' (Sun of the Hindus) was their most coveted honorific. It signified Mewar's place of honour at the head of Rajput clans not only due to their refusal to marry their daughters to the Mughal emperors and their struggle against the Muslim invaders but also as a mark of respect for the antiquity of their clan. This illustrious title inspired awe and respect for the Sisodiyas even amongst the British who were induced to give a superior rank and placement to the Maharana of Mewar. Due to their legendary association with Chittor and its chivalrous defense, the Mewar rulers were proud of their epithets like '*Chittora*' or Lord of Chittor, the ornament of the 36 royal races. They were not addressed by the commonly used prefix 'Maharaja'; instead they styled themselves as Maharanas. Within their domain, the Maharanas were, however, popularly addressed as '*Diwan*', i.e., representative of Lord Shiva – the presiding deity of Mewar.

While the Mewar potentates duly cherished their own dynastic and ancestral titles, they resisted the imposition of any external symbols and appellations that were bestowed upon by superior powers or foreign rulers whom they denounced as *Mlechchas* – the impure ones. The rulers of Jaipur took great pride in their title 'Sawai Maharaja' (denoting one and a quarter) – a title conferred on them by Emperor Aurangzeb. The Mewar rulers, however, considered it below their dignity to accept legitimizing symbols from external sources of authority. At a time when native rulers all over India sought to establish legitimacy through the meaningless *firmans* of the decaying Mughal empire, the state of Mewar abhorred and looked down upon such borrowed symbols of legitimacy.

The most enduring symbolism associated with he Sisodiyas pertains to their ideology of resistance which was rooted in the concepts of love for one's land (*dharti-prem*), sense of one's duty (*swadharma*), individual honour and self-esteem (*swabhiman*). To a large extent, it was the resistance of Mewar against the Muslim conquerors for preservation of prestige and honour that not only shaped the image of a Rajput as a chivalrous suicidal warrior but also defined the paradigm of honour commonly associated with the Rajputs. The annals of Mewar are studded with powerful and inspirational symbols in the form of heroes, heroines, monuments and even the battle-fields, which till date exercise a tremendous hold on the psyche of the Indians. For example, the embodiments of undaunted determination and fierce struggle for preservation of independence - Rana Sanga and Rana Pratap; of supreme sacrifice - Jaimal and Patta; of loyalty - Pannadhai and Chetak (Rana Pratap's horse); of *bhakti* and rebellion - Meerabai; *virangna* like Padmini, monuments like the fort of Chittor and Kirti Stambh and the arena of war - the Haldighati. These have emerged as metaphors for values of resistance, sacrifice and pride in one's independence through which generations of Indians have derived strength and inspiration for their struggles.

II

The establishment of British rule over Mewar produced significant changes in the political situation of this premier state of Rajputana. The British approach towards the domination of this illustrious state led to curtailment of the real and sovereign powers of the Maharanas while maintaining their public honour through symbols, rites and rituals within their possessions. The response of the Maharanas too was characterized by ambivalence, i.e., their desire for British protection was accompanied by assiduous attempts to preserve the visibility of their supreme status in their kingdom. The period of British paramountcy was, thus, marked by a subtle interplay between the virtual authority of the British and the projected authority of the Maharanas. In these changed political circumstances, the symbols and rituals acquired a renewed significance for both the British as well as the Maharana.

We find that scramble for appropriation of superior monarchical symbology assumed extravagant proportions after the Rajputana states entered into treaties with English East India Company, and later on directly with the Crown. A treaty of so-called friendship, alliance and unity was concluded between Mewar and East India Company in 1818 by which the British government engaged itself to protect the territories of Mewar and restore those which had been seized by others during the years of turmoil. The Maharana agreed to act in subordinate cooperation with the British government and acknowledge the latter's supremacy. Consequently, Maharana had to surrender his external independence and the right of negotiations. However, the internal sovereignty along with outward symbols of authority, as also their prerogative as the fountain of honour for their own subjects, was preserved. With the direct assumption of sovereignty by the Crown, after the revolt of 1857, was inaugurated an era of political emasculation of the native states. The Crown was proclaimed as the paramount power on whom the status, rank, dignities, privileges and jurisdiction of the rulers were dependent. The Indian states, irrespective of their treaty stipulations, were now unmistakably brought under the supreme authority of the British Crown. Disregarding the terms of the treaty, which promised to adhere strictly to a policy of non-intervention in internal affairs, the royal prerogative of the Queen and her representative, the Viceroy was expanded to include right to recognize succession, assume guardianship of minor princes, confer or withdraw titles, decorations and salutes, grant passports, sanction acceptance of foreign orders etc. This led to effective intervention in the internal sovereignty of the Maharanas with little or no resistance from the latter, thus enabling the British to assume control over court politics.[15]

Paradoxically, the Crown, however, sought to maintain, at least, theoretically and apparently, the undisputed sovereignty of the rulers in their respective kingdoms. To that extent, they were permitted to retain their outward symbols, rituals and rites for projection and legitimization of authority. At the same time, insignia and honorifics of the British Crown were held supreme and sacrosanct, which necessitated superimposition of the superior symbology of the Crown over the monarchical emblems of the Indian ruling families.

The Rajputana princes, who could no longer derive honour through success and sacrifice in the battlefield, sought to establish their relative importance and status through symbols conferred on them by the British. From the British point of view, symbols and rituals were crucial for enforcement and dispersal of the whole imperial idea since the subjugation of Rajputana states had been achieved "without a single shot being fired or the exhibition of a single British soldier in the country". Hence, their supremacy did not receive that visibility and public recognition which a conquering power acquires after armed warfare. Moreover, the vast distance between the actual seat of the paramount power, the English monarch and his subjects necessitated powerful symbols in order to build up in terms of prestige and grandeur, so that people of native states could consider British as the paramount power. Through ritualized attempts like elaborate rites of allegiance, conferment of titles and honours, creation of an order of precedence, prescription of gun salutes for each prince etc., the people were encouraged to identify themselves with the nebulous concept of the distant British empire.

Historically too, Great Britain has acquired a distinctive status as a nation that has conceded vital spaces to ceremonial pomp and elaborate ritualistic details in their political culture. Despite transition to a democratic polity, political culture of Britain has retained the institution of kingship replete with its symbols, rites and relics. The whole monarchical idea has remained a significant element in the popular psyche of British society. The democratic way of life has not weakened the respect and bonding of the Britons for the monarch. That's why, even in their relationship with the Indian native states, their excessive emphasis on symbols, both at the level of conferment on the native ruler and retention for the Crown, is quite noticeable.

The British penchant for a superior symbolic placement was reflected even in the vocabulary that was carefully drafted so as to project the pre-eminence of the Crown. The native rulers were designated as 'princes' or '*durbar*s' who sat on *gaddis* or *masnad* and not as 'kings' who occupied the thrones. Their administrative set-up was also called '*durbar*' and not 'government', which was looked upon as a superior and honourable nomenclature and was to be strictly used in reference to the British government. Any attempt to appropriate monarchical symbols like the arched crown or terms like king, kingdom, royal, throne, etc., was carefully discouraged. These terms and symbols signified the authority of the British Crown and were thus their exclusive privilege. The task of governing these delicate relations between the Crown and the native princes, which involved a minute scrutiny of the royal symbolism, rested with a small group of British officials who belonged to the Foreign and Political Department of the Government of India, and later on, came to be known as Indian Political Service (IPS).

The British defended their superior ritual positioning by maintaining that Indian rulers had never enjoyed the status of sovereign kings in the real sense of the term. "They were never at any time monarchs. What we call Indian Princes had never before the coming of the British been in the position of exercising any of the prerogatives of royalty. If there was anybody entitled to these prerogatives, it was the various dynasties at Delhi... At no time was the word *Badshah* which is the Persian equivalent of king, ever applied to Indian princes."[16] The assumption of the paramountcy was based on the theory that the rights and prerogatives of the Mughal emperor had accrued to the British as a result of the displacement of the former. The title of 'Kaiser-e-Hind' assumed by the Queen in 1876 immediately after the death of Bahadur Shah, the last Mughal emperor, was a symbolic expression of the same theory. The Crown was projected as the "apostolic or testamentary heir of the Mughal throne".[17]

The most prominent and conspicuous determinant of the ruler's status after the Queen's proclamation was the table of salutes which was drawn up in 1857 and published in 1867. As a result of the attempts by British Viceroys, beginning from Curzon, to bring the treaty states and petty principalities under one uniform category, the salute list, although arbitrary and meaningless, remained the only basis of distinction and classification among the native states. Additional grants, withdrawal and advancements subjected this salute table to minor modifications from time to time. A distinction was made between dynastic salutes, which in most cases remained constant, and personal salutes, which were an addition to dynastic salutes and a particular ruler was entitled to them for his own lifetime due to his individual accomplishments or special favour of the British. The unusually higher number of gun salutes for the Viceroy and the king of England, which were 31 and 101 respectively, signified the marked inferiority of the native states in relation to the paramount power. The state of Mewar fell in the second category and was entitled to 19 gun salutes. During Maharana Fateh Singh's and Maharana Sajjan Singh's reigns, these were further raised to 21 salutes.[18] The whole question of gun salutes assumed an inordinate importance among the rulers of Indian states who desired a ritual placement above their compeers and it became a prime arena of conflict and personal jealousies amongst themselves. The British succeeded in engrossing the native rulers in such petty trivialities when they should have paid attention to more serious matters of the diminishing virtual authority.

A further effort to impose the British Crown's distinctive symbology on the native princes was the introduction of coat of arms devised by an expert in British heraldry in 1877 on the occasion of the proclamation of Queen Victoria as empress of India. The 102 treaty states were provided with coat of arms complete with supporters of cows and elephants, scrolls often with English mottoes and crests that had helms but no crowns. Maharana Sajjan Singh, at the imperial *durbar* of 1877, received the coats of arms along with British flags.[19]

The bestowal of titular designations, honorifics and dignities formed yet another sphere where royal prerogative of the British Crown over the native princes was asserted. The Crown tried, as far as possible, to restrict the assumption of new and pompous titles by the rulers. A *khareeta* (document recognizing the ruler's accession) from the Viceroy enumerated the specific and precise style of address and honorifics of each ruler in full and any further addition to the same had to be approved by the Government of India.[20] From 1870 onwards, the title of 'His Highness' was restricted to important rulers and their consorts. The Maharana of Udaipur as the 'Sun of the Maharajas' was entitled to the prefix 'His Highness'. Although, within the kingdom, the title could be loosely used to address other members of the ruling family, the same could not be used officially outside the state for them. The government scrupulously avoided the use of word 'prince' for the heir apparent and the usual practice was to recognize the local little.[21] Accordingly, the Crown Prince in Mewar was styled as 'Maharaj Kumar' or 'Kuar'.

The grant of orders to Indian rulers from time to time was yet another means to re-assert the supremacy of the Crown. The two Indian 'orders' were the 'Most Eminent Order of the Indian Empire' and the 'Most Exalted Order of the Star of India'. The king was patron and the Viceroy, Grand Master of both. Each order was divided into three sections: Companions, Knight Commander and Knight Grand Commander. The first class princes were invariably granted the highest distinction of

Grand Commander. A smaller distinction conferred upon the native ruler implied punishment or insult due to serious displeasure of the Viceroy or AGG.[22]

The Maharana treated the conferment of such honours as a violation of their own supreme honour as the 'ornament of the 36 royal races'. When the British government decided to confer on Maharana Shambhu Singh the order of the 'Grand Commander of the Star of India' (GCSI) in 1871, the Maharana and the nobility of Mewar expressed their disapproval of the same on the plea that the title of the illustrious Sisodiya clan has been '*Hindua Sooraj*' and it was considered derogatory to accept the title of 'Star'. The Agent to the Governor General (AGG) did a great deal of convincing and was able to impress upon the Maharana that such titles were given only to the equals. Ultimately, the honour was conferred in a *durbar* held on December 6,1871. Similar reluctance was expressed by Maharana Sajjan Singh when he considered it against his dignity and status to accept the order of GCSI. He agreed to accept it on the condition that he should be formally invested with the insignia by the Governor General Lord Ripon himself in a *durbar* to be held in Chittor. In his speech, Ripon justified the grant of the order by stating that this particular decoration had been worn from time to time by the British monarchs themselves as a proud distinction. Maharana Fateh Singh was created Grand Commander of both the orders. Apart from the Maharana, members of the nobility were granted junior distinction of Companion of the Indian Empire (CIE).[23] Conferment of such distinctive decorations asserted the supremacy of the symbolism of the British Crown and, by implication, consolidated its entity as front-ranking and paramount political power.

The imperialist powers have universally sought to demonstrate their aura and authority through construction of magnificent and imposing monuments that served as formidable symbols and perpetual reminders of imperial authority. The construction of architectural memorabilia by colonial masters emerged as decisive imperial statements for bolstering and projecting the authority of a distant monarch. In Mewar too, various monuments were erected during the period of British paramountcy by the Maharanas, which were named after the English monarchs and the Viceroys to symbolize their supremacy over Mewar and register their presence. In commemoration of Queen Victoria's jubilee celebrations in 1877, Maharana Fateh Singh announced the construction of a museum which was named Victoria Hall Museum and in front of it a marble statue of Queen Victoria was installed which was unveiled by Prince Albert Victor, the heir apparent to the British Crown, on his visit to Udaipur, on February 8, 1890.[24] However, it needs to be emphasized that while the Maharana constructed these monuments, they continued to preserve and project their own aura by building monuments, lakes, institutions and gardens, which were named after their own person.

The British not only strove to establish the supremacy of the British Crown, but they also tried to erode the aura and authority of the Maharana in his kingdom by restricting certain practices which symbolized his revered position amongst his subjects. In Mewar, the most powerful oath of the Maharana's subjects was *gaddi ki aan* (oath in the name of the sovereign's throne) or *Maharana ki aan* (oath in the name of the sovereign's honour). Imposition of *gaddi ki aan* was a practice wherein a person was stopped from doing certain unpleasant activities. Whenever two individuals had a difference of opinion or a dispute, anyone so wishing could impose *durbar ki aan* or *gaddi ki aan* on the other. The latter was then constrained to act. This rite reveals the immense devotion that the Maharana was able to command from his subjects. The British abolished the practice of imposing *aan* in 1863 under the plea that it was misused by traders and wealthy classes to exploit and harass the poorer classes.[25] These attempts to deglamourize the Maharana's image met with widespread resentment. There were massive protests and general strike in the city of Udaipur against this order.

There were numerous occasions when the representatives of Maharana and the Crown struggled for supremacy on the ritual turf. On the occasion of the *durbar* to bestow the order of Grand Commander to Maharana Shambhu Singh in 1871 the AGG had asked the Maharana to make some changes in the usual arrangements of the *durbar*. It was suggested that the Maharana should not sit on the silver throne and also, no canopy should be raised over his seat. The AGG used to occupy a gilded chair placed lower than the Maharana's seat. The Maharana considered these changes as derogatory to his dignity and he informed the AGG that his chair would also be of silver and raised high to the level of the Maharana's throne. Hereafter, this spatial symbolism was adhered to in all official functions and ceremonies.[26] Maharanas, on more than one occasion, had to accept transgression of their previously held privileges in the protocol.

The most crucial intervention of the British, at the level of rituals, was the coveted role they appropriated for themselves in the *rajyabhishek* (coronation ceremony) of the Maharana. As far as interference in the internal affairs of native states was concerned, regulation of succession formed one of the earliest areas where British sought to assert their supremacy. They were not silent observers of the process of succession but played an important role in choosing the heir to the throne both in the actual process as well as at the ritual level. As a *samskara* or ritual, it was the most important of the *raj karma* (royal rituals) since it was "not simply a public act of affirmation or confirmation, a symbolic display of royal pomp and power. It was, to the contrary, held to be 'effective' or 'constitutive' ritual by which men were transformed into kings."[27] The *rajyabhishek* ceremony of a paramount or independent ruler excludes external sources of legitimization, since if the person became a king through a ritual performed by others, he was dependent on others for his power. Rites administered by the Brahmins and the Bhils had traditionally crowned the rulers of Mewar. However, due to clear demarcation of their respective spheres, and the Maharana's own supreme political status, these rituals did not reduce his status as the direct representative and appointee of the divine forces nor did it adversely affect his political supremacy. The British not only gave a theoretical confirmation to the succession of the new Maharana but also sought to demonstrate their supremacy visually and ritually through participation in the installation ceremony. In the *durbar*, which was held to commemorate Fateh Singh's succession, the AGG Col. Bradford, the Resident Col. Walter and some other Englishmen were also present. The *durbar* was addressed by AGG who on this occasion advised the Maharana on various political and administrative issues. The conclusion of the speech was followed by the presentation of the Governor General's *khareeta* to the Maharana, which the latter placed on his head as a mark of gratitude. The *khareeta* was read to the assembled *durbar* who paid homage to the document by standing in its honour. The AGG then presented the Maharana with a *khillat*, consisting of robes and jewels.[28] While the *khareeta* itself as a document was a symbol that confirmed the British paramountcy, the ritual drama associated with it seriously understated Maharana's independent status.

Imperial *durbars* emerged as the most visible symbolic device for a ritual display of the invincibility, glory and might of the British empire not only to the ruling classes but also to the wide cross-section of people ranging from powerful jagirdars to the ordinary peasants. The British used the word '*durbar*' for these imperial assemblages to justify their stand that they were simply emulating Indian tradition by holding such congregations. As one Political Officer Thomas Cotton summed up: "We innovated nothing. The institutions, titles, customs, ceremonials were all part and parcel of what the British had inherited from the former masters of India, the Emperors of Delhi."[29] The British, thus, strove to borrow legitimacy for their political domination by nurturing the old ritual forms and redirected them to new purposes. *Durbar* was now an occasion when the British monarch received obeisance and gratitude of the hundreds of the Indian Maharajas who owed the preservation of their monarchical emblems and antiquated rights to the might of the imperial army. These imperial *durbar*s were held on a vast and opulent scale and resembled a carefully arranged dramatic production heavily laden with well-choreographed symbols. The organization of this grand spectacle sparked off a desperate race among the Indian Maharajas, each one of whom wished to rank above his compeer. The rulers competed for a higher ritual placement particularly regarding precedence in the order of seating. It also brought out clearly the immense significance attached to symbols and their ritual accompaniments by both the British Raj and their subordinate partners – the native rulers.

The Maharanas of Udaipur, on account of their widely admired valiant saga of centuries of independence from the overlords of Delhi, had claimed precedence over all other chiefs of India on the occasion of such imperial assemblages. The British accepted their supreme position amongst the princes of Rajputana. In 1832, when Lord William Bentinck, as Governor General of India, visited Rajasthan, he stated: "His Highness, the Maharana of Udaipur being lineally descended from one of the greatest families in the country, his rank and dignity have been highest amongst the Rajas of Hindustan and will continue to do so."[30] When Shambhu Singh, Maharana of Udaipur, was invited to the Viceregal *durbar* of Rajputana princes held by Lord Mayo in Ajmer in 1870, it caused serious consternation among the Mewar nobility, who were appalled at the idea of their ruler paying homage in a public *durbar*, which they considered incompatible with their tradition and honour. Ironically, loss of virtual power was not so much resented as the affront caused to the projected honour of the Maharana. Protracted negotiations regarding the appropriate ceremonials for the Sisodiya rulers were conducted with the AGG and the Governor General but they could not obtain exemption from appearance of Maharana in the open *durbar*. The Maharana, however, received an assurance that he would take precedence over all other chiefs of Rajputana at the assemblage, that he would not be required to pay *nazar* (obeisance) and his reception would be marked by all the honours to which he is entitled due to his exalted rank.

The imperial *durbars* for native states all over India were held on numerous occasions after timely intervals to reiterate the imperial preeminence over native states. In 1875, an assemblage of the princes was convened at Bombay to give a royal reception to H.R.H. Prince of Wales Edward Albert. The subsequent imperial assemblages were held in 1877 to proclaim the assumption of the title of 'Empress of India' or '*Kaiser-e-Hind*' by Queen Victoria, in 1903 to commemorate the accession of Edward VII as the Emperor, and in 1911 to mark the visit of Emperor George V to India. The question of ritual precedence and order of seating of Udaipur Maharana was raised on all these occasions. Maharana Sajjan Singh, after initial reservations, attended the *durbar* along with nine of his nobles. In 1903, Maharana Fateh Singh, known for his bold demeanour and subtle maneuvers for resisting British interference in Mewar, raised the issue of placement in the *durbar* more vigorously and categorically. He left Udaipur for the pageantry at Delhi only after receiving an affirmation of highest precedence in the order of seating. However, the failure of the British to keep their promise prevented the Maharana from attending the *durbar* on the pretext of illness.[31] In 1911, Maharana Fateh Singh again demanded the same order of precedence that placed him above all his compeers. Although the Maharana did not confront the British directly over the issue, he used some pretext or the other to avoid offering obeisance in a *durbar* to an external authority.

These rites of allegiance evolved by the British, at times, through a re-adaptation of traditional rituals remained central to the assertion and sustenance of British paramountcy. In fact, the whole effort of replacing and replenishing the old symbology with a new and dominant one was pertinent to the creation of a distinctive imperial phenomenon. From the perspective of rulers the projection of authority through rites and rituals sought to compensate and conceal their loss of virtual authority.

III

Symbols and rituals form an important instrument of political struggle, wherein the contestants seek to overthrow the established source of authority. Leaders of revolution and resistance indulge in devising new symbols and reversal of established rituals to discredit and undermine the political system they seek to destabilize or alter. The Indian freedom struggle, under the charismatic leadership of Mahatma Gandhi, achieved the distinction of being the largest non-violent mass movement ever witnessed in history. Gandhi's success in mobilizing the masses against a colonial regime lay in his ability to choose the appropriate symbols based on truth, non-violence and concern for the masses. The symbolic gestures popularized by him had a dramatic effect and touched the emotional chord of the masses. He adopted indigenous symbols with which people were familiar, viz., *khadi* (coarse hand spun cloth), salt, loin cloth, simple living in *ashrams* and *yatras* (travels on foot). His decision to dress himself in the attire of ill clad farmer after his visit to Orissa sought to achieve his ritual identification with the distressed, lowly and the deprived. His insistence on wearing of *khadi* and the plying of *charkha* (spinning wheel) evolved as potent symbols of resistance against the British and also spread political consciousness among the people. Through this system of symbols and rituals he forged unity among scattered and diverse groups.

Dandi March was one brilliant example of the appropriate choice of symbols by Gandhi. On 12 March 1930, he set off on 26-day march to cover 240-mile pilgrimage to the town of Dandi where he picked up salt from the sea coast. Gandhi's own followers had looked down upon his selection of salt as a symbol of protest with skepticism and even the British government, not anticipating the powerful effect of the march on the masses, ridiculed the strategy. During this march, Gandhi employed various ritual precedents and made use of all the symbolism at his disposal. During his famous *yatra*, Gandhi captivated people's imagination with every step towards Dandi and when he symbolically picked up a few crystals of salt, he ritually attacked the salt tax and challenged Britain's right to rule.

Gandhi thus emerged as a master in designing symbols and devising rituals. The periods of struggle are those historical moments when the established symbol system is discredited to delegitimize the existing regime. The Gandhian symbology introduced a shift in the political values and created space for the rise of a new political structure based on democratic principles. It also marked a change in the ideas and paradigm that shaped legitimacy and honour in political culture. The introduction of new symbology, however, did not displace the distinctive classical symbols of the erstwhile kingdom of Mewar and the Sisodiya clan, which continued to be venerated during the period of Indian renaissance and the freedom struggle. These could be traced to the illustrious saga of Mewar pertaining to ideology of combat that reflected the notion of individual honour and valour.

The restatement of the sacrifices of Mewar by the creative writers in their novels and stories during the 19th century were crucial in restoring self-confidence among Indians suffering from political subjugation and loss of faith in their own abilities. During the struggle against British imperialism, the symbols of Mewar provided a statement of courage, independence and strength for Indians. The relics of Mewar in the form of monuments, rites and personalities are not only reminders of their chivalrous saga but their value as perennial sources of inspiration transcending boundaries of space and time has been remarkable. During the freedom struggle, new meanings were ascribed to these classical symbols for generation of the new political consciousness.

A potent symbol of Mewar's resistance to foreign domination was the fortress of Chittor, an extensive ruin on a mountain top, 72 miles east of Udaipur, which continues to be revered by all for the courage of many thousands of men and women who perished there in the three historic and tragic *sakas* or mass sacrifices and *jauhar* – first in 1303 and the last in 1567. The Maharanas themselves upheld Chittor as a relic of their glorious heritage. Even their subjects attached great significance to Chittor as a symbol of glory and pride of the state. The Gaduliya Luhars a tribal community wandering on the wheels – was so distressed at the loss of Chittor and the shifting of the capital to Udaipur that they vowed to return to Chittor only after it was retrieved from the conquerors. After independence, on April 6, 1955, a ceremonial welcome was organized for them by the efforts of the veteran leader of the state, Manikyalal Verma and Prime Minister Jawaharlal Nehru had presided over the function.[32] Till then, the Gaduliya Luhars wandered from one place to another and did not lead a settled existence. Similarly, the Kirti Stambh built by Rana Kumbha was a venerated monument. Freedom fighters from all over India flocked to these monuments to seek inspiration and strengthen their commitment to the freedom struggle. The historic battlefield of Haldighati surpasses all monumental relics as an emblem of chivalry and sacrifice. Haldighati, its imagery and symbolism have continued to inspire and attract generations of Indians. Tod conferred upon it the epithet of Thermopylae of Mewar. As the popular saying goes:

> "*Ka Ganga Jamuna Karo, Kahan Gomti Snan,*
> *In Dhara Teerath Karyo, Haldighati Maan.*"[33]

(Why talk of pilgrimages to rivers Ganga and Jamuna and of bathing in the holy waters of river Gomti? For a warrior, a battlefield like Haldighati is the best pilgrimage site, where a heroic death bestows honour and salvation.)

During the period of freedom struggle enormity of its impact even created fear amongst the Maharanas who made visits to Haldighati a punishable offence. The students who visited the historic battlefield were punished in schools.[34] Even in the post-independence period, rival political parties have competed with each other to appropriate the symbolism associated with Pratap and Haldighati. Various incidents of the battle have not only survived as metaphors of sacrifice but have defined a set of values for correct political behaviour even in democratic polity. Similarly, *ghas ki roti* (bread made of grass) which Pratap and his family had to supposedly consume during the adversities that followed the battle has come to epitomize suffering in political struggle. The present-day politicians often resort to the cliche *ghas ki roti* to demonstrate their deprivations in the course of the struggle.[35]

The popular devotional cry of the Mewaris 'Har Har Mahadev', which symbolized their faith in Eklingji, the presiding deity of Mewar, was adopted for mobilization during the freedom struggle. Pratap's camaraderie with the jagirdars reflected in their sharing of meals during the course of the legendary battle of Haldighati came to symbolize solidarity between the Maharana and the nobles. Later on, the Maharanas adopted this as a ritual when he sat down with his nobles for his meals as a mark of respect and gratitude for their contribution to the kingdom of Mewar. Sharing of food has emerged as a ritual signifying egalitarianism and solidarity in democratic political culture. Political actors in democratic polities often resort to sharing of meals with tribals and villagers. Through this rite of equalization, they seek to establish their close identification with the poor and the marginalized groups. The rich inspirational symbolism of the Sisodiya clan well-known in Indian history for their chivalry, sense of honour and fierce pride in one's independence and *dharma* was thus re-adapted to the new political needs and environment.

The foregoing discourse on the nature of symbols and rituals in the political culture of Mewar is a confirmation of their centrality in a variety of political contexts. The preoccupation with symbols that was manifest in the native states in the pre-colonial era literally became an obsession with the establishment of British paramountcy. Pertinently, this fetish for illustrious symbols amongst the native rulers was perhaps to cover a severe curtailment in their real authority and power. Erosion of power was sought to be concealed by the splendour and glamour of ostentatious rituals. This was, perhaps, a psychological effort through which they tried to get over their loss of power by exhibiting their power through symbols.

Interestingly, British response to appropriation of symbols was equally fastidious. Although, they conceded a major allowance to the native sovereigns when they were allowed to flaunt their arsenal of monarchical symbolism. Nevertheless, this was probably a ploy to keep them engrossed in trivialities of intricate protocol and detailed ceremonies, thereby diverting them from serious matters pertaining to actual exercise of authority. While the British permitted the rulers to maintain a show of public dignity within their kingdom through symbols and rituals, they sought to replenish the native state's symbolism with the superior royal symbols of the British monarch. This was done to assert, emphasize and project their own paramountcy over the native states. The excessive concern over the choice and imposition of symbols was not peripheral to the process of empire building but it formed a major element in the crystallization of the imperial idea and significance and superiority of the crown among the native rulers and their subjects.

Whatever may be the gap between exhibited and real authority, inherent and projected power of sovereignty, nevertheless it appears that symbols were of seminal significance in the polity that emerged during this period and also to the status and honour of both the political parties the British as well as the Maharanas.

A major shift in the nature of political symbolism took place with the onset of freedom struggle. The freedom struggle derived strength and momentum from a new set of symbols. The sharp contrast between the symbolism of these two political contexts suggests not only fresh political developments but also convey a totally new sense of honour and status in political culture. The Gandhian impact ushered in an era of democratic values and symbols which sought to bridge the gap between the classes and the masses. Significantly, even during the freedom struggle, along with a new set of symbols drawn by the national leadership particularly Gandhi, traditional symbols associated with Mewar remained significant within the state as well as at the national level. They were adapted and endowed with new meanings to suit the changed political context. After more than 50 years of independence, these symbols from Mewar have not only survived in collective memory but also they retain their original potency and far reaching impact. Contemporary decline in political culture has further reinforced the relevance of traditional symbols in individual as well as political life. In times, when values and ethics have given place to psychophancy, unethical submission for self-promotion, opportunism coupled with disregard for principles, it is not uncommon to refer to Rana Pratap, Meera, Panna and Padmini.

Notes

1. Ronald Iden, 'Ritual, Authority and Cyclic Time in Hindu Kingship', in J.R. Richards (ed.), *Kingship and Authority in South Asia*, p. 53.
2. Koertzer, *Ritual, Politics and Power*, p.25.
3. Wearing saffron robes (*kesariya bana*) is a symbol of warrior's preparedness for the battle and at times, implying fight till death.
4. G.N. Sharma, *Glories of Mewar*, pp.56-58 & 107.
5. A.C. Banerjee, *The Rajput States and British Paramountcy*, p. 43.
6. R.P. Kathuria, *Life in the Courts of Rajasthan*, pp.149-150.
7. Mahendra Bhanavat, *Kavad*, pp.7-12. Mahendra Bhanavat, 'Kavad: Ghar Ghar Banchti Ramayan Patri', in *Chaumasa Pustaka*, July 1991.
8. Mahendra Bhanavat, *Mewar Ke Rasdhari*, pp.1-14.

9. James Tod, *Annals and Antiquities of Rajasthan* (henceforth, *Annals*), p.184. The legendary sword is worshipped by the Sisodiya Maharanas during *Navratras.* Laxmi Kumari Chundavat, *Sanskritik Rajasthan*, p. 34.
10. Charles Allen & Sharda Dwivedi, *Lives of the Indian Princes*, p. 170.
11. Tej Kumar Mathur, *Feudal Polity in Mewar*, p. 217.
12. Kanhaiyalal Tank 'Mewar Mein Samantvadi Vyavastha', unpublished M.A. dissertation, Mohanlal Sukhadia University, Udaipur. The royal insignia and protocol for every jagirdar was specified in a document called *Rah Marjad.*
13. R.P. Kathuria, *op.cit.*, p. 55. This custom was probably abolished after Maharana Jagat Singh II (1734-1751). There is no reference to the practice in the records of the coronation of Maharana Hammir Singh II (1773 AD), *ibid.*, p.55. While according to G.H. Ojha, the practice does not find mention after Maharana Amar Singh (II)'s reign (1698-1710 AD), G.H. Ojha, *Udaipur Rajya Ka Itihas,* Vol. II, pp. 114.
14. Tod has observed that descendents of Manah retained Sadri and all the privileges and marks of honour obtained on this occasion. Their kettledrum beat upto the gates of the Maharana's palace, an unusual honour allowed to none else and they were addressed by the title of *Raj* or royal, *Annals,* p. 270.
15. A well-known instance of British intervention in internal affairs was the manner in which the assertive, at times, defiant and fiercely independent minded Maharana Fateh Singh (1884-1930) was forced to delegate his ruling powers to Maharaj Kumar which in fact, amounted to his virtual deposition. For details refer, D.L. Paliwal, *Mewar and the British 1857-1921 AD*, pp.180-265, and K.M. Pannikar, *Indian States and the Government of India,* pp. 69-70.
16. Charles Allen & Sharda Dwivedi, *op.cit.*, p. 68.
17. Pannikar, *op.cit.*, p.40.
18. *Ibid.*, p. 40; D.L. Paliwal, *op.cit.*, pp. 14, 133 & 206.
19. Charles Allen & Sharda Dwivedi, *op.cit.*, p.69.
20. K.M. Pannikar, *op.cit.*, p. 72.
21. K.R.N. Swamy, *Mughals, Maharajas and the Mahatma*, p. 75.
22. K.M. Pannikar, *op.cit.*, p. 73.
23. The other titles which the British conferred upon the nobility and senior officials of the *Durbar* were Rai and Rai Bahadur. K.M. Pannikar, *op.cit.*, p.75; D.L. Paliwal *op.cit.*, pp.121, 177, 168.
24. Similarly, to honour the first visit of a English Prince, the Duke of Cannought to Udaipur in 1889, the Maharana constructed a dam named Cannought dam on the Dewali Lake outside Udaipur. Similarly in 1909, Minto Hall was constructed in the Kunwarpada Palace to commemorate Lord Minto's visit to Udaipur. D.L. Paliwal, *op.cit.*, pp.183-184.

25. Prakash Vyas, *Adhunik Mewar Ka Itihas*, pp.297-298.
26. D.L. Paliwal, *op.cit.*, p. 122.
27. Ronald Iden, 'Ritual, Authority and Cyclic Time in Hindu Kingship' in J.R. Richards (ed.), *Kingship and Authority in South Asia*, p.54.
28. D.L. Paliwal, *op.cit.*, pp. 181-182. For a comprehensive understanding of the custom of *khillat* and its importance, refer Stewart Gordon (ed.), *Robes of Honour: Khil'at in Pre-Colonial and Colonial India*.
29. Charles Allen & Sharda Dwivedi, *op.cit.*, p.170.
30. K.R.N. Swamy, *op. cit.*, pp.133, 155 & 108-110.
31. It is widely believed that Maharana Fateh Singh was dissuaded from attending the *durbar* in 1903 by the stinging verses of a poem "Chetavani ra Chungtia" composed by Barhat Kesari Singh. The poem was presented to him first as he was preparing to leave for the Imperial Assemblage. The composition accused him of deviating from the heroic traditions of his dynasty.
32. For details regarding the rehabilitation of the Gaduliya Luhars, refer, Narendra Sharma 'Kusum', *Manikyalal Verma*.
33. Rajendra Joshi, 'Charans: The Contextual Dynamics of Caste in the Rajput System', in N.K.Singhi & Rajendra Joshi, *Religion, Ritual and Royalty*, p.307.
34. Interview with Rajendra Singh Chaudhary, a prominent leader of the freedom struggle in Mewar.
35. The Government of Rajasthan had organized a commemorative function in Haldighati in 1997 projecting the erstwhile battlefield as a symbol of suffering and patriotism. Recently, in 2003, the Indian Army officials' function was organized at Haldighati by M.M.C.F. (Maharana Mewar Charitable Foundation).

II

Honour and Socialization

5

Honour and Gender Construction

The idea that honour of men lies in their women and can be violated by their conduct is widespread in human societies. In Indian society this mindset evolved over a period of centuries and resulted in a differential paradigm of honour for women. The free moving damsels of the Vedic period (2500 BC to 1000 BC) were transformed into restrained and submissive women requiring control and protection, around 2nd century AD, when *Smriti* writers, especially Manu, reinforced the basic theme of women being unfit for independence.[1] With the crystallization of these ideas, a distinctive notion of honour for women took shape in which women's bodies became central to the dynamics of personal honour and dishonour. More significantly, female sexuality transcended individual connotations and hitherto, became pertinent to the preservation of the ritual status and honour of the entire group to which she belonged – family, caste clan, and community. Multifarious social practices and customs, especially those associated with marriage, derive their justification from this concern with female purity.

The differential paradigm of honour resulted in developing control mechanisms and processes of socialization severely restricting women's mobility and work sphere. It imparted a special character to the growing up of girls and their sexuality had to be protected and contained at all times. This is sought to be achieved through the formulation of stringent ethical standards, behavioural pattern and code of conduct that governed them in all life stages. Non-conformity or deviation from the prescribed norms invited harsh sanctions from the groups such as ex-communication, social ostracization, and at times, even death. However, the particular code that governs women's status and honour is not uniform and one can discern variations across caste hierarchy and regional differences. Similarly, there are extraordinary situations, particularly, periods of political strife and military warfare and challenge from alien cultures and religions when the mechanisms to contain and protect female chastity and honour acquire urgency. Indian history offers numerous examples when female virtue and roles acquired a special character and became more inextricably linked with the group's honour.

The various Rajput clans dominated the polity of the erstwhile Rajputana states from the 7th century onwards and this period represents an interlude in Indian history that evolved beliefs and practices that endowed a distinctive character to female honour. The Rajputs were essentially a martial race involved in incessant warfare amongst themselves or with foreign invaders – the Turks, the Mughals, and later on, the Marathas. In such a warrior culture, characterized by volatile and uncertain political conditions, not only men, but women were also obligated to inculcate the virtues of fortitude, bravery, discipline and sacrifice. In fact, women played an important role as wives and mothers of warriors in sustaining and preserving the chivalric ethos of the Rajput polity. To some extent, the system of values cherished by the Rajputs led to their sensitive attitudes towards women. A major component in the traditional Rajput ethic of protection is the responsibility for guarding the safety and virtue of women. According to a popular saying associated with the Rajputs,

> "*Ghar jatan dharm palatan, tiriya padta tav,*
> *Yeh tinuhi din maranra, kaha rank kaha rao.*"[2]

(When the home and hearth is in danger, when religion is at stake, when women folk is in distress, these are three days for all to die, whether pauper or a prince.)

Protection of women also envisaged their conformity to a strict moral code so that they did not indulge in indecent behaviour that would be injurious to the clan. This perception and image of women is inadequate and overlooks the fact that women had a definite role to play in the glory that history has associated with Rajputs. Socialization process, coupled with cultural practices, art and literature, reveals an elaborate and distinctive process for construction of women's honour. In folklore and Charan literature, women's ornaments and attire were linked to the spirit of chivalry and sacrifice that pervaded the contemporary political culture. In Rajputana states, the brides wore *saris* or skirts of red or saffron colour, which signified a readiness to sacrifice. Similarly, ivory bangles worn by Rajput women meant that their husbands were so brave that they could kill an elephant.[3] There are numerous tales that depict a woman's contempt and intolerance for a coward husband and son. A son who was an unwilling warrior brought shame to his mother's milk (*doodh lajana)* and a coward husband brought dishonour to his wife's bangles (*choori lajana).* In the Rajput ethos, women, on the one hand, had to conform to the predominant ideal of *pativrata* (devoted wife) which is inspired by the desire to remain a *sada suhagan* (eternally married), on the other hand, they had to contend with situations, which saw a reversal of the *pativrata* paradigm, i.e., they had to inspire their husbands for preservation of freedom and attain *vir-gati* (warrior's death).

Among the Rajputana states, the erstwhile state of Mewar, ruled by the illustrious Sisodiya clan, came to be associated with a distinctive sense of honour derived from its undespoilt history due to its relentless struggle against the Mughals for preservation of *dharma* and independence. In addition to heroism, valour and imprudence, an integral aspect of their ethic of honour was the manner in which purity and honour of the clan was intimately linked with women's sexuality. The traditional restrictions on women and the various socio-religious practices that sought to enhance and preserve women's honour and by extension, that of the state, were much more pervasive in Mewar. The erstwhile scions of the Sisodiya clan viewed the customs like hypergamous marriages, *purdah*, *sati* and *jauhar* as integral practices of their identity and any erosion of these conservative traditions was viewed as derogatory to the specific cultural ethos of the state. The Sisodiyas, unlike other Rajput states, refused to give their daughters in marriage to the Mughals. Similarly, they refused to cooperate with the reform endeavours of the British authorities and Mewar was the last Rajputana state to prohibit *sati*. While it is true that Mewar had resisted any kind of relaxation as far as practices of *sati* and *purdah* were concerned, but the rulers of the erstwhile state have been incorrectly projected as rigid and retrogressive in every sphere. Pertinently, they had adopted a progressive stance on other social issues affecting women. Maharana Jawan Singh had issued a proclamation prohibiting the practice of infanticide among the Meenas of Jahajpur as early as 1831. On 27 December 1843, Maharana had agreed to prohibit infanticide throughout Mewar and in 1844 issued an order that "whoever commits female infanticide will be hanged by the neck for the offence". The Maharanas also strove to restrict the *tyag* (alms or grants given to the Charans or Bhats on the occasion of marriage and other festive occasions) as it was inextricably linked to the practice of female infanticide. Such prohibitory orders were issued in quick succession, which is a further indication of the rulers' earnestness towards removal of these evils. Above all, it was Maharana Sajjan Singh of Mewar who initiated the formation of Desh Hiteshini Sabha in 1877 which aimed at regulation of marriage expenses, restriction on polygamy and unequal marriages as well as *Tyag*.

The Sabha formed the earliest organizational endeavour to consciously involve the rulers of the Rajputana states in the process of social reform. Such initiatives need to be commended, as contrary to popular perceptions, these were undertaken without the persuasive tactics or intervention of the British officials. Interestingly, it was a decade later when the more well-known reform organization, Walterkrit Rajputra Hitkarini Sabha, was formed at the initiative of the British with more or less similar objectives.[4]

The fiercely protective attitude of the Mewar rulers towards women was also necessitated by the fact that, unlike other Rajput states, they were involved in longer periods of continuous warfare. The concept of honour as it evolved in Rajputana states and particularly in Mewar, imparted a special character to the lives of women. Their upbringing, marriage, education, day-to-day life and social endeavours digressed from the normative pattern of women's lives. A brief perusal of women's lives and activities illuminate the significant and conspicuous manner in which they enriched the Rajput value system.

I

The socialization of young men and women, especially in families of ruling class and the *thikanas,* was meticulously worked out. Interestingly, women were subjected to a dual process of socialization. On the one hand, they had to be instilled with a discipline and skill required to meet a military exigency, on the other, their socialization conformed to the normative pattern, wherein training in domestic female roles and household activities was deemed imperative. Preparation of a Rajput girl for the exigencies of battle formed an intrinsic part of her education which, in most cases, comprised of informal training within the *zenana*. The ethos of sacrifice and valour was inculcated amongst girls through several methods. They were endowed with pride in the legacy and exploits of their clan through the numerous tales that were narrated to them by the Charans and Bhats of their particular families. Through their effective narration and musical rendering, they inculcated amongst young girls a strong craving for courageous husbands and valorous sons who attain either victory or *vir-gati* (death of a warrior). Women figure prominently in Charan poetry as heroic individuals, inspirational figures for men and upholders of Rajput *kulreeti* (clan tradition). In one of the Charan verses a Rajput woman enumerated the attributes of a true Rajput in the following words: "Oh, friend, by taking a royal umbrella and *chanvar* (whisk made out of tail of yak,) one cannot be called a Rajput, nor by inheriting the title of Rajput. Only he is a true Rajput who sacrifices himself for the benefit of the country." Similarly, on seeing her husband acting cowardly, she says: "My dear, even though you desire to show Kshatriya values, yet you are not able to escape emotional involvement. Till the time your head is placed on your body, till then think that *Kshtriatva* is beyond you." Similar sentiments are expressed in Meghraj Mukul's famous composition, *Senani*.[5]

Rajput women imbibed ideas of valour, bravery and heroism through such compositions. In addition, there were *vartakars* (storytellers) and *baatposhis* (narrators) in the *thikanas* as well as in the city of Udaipur who specialized in highly evocative and fascinating rendition of stories of the exploits and battles in which their ancestors had participated. According to an erstwhile Yuvraj of Dungarpur, "these stories were much more than bedtime stories or history lessons. They enshrined examples of princely virtue and good behaviour which princes and princesses were expected to follow, so that you didn't forget who you were, what your family tree was, that you were born in Bhagwan Ramchandra's family and that you were never to put a blot on the name and tradition of your family."[6] This kind of indoctrination imbued women with a strong sense of superiority of the clan to which they belonged. There are numerous examples when a 'Rajputani' would not sit at ease until any offence to her clan or relatives on her father's side was avenged. The Rajput women were fluent with their natal genealogies that they had to recite on arrival as young brides in their marital home.

Apart from this oral indoctrination, women received training in the use of arms, especially guns and swords. In times, when men had to respond to the call of the battlefield, it was imperative to impart military training to women for self-defence, in case it was required during exigencies. At times when men used to be away, there were occasions when *Ranwas* was attacked. In such an eventuality, women had to use arms for self-defence. It is a lesser-known fact that Padmini had abandoned the confines of the *zenana* to lead her husband's army when Alauddin Khilji had taken him as a hostage and had demanded Padmini as ransom. Padmini masterminded a strategy to liberate her husband. She ostensibly agreed to his terms but demanded that she should be allowed to bring along her attendants and belongings. Queen, on the pretext of carrying her maids hid soldiers in curtained palanquins who, in a surprise attack, sprang upon Muslim soldiers. In the confusion that followed, Padmini and her husband Rana Ratan Singh fled to safety. It was only during a subsequent confrontation between the Maharana and the Khilji Sultan, when defeat became imminent, that Padmini led large number of women who committed *jauhar* along with her. These heroic actions not only project her as a trained warrior but also established her as a master strategist. There are numerous such examples when women faced the ravages of the battle thereby confirming the fact that military training formed an integral part of their socialization process as well as their normative code of behaviour. This tradition of military training to daughters survived in some of the *thikanas* of Mewar until the 20th century although the expectation that women will have to participate in a battle became minimal. The daughters had to make weekly visits to the *silahkhana* (weaponry), in order to reinforce their familiarity with the arms and ammunitions. In fact, shooting and fencing formed a part of the leisure activities of the daughters of elite families. The women of the erstwhile ruling Rajput class in Mewar at times indulged in hunting. As young girls, they were allowed to join hunting expeditions in which they enthusiastically participated. Lakshmi Kumari Choondavat, daughter of the erstwhile jagirdar of the illustrious Choondavat clan in Devgarh, recalled how as a young girl she was allowed to kill pigs or leopards during hunting expeditions. Horse riding was also taught to the girls, as a part of their military training and, later on, as a time-honoured tradition. *Ustaads* (trainers) were appointed for each child to teach them horse riding.[7] This pattern of socialization was, however, largely confined to the daughters of the upper strata of society, i.e., those who belonged to the ruling family and the nobility. In addition to this, conventional feminine socialization pattern was a part of their training.

In the erstwhile states of Rajputana, the daughters were specially moulded to a lifestyle of *zenana*. *Purdah* was perceived by Rajput women as an intrinsic and integral part of their lives, and a predominant means by which their *sat* (purity, goodness, truth, character) is generated and preserved. It helped in the preservation of their 'inherent modesty'. In fact, it "functioned as the pre-eminent symbol of the their ethos and identity."[8] Moreover, it was considered extremely important that from an early age girls were carefully nurtured into the discipline that strict *purdah* required since "no one who enjoyed unlimited freedom even as a child could later accept confinement."[9] *Purdah* and the etiquette that went with it was much more rigid in Mewar and its demand of conformity much more exacting. The state even prescribed the clothes to be worn by women of different social strata. Women of the upper and middle classes could not go without covering themselves with a large sheet of cloth, which was carried by maid servants. While in other Rajputana states the restrictions on women's mobility and *purdah* became considerably relaxed towards the end of the British period, in Mewar women connected directly or indirectly with the ruling house or governing classes were expected to conform to the practice with the same rigour.

Although, it is true that there were some *thikanas* like Devgarh, Shahpura and Banera, which under the influence of Arya Samaj did not adhere to this strict interpretation of *purdah*. These *thikanas* were sarcastically referred to as spoilt or deviant *thikanas*. The women of the families of these *thikanas* could freely roam on the terrace of the palaces whereas in the royal palaces in Udaipur, there were high walls on the terrace that blocked the view from within and outside. In Devgarh, the young girls had easy access to various parts of the palace and could play around freely.[10]

Dress norms for women of the lower and tribal classes were different. They wore shorter *lehangas* (skirts) and *sarees* or *lugda* (a long piece of cloth worn over the blouse and *lehangas*). Apart from state regulations, these restrictions and conventions regarding dress were also a part of caste rules. While severely restricting women's choices regarding attire, these entrenched conventions also had an implied sense of honour or lack of honour associated with them. The length of dress worn by women was a significant status parameter and indicated the extent of freedom and mobility allowed. The longer skirts were indicative of an affluent and elite lifestyle and were worn by women of the upper classes. Moreover, longer dresses also inhibited mobility and perhaps, symbolized severe restrictions on their access to outside world. Conversely, shorter skirts worn by tribal and peasant women allowed free movement which were perhaps necessitated by their rigorous life in the farms and forests but they also signify the greater sense of liberty allowed to them. Similarly, women of the upper classes could not wear shoes in the presence of elders and men, as it meant disrespect towards them. Women of lower classes could not put on shoes in the *thikanas* and *jagirs* as a mark of respect to the governing classes.[11] The intricate prescription of dress norms was a part of an elaborate system of control mechanism which restricted women's lives and at the same time it shows caste based compartmentalization in cultural construction of gender.

II

Marriage constitutes one of the most significant events in a girl's life as it not only marks her departure from her natal to the conjugal home but also involves a total transformation in her lifestyle. In a caste society, marriage norms were governed by endogamy, which ensured that marriage took place within a *jati* or *jati* cluster leading to highly restricted choices for girls. The ruling elite amongst Rajputs conformed to the dual restrictions of caste endogamy and clan exogamy. While the first obligated them to marry within their caste group, the latter precluded them from taking wives from within the clan. Conforming to this normative pattern, broadly two types of marriages took place amongst the Rajputs: hypergamous marriages, wherein daughters were married into a superior family or clan; and the second type were equal status marriages variously called exchange or *atta-satta* form of marriages, which took place in families in which daughters could be given and from whom wives could be taken. Such exchange marriages were however not very frequent.[12] Within these broad restrictions, the Rajputs evolved a clearly defined and stratified system that resulted in hierarchical categorization of states in the context of marriages. In the traditional political and kinship system of the Rajputs, the clans were clearly ranked. One of the criteria that underscored a particular clan's superiority over the other was that a higher clan may accept girl from the lower clan but it could not give a girl in marriage to the lower clan. The rulers of Jaipur, Udaipur, Jodhpur, Bundi, Kota and Bikaner were of the same status and always gave their daughters to each other. Some Rajput families evolved special relationship with each other that were further strengthened by marriages. The rulers of Jaipur had a long-standing commitment to the state of Jodhpur, whereby the former accepted daughters from the Rathore clan. The last ruling Maharaja of Jaipur, Sawai Man Singh was married off as a boy of 12 to a Jodhpur princess considerably older than he was and, nine years later accepted her niece as his second wife.[13] Thus, Rajput system of marriages, more or less, operated within the restrictions that were applicable to the caste-bound society of the Hindus. In such a system, where social and ritual statuses of the group were the motivating factors in the settlement of marriages, individual choices and personal qualities of men or women had little space.

Amongst the royal elite of the Rajputana states, comprising the erstwhile rulers and the nobility, the system of marriages was much harsher on women due to a variety of reasons. Among the ruling classes, the institution of marriage was not limited to the social realm. In fact, it transcended the specific socio-religious purpose and was used as a political device for preservation, consolidation and expansion of authority. Marriage alliances had an important function in providing trusted allied, mobilization of military assistance and forging of political links and for ensuring peaceful relations. Qanungo has noted, "In medieval Rajput society, no money compensation could atone for bloodshed; only *dharti* and *dulhan* (territory and bride) from the guilty clan were acceptable as peace offering."[14] According to the scion of an erstwhile royal family, "society did not consist of individuals but of houses and it was important for houses to maintain alliances. This applied ten-fold among the royal houses, where a matrimonial alliance was the next best thing to a military alliance."[15] In such a system, where political considerations remained supreme, women were reduced to objects of transaction, who could be given or taken for buying peace, raising status and enhancing the honour of a particular clan.

Apart from clan exogamy and caste endogamy, the ruling families had evolved certain norms for safeguarding their honour and status within the clan hierarchy that further restricted the matrimonial choices. The daughters of the royal families had to be married to either a ruler or an heir apparent but the number of rulers remained constant and polygamous marriages provided a solution to this dilemma. Each ruler or a *yuvraj* contracted a series of matrimonial alliances with the daughters of the ruling clans of Rajputana. Life in a polygamous household, that too, within the confines of the *zenana*, with no legitimate or institutionalized position in the political set-up, could not be termed as a very congenial state of affairs for women. Even within the *zenana*, their hierarchy and status were determined in accordance with the ranking of their natal clan among the Rajputana states. Although a Rajput girl was socialized right from her childhood for a married life in a polygamous *zenana*, yet it was not easy to accept the distressing situation, especially when a ruler was fond of a particular wife whom he considered his favourite.

Maharana Hammir used matrimonial alliance to regain his territory. In the 14th century, when Alauddin Khilji defeated the Maharana, he handed over Chittor to Maldev Songara. Rao Maldev found it difficult to retain Chittor and returned to his ancestral *jagir* at Jalore. He decided to conclude peace with Maharana Hammir Singh by giving his daughter in marriage to him and in turn, the Maharana regained eight hilly areas of his lost territories in dowry. Even though it was later known that Maharani Songari had been a child widow and was earlier married to the Bhati ruler of Jaisalmer, which was indeed very humiliating, the Maharana accepted her since she gave him political and military clues to regain the fort of Chittor.[16]

Similarly, a vast difference between the ages of the individual partners was overlooked as far as it assisted in the furtherance and consolidation of political status. Maharani Hansa Bai, princess of the Rathore clan of Jodhpur, was married to Maharana Lakha, the aging ruler of Mewar at a relatively young age on the condition that son born to her would ascend the throne. It was fait accompli that Hansa Bai was widowed at a very early age, but, alas, such tragedies in the lives of women were considered secondary to political gains and status. Not only did Hansa Bai acquire the coveted political status of *Rajmata* (the ruler's mother) which otherwise could not have been possible since she was the youngest wife of the

Maharana, but even the Rathores gained tremendous political clout in the court of Mewar.[17]

The ruling clans of Rajputana had extremely sensitive attitudes towards matrimonial alliances that involved serious issues of honour, dishonour and shame. Among the Rajputs, a girl once betrothed to a member of any family was called the *mang* (fiancée) of that particular prince. If the *mang* of any prince was then betrothed or married in some other ruling family due to certain untoward development or mishap, it was considered derogatory to the honour of that clan. Even, until the 19th century, such issues could easily offend the sensibilities of the rulers. The famous Krishna Kumari episode gives an insight into the tragic and helpless predicament of Rajput women in such situations. Krishna Kumari was the daughter of Maharana Bhim Singh of Mewar who was betrothed to Maharaja Bhim Singh of Jodhpur. Nevertheless, he died before the marriage took place. Her father then wanted to get her married to Mahraja Jagat Singh of Jaipur. However, the events took a tortuous turn when Maharaja Man Singh who succeeded Bhim Singh as ruler of Jodhpur staked his own matrimonial claims over Krishna Kumari, as she was the *mang* of member of his family. Her proposed marriage with the scion of the Jaipur state was considered a deep offence to the honour of Rathores of Jodhpur. Daulat Rao Scindia, the Maratha chieftain, upheld the claims of Marwar. Meanwhile, Man Singh collected 60,000 soldiers near Merta and threatened Maharana Bhim Singh with dire consequences if he did not recall his emissaries from Jaipur who had gone there to perform the betrothal ceremony. Daulat Rao Scindia also attacked Udaipur. Krishna Kumari became a cause of disagreement among the houses of Jaipur, Jodhpur and Mewar. To avoid calamities, Krishna Kumari was administered poison on 21 July, 1810.[18] This explains how Rajput women were sometimes forced to end their lives as an act of political self-sacrifice at the altar of clan honour.

The ruler's desire to derive political gains from matrimonial alliances was so compelling that it even led them to violate the norms of caste endogamy and clan exogamy that governed the Rajput system of marriages. One of the most blatant disregard for traditional norms took place in the 16th century when Mughal emperor Akbar concluded treaties and established matrimonial alliances with Rajput rulers. Raja Bharmal of the Kachchawa clan of Amber (later the state of Jaipur) has been recorded as one of the earliest Rajput rulers to make matrimonial alliances with the newly emergent Mughal dynasty in 1562. He was followed by the Rathores of Jodhpur under Udai Singh (1581) who followed the 'politically wise but socially condemned' precedent laid down by their Kachchawa rivals. Bikaner under Kalyan Singh (1541-71) and Jaisalmer also followed the 'politically correct' policy of marrying their daughters to the Mughal rulers and princes.[19] This extensive network of marriage alliances with the Rajput rulers and jagirdars formed the important plank of Akbar's Rajput policy. These politically inspired marriages were motivated by the primary objective of securing political ascendancy.

Running paradoxical to the policy of collaboration with the Mughal emperor was the opposing trend symbolized by the rulers of Mewar. They persisted in following a policy of armed resistance to the expansionist designs of the Mughals and outrightly rejected the marriage policy of Akbar in Rajputana. Despite numerous adversities, leading to loss of power and territory, the Mewar Maharanas could not reconcile themselves to the 'dishonourable' alternative of sending their daughters to the harem of the Mughal emperor.

Without delving into the political significance of the Mughal-Rajput marriages and the way they impinged upon or enhanced the honour of the various clans of Rajputana, one needs to look at the way these opposing perspectives impacted the lives of women. Women were, perhaps, the ultimate sufferers in a political culture where overarching political ambitions and compulsions transformed them into objects of transaction. Although it is true that Akbar was endowed with a liberal outlook and sought to promote a joint Islamic-Hindu culture. In keeping with this spirit, the marriages with Rajput princesses were celebrated with a mixture of Muslim and Hindu ceremonies. The Hindu wives and their entourage were allowed to practise their own customs and religious observances. The Rajput queens had their own temples in the *zenana*. However, the space conceded to these women should not detract observers from the distressing moments in their lives, when they were placed in an environment which was totally alien to their own cultural milieu.

For the ruling house of Mewar, honour of the Sisodiya clan was the paramount consideration. They not only desisted from giving away their daughters to the Mughals but also decided against marrying them to rulers and princes of other premier Rajputana states who had given their daughters in marriages to Mughal emperors. In contravention of the established norm of hypergamy, the Maharanas had been compelled to marry their daughters to the subordinate chiefs. For the Sisodiya princesses, who had imbibed the notion of supremacy and honour of the clan through meticulous indoctrination since their childhood, it was particularly difficult to accept a subordinate position in a family which occupied a lower status than their own clan. For instance, when Maharana of Mewar married his daughter to the chief of Sadri, it led to marital maladjustment. The Sisodani wife of Sadri chief could not reconcile herself to a situation where she had to receive orders from her husband. It led to serious differences between the couple that could be resolved only after Maharana's intervention.[20]

In a system, where military and political considerations dictated the matrimonial relations, there was little scope for women's own choices. However, there have been extraordinary women who refused to succumb to the demands of the political system and, instead, demonstrated exceptional courage and determination in deciding upon matrimonial alternatives that they found more honourable and conducive to their personal happiness. One of the better known instances is the marriage of Princess Charumati of Roopnagar with Maharana Raj Singh-I. After the death of Roop Singh, his son became the ruler of Kishangarh, at the young age of five. His sister Charumati, who had acquired a reputation for her beauty caught Aurangzeb's attention who expressed his desire to marry her. The princess, therefore, herself wrote a letter to Maharaja Raj Singh of Mewar, "Aurangzeb has expressed a desire to marry me and I do not want to marry a Muslim. In my heart, I have married you, therefore if you do not marry me, I will kill myself."[21] Maharana Raj Singh, who had consciously cultivated the image of the defender of Hindu *dharma* and upholder of the Rajput system of values fulfilled her wish even though he already had fifteen wives.

Yet another dimension of the prevalent system of marriage shows that, at times, exceptional individual abilities of a girl were given primacy over rules of hypergamy and clan honour. As the story goes that once when Maharana Laxman Singh's eldest son Ari Singh had gone in the direction of Kelwara (in Mewar) for hunting, he saw a young woman shooting a boar while guarding her father's farm. He was duly impressed by her bravery and felt that sons born from such a woman would be equally courageous. The girl was a Chandana Rajput. The Maharana called for her father and proposed to marry her.[22] The offspring of this marriage was the brave Hammir who not only occupied the throne of Mewar but is cherished in the Mewar saga for his exceptional abilities as a ruler.

Largely, the nature of matrimonial alliances amongst the political elite of the Rajputana states had impinged adversely on the lives and happiness of women. A Rajput prince candidly confessed the ruthlessness with which daughters were offered to fulfil political and military objectives: "There were many marriages of alliance in the past, where somebody gave you his daughter saying, 'Don't attack me next week,' and Rajput girls were often given away without much thought beyond prestige and the right kind of home."[23] Women were exchanged for raising political status, regaining territories, extract promise of military support in case of exigencies and it was considered the best way to end political rivalries and military hostilities. As Zieglar observed, "when Rajputs of different clans and *gotras* were involved, they usually confirmed hostilities through gifts of daughters in marriage and the formation of alliances, thus creating a new pattern of relationship amongst themselves."[24] In fact, preoccupation with clan honour was so engrossing that women's wishes and personal choices were rarely considered important in deciding matrimonial alliances. In Mewar, the women of the ruling family had to face a more precarious situation at the personal level, when Maharanas refused to marry them into equal status ruling clans, which had married their daughters to Mughal emperors and princes, to preserve the purity and honour of their own clan. Consequently, they were given in marriage to jagirdars within the state whose status was inferior to that of the Maharana's clan. Ironically, the violation of traditional clan hierarchy for preservation of the honour of the Sisodiya clan had adverse implications for women's own personal honour.

III

The most flagrant violation of the Rajput notion of honour as exemplified by proper feminine behaviour took place within the precincts of the palace of the Mewar Maharana. Meera Bai, the daughter-in-law of Rana Sanga and wife of his eldest son and heir apparent, Bhoj Raj, articulated this rebellion against conventional restrictive norms for controlling and regulating women's lives. Meera emerged as a shocking aberrant flouting the meticulously prescribed stringent behavioural code for royal women. In feudal society, such deviants were surely condemned, yet Meera is honoured and revered and until date, survives in the collective cultural consciousness of the people. Meera's personality is enshrined in public memory as a saint, a mystic, a fervent devotee of Krishna, an itinerant singer and above all, a courageous rebel.

Over the period, various legends have been woven around Meera Bai which have, to some extent, obscured true facts concerning her life history. Meera, born in 1498 AD, was the daughter of Ratan Singh of the Medtiya Rathore clan. Tradition has it that as a young child Meera had considered herself wedded to Lord Krishna. Her attachment to this particular deity of the Hindu pantheon, an incarnation of Lord Vishnu, was partly due to the fact that her natal family was Vaishnavite. She was married into the royal family of the Sisodiya Rajputs of Mewar who had become legendary as upholders and defenders of Rajput system of values and traditions. Even after her arrival into the royal family, Meera continued to venerate Lord Krishna as her husband. She refrained from sexual contact with her husband, Raja Bhoj Raj. Not only did she refuse to revere the family deities, her irrepressible urge for *bhakti* led her to indulge in behaviour considered highly inappropriate for a Sisodiya Rani. Due to contradictory and varied versions handed down by popular traditions, it is difficult to establish the nature of Meera's relationship with her husband and father-in-law. In some literary works Meera'a relationship with both these men has been described as cordial. In fact, she was even able to persuade her husband to build a temple for her. But, after her husband's death, her brother-in-law Vikramaditya, who succeeded to the title of Maharana, resented her lifestyle and particularly, her unwillingness to conform to the norms of the royalty. It is popularly believed that he even plotted to kill her many times.[25]

To escape the inhibiting lifestyle of the palace, Meera left Chittor, intermingled with male ascetics and danced and sang *bhajans* (devotional songs) for Lord Krishna in the temples, forests and on the streets. She spent the rest of her life in the temple at Dwarka where she attended to and worshipped Krishna. There are many fables about her death, the most popular being her final absorption in Krishna's idol.

In the course of her unswerving devotion to Krishna, Meera disowned, defied and subverted the normative pattern of values associated with powerful and entrenched institutions – family, marriage, caste, clan, royalty and even the realm of *bhakti*. Despite her disregard for societal norms, she was able to acquire a special kind of honour and reverence – distinct from the honour derived through adherence to predominant norms laid down by the contemporary political, social and religious elite. Meera's emergence in the realm of *bhakti*, her subsequent acceptance by the people, accompanied by her widespread popularity and more surprisingly, her long-lasting survival in the cultural ethos, goes to prove that an alternative paradigm of status and honour existed in opposition to the Rajput notion of honour, *izzat* and *maryada*. In fact, a perusal of Meera's life shows that there is a continuous conflict and confrontation between Meera's fiercely independent and single-minded devotion to Krishna and the code of honour cherished by the society and polity in the erstwhile Rajput state.

At the outset, Meera denied to herself the status of a wife by proclaiming herself as wedded to Lord Krishna. Further, by refusing sexual relations with her husband, she also deprived herself of the most honourable and lofty status a woman enjoyed in Indian cultural milieu, i.e., of a mother. This constituted a rejection of the primary status roles that have been cherished as the most appropriate roles for women, e.g., devoted wife and a loving mother. These ideals continue to be predominant amongst Indian women even today. She discarded the symbols that signified marital status. In her poetry, there is repeated reference to her aversion for symbols of *suhag* (marital status), i.e., *sindoor* (vermillion), head ornament, bangles, *kajal* (collyrium) etc. As a member of the royal family, acceptance of wifehood would have meant a special honour in addition to pleasures and luxuries that were not accessible to ordinary women. Meera refers to the "gem studded ornaments, *kheer* (a sweet dish prepared from milk and rice) sugar, southern silks" in her songs as luxuries for which she had no temptation. For a married woman of the royal family, such streaks of asceticism wherein symbols of *suhag* were discarded was considered highly disgraceful and improper behaviour. Such ascetic women were called '*Bhagtin*', a derogatory epithet for aristocratic and upper class women amongst Hindus.[26] thus, the first major confrontation of Meera occurs with the whole ideological construct of *pativrata* – the most acceptable duty of a woman (*stridharma*) in the cultural construction of womanhood.

For women of the royal family, compliance with the traditions and norms of the kinship group was even more obligatory and rigorous. One of the most important traditions amongst the Rajput clans, which marked the initiation of the daughter-in-law into the conjugal family, was the worship of the *Kuldevi* – the family deity – who is protector of the *kul* (clan) and of the *suhag* of women.[27] The legend goes that Meera refused to worship her in-laws' family deity and, in turn, proclaimed her exclusive devotion to Lord Krishna. She not only repudiated one of the most cherished traditions of the royal family but also outrightly refused to be moulded into the role of a daughter-in-law of the illustrious Sisodiyas.

In Rajput culture, especially in Mewar, restrictions on women's movement were particularly stringent. Their contact and communication with outside world was strictly monitored and restricted. It may be mentioned that within the *zenana* (female quarters), their lives were not so monotonous, oppressed and drab as they are frequently projected, yet women's involvement in cultural, religious, political and recreational activities had to be achieved within the confines of the *zenana*. Meera overstepped the family *maryada* (one of the words used as honour emphasizing the limits of freedom) when she refused to accept restrictions on her movement. It is widely believed that Meera's *bhakti* for Lord Krishna would not have provoked hostility from members of the royal family had she persued it within the seclusion of her palace. There are instances of queens in Mewar when they persisted in worshipping their natal deities in addition to the worship of

Eklingji – the *ishtadeva* (presiding deity) of the Sisodiyas and the *Kuldevi.*[28] However, women belonging to the Rajput aristocracy were expected to perform all regular worship and religious ceremonies within the *zenana.* They could not even visit the temple in the palace and of course visiting public temples was a taboo for Rajput princesses and queens. Even on pilgrimages they travelled in totally covered *palkies* (palanquins) duly chaperoned by guards, away from public gaze. They had to conduct themselves in public with regal dignity but Meera tied jingle bells in her feet (a highly objectionable ornament for women as it is associated with dancing girls and prostitutes) and indulged in devotional dances in the public temples, roadside, forests, etc., in full public view. This transgression of spatial sanctity, a rigid behavioural norm cherished as part of the female paradigm of honour, was construed by the Maharana as highly disgraceful for royal honour. Not only this, Meera freely mingled with the male *bhaktas* and ascetics. Her association with male company must have outraged royalty beyond measure.

On her husband's death, Meera refused to acknowledge the community's prohibitory norms, customs and way of life prescribed for the widows. By refusing to commit *sati,* Meera not only repudiated the *kulreeti* (cultural values and norms that are evolved over centuries to sustain and preserve the honour of the clan) but also forsook a custom that was effectively linked to a woman's own personal honour and an exaltation of the conjugal and natal clan. Some of the verses of Meera make it clear that she herself was actually conscious of the disrepute that she was bringing upon her own person and the Sisodiya clan but also expresses her callous disregard for such societal norms of honour. In the following verses Meera is confiding in her friends how she is possessed by her love for Lord Krishna, regardless of public perception:

> "*Meera Girdhar hath bikani,*
> *loga kahaim bigari.*"[29]

(I am sold to Lord Krishna
But people think that I am spoilt.)

(Free translation)

In yet another verse she writes:

"Sisodyau ruthyo to mhamro kaim karalesi
Mhei to guna govinda ka gasyam, ho mai
Rano ji ruthya, varo desa rakhasi
Hari ruthya, Kumhalasyam, ho mai
Loka laja ki kana na manu."

(If Sisodaya is offended, what will he do to me,
O' mother, I will sing about the virtues of Govinda,
If Ranaji is angry, he can keep his kingdom,
But if God is offended, O'mother I will wither,
I am not bothered about public honour.)

(Free translation)

Meera's callous disregard for clan prescriptions was accompanied by a similar rejection of caste norms. One of the most significant features that the *bhakti* movement sought to emphasize was the equality of all devotees, irrespective of caste. The exponents of the *bhakti* movement in the realm of religion advocated humility, simplicity and equality. Not surprisingly, a number of *bhakti* saints belonged to the lowest rungs of the caste hierarchy.

Meera broke clan and caste boundaries when she became a disciple of Raidas – a *Chamar* saint. As she intermingled freely with the *bhakta* community, she transcended the class and caste boundaries. In fact, she aroused the ire of her family, who resented her association with low-caste people. It has been contended by some scholars that Meera owes her popularity and survival in public memory to her following amongst depressed and downtrodden sections of peasants and artisans, who through the singing of Meera's *bhajans* seek to flout symbolically the authority of the Rajput ruling family of

Mewar. However, it needs to be emphasized that Meera was adored because she was a *sadguru* (a righteous teacher) and a *bhakta*. Singing of her *bhajans* or devotion to her never implied an attempt to subvert or challenge Rajput dominance. It was natural attraction towards Meera's intense *bhakti* that drew people to her. She was able to command respect from both – the princes as well as peasants. The author of *Bhaktmal* has mentioned the names of chiefs and chieftains who were Meera's devotees, prominent amongst them were Abhay Raj of Idar, Prithviraj of Bikaner and Jai Singh of Jaipur. He also mentions the names of some princesses like Ranavati, wife of Prithviraj and Kichani of Marwar as women *bhaktas* who came in continuity after Meera passed away and were, possibly, inspired by her. A small sect of Brahmin and other caste widows called 'Meerabais' has been existing in Mewar from 17th century onwards. More significantly, women of this sect have maintained themselves on charity by Mewar state.[30]

The lyrical musical quality of Meera's compositions is well-articulated in folk as well as classical music. More singers have recorded her songs than those of any other *bhakta* poet. Prominent male and female singers from both the genres have sung Meera's *bhajans* and received popular acclaim. Some of the well-known names are Subhahlakshmi, Lata Mangeshkar and Anoop Jalota. In fact, her popular image is far more acceptable and diffused when compared to other *bhakti* saints. Meera's verses still survive as delightful *bhajans* recorded and available in cassettes and discs. In this context, Kiran Nagarkar has rightly observed: "The measure of life in India is the commercial cinema. Indian cinema keeps going back to the Little Saint (Meera) time and again.... The other great *bhakti* saints may have been intellectually more robust than her but their fame is mostly regional. Her name is on almost every Indian's lips."[31] In the context of Meera's utter disregard for established institutions and norms, it need to be underscored that it was not their irrational or exploitative nature that compelled her to subvert these structures. It was not an act of deliberate rebellion but sheer intoxication of her intense spiritualism that drove her to trample upon the societal proscriptions. Meera's spiritual experiences were a process of empowerment that endowed her with reservoirs of indomitable inner strength, self-confidence and determination to transcend worldly impositions.

As a *bhakta* too, Meera's spiritual experience distinguished her from the *bhaktas* of her genre. In the Indian *bhakti* tradition, there have been various forms in which God is visualized, worshipped and approached by his devotees. These *bhavas* and *rasas* of *bhakti* are: *Madhuryabhava*, which posits God as lover and husband; *Dasyabhava,* where the devotee assumes the role of a servitor to the God implying complete surrender, humility, service and a sense of belonging; *Shantbhava,* wherein the devotee contemplates the incarnate form of God; *Sakhyabhava,* wherein God is approached as a friend and companion; and *Vatsalyabhava,* wherein the devotee envisions God as a child and while identifying with the role of a parent or an elder finds joy in his childlike innocence. While most of the male *bhaktas* of the *bhakti* movement, especially so in the northern region, sought bliss by surrendering themselves in the service of God as *das* or subordinate, in Meera's *bhakti* there is predominance of the *Madhuryabhava* as she approaches her God as her husband and lover. However, Meera is not a votary of *Madhuryabhava* only. Her devotion to Lord Krishna encompasses all *bhavas* except *vatsalya.* She visualizes Krishna in varied forms – as a Lord Creator, saviour of the people of Braj, beloved of the women of Braj, a cowherd, a flute player, a companion and a lover. Meera surrendered both her mind and heart to Krishna and lost herself in the ecstasy of his devotion. Her acquaintance with music and dancing gave her songs a divine fervour. She found presence of Krishna in the entire world.[32] Unlike other male *bhaktas,* who refer to a conscious process of self-control in their poems, Meera's *bhakti* has been defined as "natural, spontaneous and so strong that it enables her to break all bonds, confront all opposition... Meera represents her love of God as something perfectly natural in comparison to which family ties, norms of honour and material luxuries appear artificial impositions."[33] Meera, in fact, was among the chosen few saints whose spiritual experience was blessed by the vision of God – such a person is said to achieve the topmost heights of *bhakti*.

Meera owes her survival in the cultural consciousness of people, especially in the northern region, to the *padas* or verses composed by her. These *padas* described Meera's unswerving devotion to Lord Krishna and her defiance of the society, clan and royal family. Scholars differ over the number of verses actually written by her. Krishnadeva Sharma's *Mirambai Padavali* has 231 verses; Vishvanath Tripathi's *Meera ka Kavya* about 100; Bhagwandas Tiwari, 103; Padmavati's *Miram Vyaktitva aur Krititva,* 601; and Chunnilal Shesh's *Mira Padavali* has 236 verses.[34] In all these compilations, it is difficult to ascertain if they are Meera's original compositions or later accretions.

Like the political and social realms, in the realm of *bhakti* too, Meera confronts and resolves various patriarchal dilemmas, as the ascetic option was considered a male domain. Culturally, a woman is perceived as an obstruction in the path of salvation. The temptation for woman is equated with lure for gold, which weans the devotee away from the journey to salvation. This image of woman as a temptress and one who is responsible for distraction is deeply rooted in religious tradition and reinforced through myths and legends. Therefore, when women themselves resort to spiritualism and devotion to God, they are viewed with suspicion and aspersions are cast on the purity of their character. Women *bhaktas* had to contend with the possibility of sexual harassment also. Priyadas in *Bhaktmal Vartik* narrates a legend when a fellow sadhu demanded to have sexual relationship with Meera saying it was an order from Lord Krishna. Meera sought to resolve this crisis by spreading the bed in broad public view in the midst of other saints. She asserted that if it was a divine order, there was nothing shameful in doing so. The sadhu hung his head in shame and fell at Meera's feet and became her devotee. Meera thus reversed the normative pattern of shame and dishonour for women. Normally, in such incidents of sexual harassment, humiliation, disgrace, and even the entire blame is shifted to a woman but Meera, instead shames and embarrasses her seducer.

Another well-known legend is associated with her meeting with Jiv Goswami, Chaitanya's disciple at Vrindavan. Jiv Goswami declined to receive Meera as he had taken a vow that he would never look at a woman lest she may lure him away from his spiritual and devotional concerns. Meera retorted by saying that she had thought that there was only one man in Vrindavan and that was Krishna and she was surprised that there was another man. The stinging comment mitigated Jiv Goswami's tough posture who hurriedly came to meet Meera.[35] Meera sought to subvert the conventional norms guiding female behaviour even in the realm of asceticism and with this singular statement sought to proclaim that gender divide was irrelevant in the pursuit of *bhakti.*

On several occasions Meera emerged as a fiercely independent-minded devotee with scant regard for recognition from any established schools of *bhakti.* Although Meera attended religious gatherings, listened to the discourses of the sadhus and interacted with them, she resisted all attempts to formally affiliate herself with any established school or sect of *bhakti.* Meera has been criticized not once but thrice in *Chaurasi Vaishnavon Ki Varta* of the powerful Vallabh Sampradaya. The reason: she refused to accept Vallabhacharya as her Guru and become a member of the sect. Even when her own priest Ram Das joined Vallabh Sampradaya, she refused to follow him and he retaliated by calling her a whore. This incident provides insights into the state of affairs in which Meera found herself. Firstly, as Meera had acquired tremendous fame and renown for her piety and spiritualism powerful sects wished to enrol her as a member. Secondly, even in the company of renouncers, Meera, despite her own status as a full-fledged *bhakta*, could not transcend her gender identity. She was the victim of slanderous comments by her fellow *bhaktas* when she refused to be subordinated. Thirdly, like the social and political structures, the world of *bhakti* too was hierarchical. The predominant and powerful sects tended to preclude or subordinate the relatively new and parallel streams of *bhakti*. Meera did not accept either institutional or human mediation in her communion with Lord Krishna. Meera's devotion to Krishna was an intensely personal experience of a relationship with a divine figure whom she regarded as her husband, master, lover and protector. She was so possessed by the idea of Krishna that she could not abide by any formal rules or regulations. Moreover, she was averse to acceptance of any restrictions and had developed a lifestyle wherein she challenged all kinds of hierarchy, authority and subordination.

Thus, in both the social realm and that of *bhakti*, Meera seeks to redefine and even subvert conventional norms, and yet, carve out an independent identity and honourable status for herself. Her compositions show that she was keenly aware of her deviant behaviour. She repeatedly emphasized her disregard for public opinion and insisted on remaining *anuthi*, i.e., unique and different. Having thus "proved herself, dared all, broken all barriers, she is still exalted and revered and regains in far greater measure the honour and repute she lost or seemed to have lost by flouting the norms of womanly behaviour."[36] In popular mind, she has a distinctive place, a more pervasive one, than other contemporary saints. She was able to create new norms of honour in male-dominated society and emerge as a legendary figure in her own right.

There are certain legendary women figures in Indian culture who are perceived as ideals by women. There are two categories of such ideals. Some of them have become role models in common parlance and emphasize the traditional women images of a devoted wife and loving mother. Anusuya, Sita and Savitri represent this particular cultural category. There is another category in the ascetic and devotional tradition. Meera stands out as the most pervasive ideal in the latter category. Her symbolic significance in Indian culture, especially for women, has been unparalleled. Meera has high inspirational value for women when they step out of the ordinary and the stereotypical and aspire for spiritual roles that go beyond their traditional roles of mother and wife.

Gandhi adopted Meera as one of his favourite symbolic figures when he wanted to initiate women into new non-traditional role of a political activist in the anti-colonial struggle. He defined Meera as 'paramount *satyagrahi*' since by resisting Ranaji's tyranny and by drinking poison she courageously endured sufferings and punishment. He raised Meera to the status of a venerable national symbol worth emulating by women.

Paradoxically, there are instances wherein Meera's character has certain negative connotations too, especially in the region of Mewar, among Rajputs and also among those groups who were associated with the ruling classes.[37] She is looked down upon as a deviant who besmirched the honour of her *kul* (*kulnasi*). The name 'Meera' is akin to contempt amongst these communities. It is contended that dominant Rajput community even exercised its authority to obliterate Meera's memory. Most of the Rajput women of this area look upon Meera's defiance of family and community, as also her rejection of her husband as outrageous and entirely against Rajput *kulreeti*.

At another level, women who show disinclination for traditional status roles conferred upon by marriage and motherhood and, instead, choose the ascetic option in the typical Meera's style of dancing and singing are proverbially referred to as 'Meera'. Nancy Martin refers to such Meera prototypes whom she located in Mathura.[38] These women renouncers have devoted themselves to the worship and adoration of Lord Krishna, and have close affinity with Meera's devotional style. They are variously called Ma Krishna, Meera etc. Women, who are not necessarily ascetics but adopt a austere and simple lifestyle, instantly conjure up an image of

Meera. She also serves as a model of creative excellence for women.

IV

Jauhar was primarily aimed at preservation of female chastity and virtue. To ensure the purity of blood and lineage, the higher castes, especially the Rajputs, exercised control over women's sexuality. During periods of turmoil, especially invasions and conquests, when the possibility of capture of women became imminent, the Rajput rulers resolved the problematic issue of protecting women's honour and the mixing of blood through the rite of *jauhar*, i.e., immolating their women before they could be ravished by the enemy. Violation of a woman's chastity not only meant dishonour and shame for the women at the personal level but it was effectively linked to the honour and prestige of the clan, ruler and the state.

The practice of *jauhar* is related to the most striking tales of valour, heroism and sacrifice pertaining to women for protection of their own and the collective honour of the clan and the state. *Jauhar* and *saka* were parallel and integral processes, which symbolized ultimate expression of protection of honour by men and women. *Saka* was the last-ditch attempt by warriors when they entered into battle with no expectation of survival or success. *Jauhar* and *saka* reflect, perhaps, the same psyche of making supreme sacrifice for preserving the honour of the clan and the state. Before men donned the *kesariya bana* for the ultimate battle, women mounted the pyre so that men could go and fight, without fearing for the violation of their bodies by the enemy. *Jauhar* symbolized the ultimate female Rajput value of courage and bravery in the sense that men were liberated from the fear of their women being exploited. This enabled the men to resist until the end. *Jauhar*, in a way, prompted and inspired martial valour and courage of the warriors. It was collective supreme sacrifice by women inside the fort when its fall had become imminent and their honour endangered. In such a situation, not only Rajput women but also those belonging to other castes performed *jauhar*.

Although capture of women after military conquest has been a usual feature in all political cultures, *jauhar* emerged as a peculiar feature of Rajput polities, especially in the erstwhile state of Mewar. Pertinently, the Mewar Maharanas were particularly keen to protect their womenfolk from the Muslim invaders and, therefore, some of the most heart-rending incidents of *jauhar* took place when Mewar was ravaged by Muslim rulers. The fort of Chittor in the state of Mewar witnessed the three most tragic massacres and mass sacrifice by women. The most memorable *jauhar*, which is well – etched in public memory and lucidly articulated in popular literature, is associated with the legendary queen of Mewar, Padmini, wife of Maharana Ratan Singh, who was renowned for her incomparable beauty. It is popularly believed that the Muslim invader Aladuddin Khilji, fell for her charm and driven by a fierce desire to possess her attacked Chittor in 1303. Since the defeat of the Maharana's forces was clear, Padmini led hundreds of women to the vaults under the palace where they committed *jauhar*.

Another tragic *jauhar* at Chittor preceded the *saka* of 1535, when Bahadur Shah of Gujarat besieged the fort. On this occasion, Maharani Karmavati, mother of Maharana Vikramaditya, led 13,000 women to the pyre of *jauhar*. The third *saka* took place in 1568, when Akbar besieged the supposedly impregnable fort. Before the Rajput warriors flung open the gates of the fort for the ultimate battle, women and children consigned themselves to the flames. Apart from these, the other occasions when this unfortunate rite was performed are those which took place at Ranthambhor (1301 AD), Siwana (1308 AD) and at Jalore during Alauddin Khilji's invasion. The *jauhar* at Jalore in 1310, when the fort was about to fall in Alauddin's hands, has been described vividly with rare sensitivity by Padmanabha in *Kanhadde Prabandh* written in 1455 AD. *Jauhar* fire was lit in 1,584 homes in Jalore. "The kith and kin, fathers, brothers, uncles and other male relatives, barely withholding their tears, stood in rows as the procession of ladies bedecked in their finest dress and jewellery, passed in front of them to jump into the raging fires to preserve their honour from the enemy."[39]

Some modern scholars have questioned the wisdom of the suicidal mindset that governs the twin processes of *saka* and *jauhar*. Professor Nizami writes: "... when imprisonment of a few hundred or thousand warriors would have solved the problem, *jauhars* were performed on a large scale and thousands of men and women were needlessly reduced to ashes."[40] However, this approach fails to grasp the Rajput paradigm of honour that motivated these supreme sacrifices, i.e., death rather than dishonour, defeat and loss of religion.

Interestingly, despite its retrogressive nature, the rite of *jauhar* is loaded with immense symbolic and inspirational significance for Indian women. Maharani Padmini until present times is cherished as a model of beauty, valour, indomitable courage and undying resistance for preservation of purity of body. During the freedom struggle, Padmini emerged as a symbol of sacrifice and fearlessness who was invoked to enthuse and inspire women for heroic action in the agitation against British imperialists.[41] In the nationalist literature that sought to refashion the meek and submissive women into heroic resisters, Rajput women are portrayed as embodiment of courage and sacrifice who cheerfully chose death rather than dishonour. R.C. Dutt, in his novel *Pratap Singh*, seeks to reinvigorate contemporary women by focussing on the indomitable courage and fierce resistance of the Rajput princesses who form the main women characters of his novel. One of the high points in his narrative is the poignant description of the rite of *jauhar* performed by women when the kingdom was surrounded by enemies.[42]

Interestingly, this obsession for protecting the purity of women and by implication that of the family, community and state persisted in Indian political culture and resurfaced in the partition and post-partition phases. There are innumerable poignant memories associated with communal riots following partition of India in 1947. There were heart-rending incidents when men killed the women of their family when they realized that their fate is to fall prey to the rioters of other communities.

Similarly, the Indian State demonstrated patriarchal attitudes when it launched the programme for recovery of Hindu and Sikh women who were abducted by the Muslims in Pakistan as also the Muslim women who had been abducted by frenzied Sikh mobs. In most of the cases, these women had been converted to Islam. They started their lives anew by marrying Muslim men in Pakistan. There were also cases of Muslim women marrying Sikh or Hindu men. There are heart-wrenching details of forcible recovery of these women when they were compelled to leave behind their husbands and children just when they had started adjusting and normalizing in the changed situation and in their new identities with new relationships. Yet again, these women were forced to relocate their lives and identities. The way national honour was treated as inextricably linked to women's bodies and their purity becomes clear from the debates in parliament around the 1949 Abducted Persons Recovery and Restoration Act. "Women's sexuality as it had been violated by abduction, transgressed by enforced conversion and marriage and exploited by impermissible cohabitation and reproduction was at the centre of debates about national duty, honour, identity and citizenship."[43] In the process of reclaiming these women, their emotional trauma and rights as citizens of the states were completely ignored in the name of national honour. These policy measures are a clear indication of the grip of feudal values of status and honour that have continued to determine attitudes towards women.

The poignancy and trauma of these women who suffered during partition has been sensitively portrayed in films and creative writings. The film *Shaheed-i-Mohabbat Buta Singh* has brought out the pathos inherent in such a situation. The film is about the times of partition when, during the inter-community riots, amongst Hindus, Sikhs and Muslims, abduction and rape of women of the hostile community had become a popular mode of humiliation and violence. The film revolves round a Muslim girl Zainab who was rescued by a Sikh youth from bloodthirsty abductors. Closeness bred amongst them love and affection for each other leading to marriage and, subsequently, birth of a child. When the girl had started finding peace, solace and happiness in her new relationship and environs, she is shifted to Pakistan in keeping with the new legal enactment. Her husband Buta Singh and the victimized girl go through a harrowing experience after the separation that has been portrayed vividly and in a realistic manner in the film.

Another heart-rending incident reminds of the bestiality and communal frenzy that had pervaded the popular psyche during these days. It relates to a Sikh family where the daughter of the family, Maan Kaur, was beheaded by her father himself to prevent her from falling into the hands of the Muslim rioters. This was deemed imperative for protection of the honour of the family. The poignancy of the incident is vividly recounted in these words: "Sant Raja Singh of Thoa Khalsa village in Rawalpindi district picked up his sword, prayed and brought it down on the neck of his younger daughter. When he did not succeed his daughter aged 16 years came once again and knelt before her father, removed her thick plait and offered him her neck. This time his sword found her neck ...and [head] rolled off." The observations of Bir Bahadur, the brother of Maan Kaur, who had observed the incident as a 10-year old, reinforces the prevalent mindset towards the entire issue of woman's chastity and the way in which it was linked to the honour of the family. Bir Bahadur expressed admiration for her sister who brought honour to the family. Ironically, his compassion and sympathy were reserved for his father when he recounted: "Imagine, a father who kills his daughter, how much of a victim, how helpless he must be...."[44] In many instances, women jumped into the wells or committed collective suicides. These mass suicides resurrect the memories and symbolism of the *jauhars* of Rajput political culture. Despite different political contexts and periods, the underlying sentiment was to protect women's virtue and chastity and to avoid the humiliation of rape and conversion.

An extreme exemplification of the concept of honour is the practice of honour-killing that is widely practised in some countries. The practice demonstrates the retrogressive and ultra sensitive attitudes towards female chastity and the manner in which it is perceived as inherently linked to the honour and prestige of the family, caste and community. The practice is derived from the idea of strict control over women's sexuality and chastity and how slight suspicion regarding the same could lead to most brutal behaviour with women, mostly resulting in their murder. Transgression of the rules of a community, caste or religion regarding marriage by young women also invites such brutalization in the name of honour of the family or the community. While the practice is pervasive in Islamic countries, many other religious communities also subject their women-folk to similar violence and physical abuse. In Islamic countries like Pakistan, Jordan, Iran, etc., despite a veneer of westernization, such a fierce and primitive code leads to murder of women. Even in India, particularly in rural areas, women who violate the rules related to caste hierarchy, while choosing their marriage partners are subjected to horrific treatment at the hands of caste panchayats. Unfortunately, those who survive these honour killings also face an appalling existence and have to deal with hostility of the community since everyone treats the fleeing of woman in distress as a matter of honour for the whole community. They are virtually ostracized as '*kari*' (black women), a stigmatized epithet for such transgressors, and forced to lead secluded and shameful lives. Norma Khouri from Jordan and Asthma Jahangir from Pakistan, both ardent and tireless crusaders against the cause of honour-killing, intensely feel that the world continues to be a place of paradox and double-standards for men and women.[45]

In the preceding discussion, distinctive aspects related to the position and status of women in the native states of Rajputana have been underscored, particularly against the backdrop of the peculiar political culture of the region. Often, there have been sweeping generalizations about women's situation in Rajasthan leading to the projection of a specific picture that is embedded in people's psyche. The explanation for this construction partly lies in the historical documentation, which either tends to romanticize the women's position, or condemns their low status and is generally portrayed in a 'victim image'. More often than not, these writings have focussed upon the upper classes and the elite groups thereby completely overlooking the women's situation in the lower and tribal groups. Such a fragmentary construction naturally led to narratives, which give a homogenous picture that ignores variations in women's situation across groups and between castes and tribes. A stereotypical image of a powerless, suppressed and constricted womanhood has been the pattern of these writings. In fact, the level of freedom allowed to tribal and lower caste women contrasted sharply with the strict and guarded privacy of the women of the ruling classes as also the upper castes.

The Rajput political system, which derived its strength and stability through involvement in continuous warfare, could not have been sustained without the active cooperation of its women. Women were not passive recipients or inactive pawns crippled by the political system. In fact, numerous channels were available to women through which they could not only strengthen the political structure but also consolidate and enhance their personal honour and that of the clan.

They participated in administration as regents and advisors, held equally ostentatious and elaborate parallel *zenana durbars* on important occasions, patronized art and literature and took a keen interest in benevolent and philanthropic activities. They had exposure, and at times, had access to areas, which are considered male domains such as hunting, armoury, training in arms and administration etc.

In the context of gender construction certain unusual and positive aspects of the cultural heritage of the state are completely overlooked. In aforementioned account, an attempt has been made to present the other side of the picture by focussing upon certain interesting facets of the cultural ethos of the state. Surprisingly, it were the conservative and feudalistic environs of the erstwhile state of Mewar which witnessed the rebellion of Meera, who challenged and subverted the most entrenched institutions of her times, yet she was able to accumulate unparalleled honour, fame and following which has made her "the most remembered and quoted woman of Indian history, right down to our times". Beyond historical construction, distinctive paradigm has been formulated around Meera's personality and her archetypal characters have become proverbial in Indian society. In fact, many legendary stories associated with gender construction in Indian culture can be traced to *Bhakta* Meera and *Virangana* Padmini.

Notes

1. For a historical overview of women's status in Indian society refer, A.S. Altekar, *Position of Women in the Hindu Civilization* and S.R. Shastri, *Women in the Vedic Age*.
2. Cited from K.R. Qanungo, *Studies in Rajput History*, p. 67.
3. Charles Allen & Sharda Dwivedi, *Lives of the Indian Princes*, p. 149.
4. Shipra Vyas, 'Social Legislation in Rajasthan related to the Problems of Women' (unpublished Ph.D. thesis, Department of History, University of Rajasthan, 2000), pp.101-120.

5. Varsha Joshi, *Polygamy and Purdah: Women and Society among Rajputs*, p.91. The poem '*Senani*' has been effectively sung by the author and is available in cassette form.
6. Charles Allen & Sharda Dwivedi, *op.cit.*, p.43.
7. Interview with Laxmi Kumari Chundavat, daughter of the erstwhile jagirdar of Devgarh, a first-class *thikana* of Mewar and a member of the illustrious Choondvat clan. Also, Laxmi Kumari Chundavat, *Sanskritik Rajasthan*, pp.109-110.
8. Lindsey Harlan, *Religion and Rajput Women: The Ethic of Protection in Contemporary Narrative*, p.72.
9. Rama Mehta, 'From Purdah to Modernity' in B.R. Nanda(ed.), *Indian Women: From Purdah to Modernity*, pp.113-114.Custom of observing *purdah* had conditioned women's mindset who accepted and continued the practice without any resentment. In fact, when some of the educated, liberal and enthusiastic reformers of the state initiated the process of elimination of *purdah* from their homes, women in the family found it difficult to walk without *purdah* in the main bazaars under public gaze. Chandra Bhandari recalled that her mother had tears in her eyes when her husband Shri Kesarilal Bordia persuaded her to give up the practice of observing *purdah.*
10. Interview with Laxmikumari Chundavat. The do's and don'ts of the *zenana* lifestyle amongst Rajputs are sensitively portrayed in movie titled '*Zubeda*'.
11. G.V. Vyas, *Mewar ka Samajik aur Arthik Jivan*, pp.229-231.
12. Francis Taft, 'Honor and Alliance: Reconstructing Mughal and Rajput Marriages', in Schomer & others (eds.), *The Idea of Rajasthan: Explorations in Regional Identity*, Vol. II, *Institutions*, p.22.
13. Charles Allen & Sharda Dwivedi, *op.cit.*, p.138.
14. K.R.Qanungo, *op.cit.*, p.69.
15. Charles Allen & Sharda Dwivedi, *op.cit.*, p.137.
16 Lt.Col. James Tod, *Annals and Antiquities of Rajasthan,* Vol. I (henceforth, *Annals*), pp.219-220.
17. J.C. Brookes, *History of Meywar*, p.11.
18. *Annals*, pp.366-368.
19. A.C. Banerjee, *Lectures on Rajput History*, pp.89 & 94-95.
20. *Annals*, p.487.
21. Shiv Charan Menaria, *Rajasthan Ke Nari Ratna*, pp.68-82.
22. Varsha Joshi, *op.cit.*, p.49.
23. Charles Allen & Sharda Dwivedi, *op.cit.*, p.143. In the political culture across the world, especially in monarchical polities, matrimonial alliances among the ruling classes were commonly motivated by political objectives. Kathryn Lasky, author of the fictional diary of Queen Elizabeth I,

the Tudor princess who ruled England from 1558-1603, has made a similar observation while dealing with the childhood of the princess. "The daughters of Kings are indeed like pawns on a chessboard ready to be offered in marriage to secure new allies against an enemy." Kathryn Lasky, *Elizabeth I (The Royal Diaries)*, p.57.

24. Norman Zieglar, 'Some notes on Rajput loyalties during the Mughal Period' in J.F. Richards (ed.), *Kingship and Authority in South Asia*, p.232.
25. Quite well known till date are some of the stories that are woven around these incidents. It is believed that Maharana Vikramaditya tried to kill her by offering her poisoned drink and then by sending her a cobra concealed in a fruit basket. According to a popular myth, Krishna rendered the poison harmless and transformed the snake into a garland of flowers.
26. Shah Alam Khan, *Meera: Loktatvik Adhayayan*, p. 34.
27. Lindsey Harlan, *op. cit.*, p. 48.
28. *Ibid.*, pp. 47-48.
29. The Hindi version of Meera's verses have been quoted from, Krishna P. Bahadur, *Mira Bai and Her Padas*, 1998, pp. 40, 57 & 58.
30. G.N. Sharma, *Glories of Mewar*, p.77.
31. Kiran Nagarkar, *Cuckold*, p. 609. The phenomenon of spiritualism as a source of strength and empowerment for women has been articulated in the article by Manjula Bordia, 'Samajik Nyaya aur Atmabal' in *Moolprashna*, April-June 2001.
32. Her disenchantment with wordly ties is reflected in a well-known *pada*, *"Mere to Girdhar Gopal, Dusara Na Koi.. .."*
33. Madhu Kishwar & Ruth Vanita 'Poison to Nectar: The Life and Work of Mirabai' in the special issue of *Manushi*, Nos. 50-51-52 on *Women Bhakta Poets*, p.88. For different schools of *bhakti*, refer, *ibid.*, pp.87-88.
34. Krishna, P. Bahadur, *op. cit.*, p. 39.
35. Sooraj Paliwal 'Bhakti Kavya Mein Nari Ki Stithi: Meera Ke Vishesh Sandarbh Mein', in Kunwar Pal Singh (ed.), *Bhakti Andolan: Itihas aur Sanskriti*, p. 242.
36. Kishwar & Vanita, *op. cit.*, p. 92.
37. 'Mirabai in Rajasthan', an article by Parita Mukta in *Manushi*, op. cit., pp. 95-97.
38. 'Mirabai: Shastron Mein Ullakhit, Jeevan Mein Roopayit', an article by Nancy M. Martin in *Rangayan*, January-March 1997, pp. 14-15.
39. V.S.Bhatnaghar, 'Women in Medieval India: A Study of Position and Images' in Pratibha Jain & Rajan Mahan (eds.), *Women Images*, p.158.
40. *Ibid.*, p.159.
41. Radha Kumar, *History of Doing*, p. 57.

42. Uma Chakravarti, 'Whatever Happened to the Vedic Dasi? Orientalism, Nationalism and a Script for the Past' in Kumkum Sangari & Sudesh Vaid, *Recasting Women: Essays in Colonial History*, pp.51-52.
43. Ritu Menon & Kamla Bhasin, *Borders and Boundaries: Women in India's Partition*, p.20; Ritu Menon & Kamla Bhasin, 'An Exchange of Women', *Outlook*, May 28, 1997, p.55.
44. Urvashi Butalia, 'The Persistence of Memory' in Kai Friese & Mukul Keswani, *Civil Lines 5*, pp. 169-198.
45. For details regarding the practice of honour-killings and their horrific nature see, Vijay Dutt, 'Murdered for honour', *Hindustan Times*, April 25, 2004; and Norma Khouri, 'Forbidden Love' *Reader's Digest*, May 2004; Sultan Shahin, 'Of Female Bondage' *Hindustan Times*, February 10, 2000.

6

Social Classification and Mewar Polity

The annals of Rajputana have been represented as a bundle of adulating chronicles of Rajput oligarchies instead of the history of the people of Rajputana.[1] It had the effect of camouflaging and undermining the seminal role played by the non-Rajput communities in the emergence, consolidation and sustenance of polity. Significantly, various communities like Bhils, Charans, Oswals, Vaishyas, Kayasthas and Brahmins were an integral part of the military, administrative, political and social system. Time and again, the Rajput rulers acknowledged their indispensability and significance to polity by conceding them vital spaces, both at the symbolic and ritual level and also in the actual sharing of authority. They were entrusted with key responsibilities in the administration and conferred upon with marks of honour to signify their contribution as makers of the history of the land. Some other well-known distinguished groups were Marwaris of Shekhawati belt, Jats of Bharatpur and Vishnois of Marwar area who have made remarkable contribution to economic growth, conservation of environment and to political structure. Interestingly, these communities too cherished a code of honour and norms of status that sought to define distinction, stratification and hierarchy in their respective social formations.

Historically speaking, the dominant ethic of the Rajput warrior-ruler that stressed feudal honour and valour without regard to consequences has captivated the imagination of a wide spectrum of people - historians, western writers, leaders of freedom struggle and the masses. The historiographical stereotype of a Rajput as a diehard hero who prized honour over death was partly due to their control of historical writing through court chroniclers, bards and genealogists. The Charans, as the hereditary panegyrists and court historians, composed *geets* (songs), *rasos* (martial epics), *vartas* (stories), *khyats* (clan histories) and *vanshavalis* (genealogies). The Charan, thus, emerged as the custodian and perpetuator of Rajput glory. Subsequently, in the 19th century, James Tod, British Political Agent for the western Rajputana states and a brilliant scholar, wrote his *magnum opus, Annals and Antiquities of Rajasthan,* one of the most extensive and trendsetting work on the history of the erstwhile Rajputana states, particularly Mewar. Through this work, Tod, a great admirer of Rajput character, sought to reinforce the image and identity of the Rajput as a chivalrous warrior. In addition to this, during the renaissance and the nationalist movement, the Rajput warrior was projected as an inspirational figure. These historical and literary works either completely overlooked the contribution of other communities or treated them in a state of dependence in relation to the ruling Rajput clan.

Even a cursory glance at the historical antecedents of the Rajputana states makes it clear that it is not merely the history of Rajput clans but of non-Rajputs as well. These groups formed the vast majority and some of whom have a much older history than ruling Rajput clans - Guhilots, Chauhans, Rathores and Kachchawas. A holistic and objective history of Rajputana states is not possible without projecting the role of these non-Rajputs, who were not only an intrinsic part of the processes of state formation but practically ruled and sustained the Rajput principalities by manning their civil administration. Hence, they have legitimate space in the glorious history of the region, which continues to be pervaded by the Rajputs. In the present discourse, role and status of five non-Rajput communities, namely, Bhils, Charans, Brahmins, Oswals and Muslims in the polity of the erstwhile state of Mewar will be underscored.

I

The Bhils, perhaps, represent the oldest stratum of population in the areas of southern Rajasthan, lying adjacent to Malwa and Gujarat. In the pre-independence era, the region comprised of five erstwhile princely states of Mewar, Dungarpur, Banswara, Pratapgarh and Kushalgarh. This tribal community, due to its distinctive cultural traditions, ethic of fidelity, fierce sense of pride in their identity and independence, has fascinated the historians, anthropologists, ethnographers and sociologists, as also the laymen. Bhils have become legendary for their bravery and courage as well as for their aversion for submission to the *vilayatis* (foreigners). The Bhil love for freedom has become proverbial. Not surprisingly, the tradition and urge for resistance against encroachment on their autonomous way of life has been a consistent feature of the Bhil tradition.

Anthropologists differ over the origin of the word 'Bhil', 'Billu' or 'Beel'. G.S. Ghurye claims that it is a generic term that is attributed to various ancient people of the land by the invaders. According to the *Cambridge History of India*, the word 'Bhil' seems to have been derived from the Dravidian equivalent of the word 'Villu' or 'Billu' meaning a bow. Since the Bhils were scarcely ever seen without a bow, they came to be known as 'Bil' or 'Bhils'.[2] The other various names by which Bhils were addressed were: *Vanputras* (children of the forest), *Mairote* (born of the mountains), *Goind* (lord of the caves) and *Pal-Indra* (lord of the pass).

The earliest reference to the Bhils is found in *Katha Sarit Sagar*, which is supposed to be a text dated between 400 AD and 600 AD. However, there is frequent mention of 'Nishad' – a term that appears to be a synonym of Bhil in many ancient scriptures like *Ramayana*, *Mahabharata*, *Bhagwat Purana*, *Shiv Purana*, *Manu Smriti* etc. According to *Bhagwat Purana*, the king named Bena did not honour the sages who cursed him to die. On his death, they created a person named Nishad with a black body like a crow and bloody red eyes. In *Shiv Purana*, they are described as the descendants of the ugly and vicious son of Mahadev (one of the names for Lord Shiva) from a forest girl, who had committed a serious crime by stealing and killing his father's favourite bull.[3]

These myths regarding origin and mythological references do not explain their actual descent, yet it is clearly indicative of the peculiar attitude that has been very common in the representation of the tribals. Except stray illustrious references in the epics and other religious classics, their origin and so-called distinctive physical appearance are attributed to an "unethical act, wicked deed, a foolish act, an incestuous union, a misfortune or a defect". These mythical references to their origin signify and underscore certain typical features associated with the status of the tribals within the broader community. The fact that these tales regarding origin are traced to the scriptures of Hinduism shows the tribe as having some relation with caste Hindus, yet at the same time, they are projected as low status inferior groups. All these myths are constructed in a manner so as to attach some kind of stigma to their descent and attitude to life. They are projected as semi-civilized and ungrateful people with lesser morals.

The ethnological origin of the Bhils is also mired in confusion and controversy. While one set of scholars considers them as original inhabitants of this subcontinent, others regard them as migrants. Tod describes them as *Vanputras* and believes that the Aryans pushed them into the forests. Russel, Hiralal and S.C. Ghurye support this view. Crookes describes them as belonging to the Dravidian stock. D.N. Majumdar considers them as somewhat distant from the pro-Dravidian but closer to the people of higher castes.[4] Despite various disagreements over their ethnologic origin, scholars seem to be unanimous over the fact that they were the inhabitants of the areas of Rajasthan, Madhya Pradesh, Gujarat and Maharashtra at the time of the advent of the Aryans and after being pushed into the interior they developed their distinctive cultural traits and forms of social and political organization.

The British administrators, ethnographers and anthropologists had projected the "tribal communities as isolates, tribals as noble savages and the primitive condition as a state of Arcadian simplicity". According to K.S. Singh, this assumption ignores the historical role of the tribal communities spread over different parts of India in the process of state formation and, later on its sustenance.[5]

In Rajputana states, there is clinching evidence to show that Bhils exercised political authority before the emergence of the Rajputs on the political scene. Many towns in Rajputana still owe their nomenclature to their Bhil masters. Kota is named after Kotya Bhil, Kushalgarh after Kushala Bhil, Banswara takes its name from Bansiya Bhil and Dungarpur is named after Dungria Bhil. According to R.C. Gunarthi, in the ancient times, Bhils were the ruling classes called Vihil.[6] The erstwhile state of Mewar provides numerous instances of collaboration between the tribals and the rulers. The establishment of Rajput rule over Mewar did not lead to the total subjugation of the Bhils. Quite significantly, they were able to retain autonomy in large measure in all spheres - political, social and religious. At the same time, they were able to play a significant role in the processes of state formation of the Guhilas of Mewar. In the early stages of the Rajput occupation, they found the Bhils to be ritually pure enough to have commensal and connubial relations with them. The marriages between Rajput girls and Bhil chiefs were quite frequent. The Girasia and the Bhilala tribes are said to be the mixture of the Rajputs and the Bhils.[7]

The Bhils were the earliest settlers of Mewar and the adjoining hilly regions. Numerous legends, which describe the origin of the erstwhile state, suggest that the Bhils held effective control over the territories that were later ruled by the Guhilots. It is believed that the Bhils of Mewar had put up a stiff resistance to Rajput aggression. Legends associated with Bappa Rawal, the founder of the state of Mewar, mention that when he was threatened by the Solanki chief, he fled to the forests with his two best friends – the Bhils Baleo of Undari and Dewa of Oguna. It was Dewa who drew with blood the ceremonial mark of installation on the forehead of Bappa on the occasion of taking over the crown from the Mori ruler of Chittor.[8] These legends may lack authenticity yet if one looks at the role played by the Bhils in the polity of Rajput rulers who had displaced them, one is forced to lend some measure of credence to these anecdotes.

The Mewar sovereigns had conceded a vital role to the Bhils in the *rajyabhishek* or coronation ceremony. The descendants of Dewa and Baleo continued to perform the *tika* during the installation ceremony. Besides making the *tika* of blood through an incision of his thumb, the Oguna chief took the prince by the arm and seated him on the throne while the Undari Bhil held the salver of spices and sacred grains of rice used in making the *tika*. It needs to be emphasized that *rajyabhishek* was the most important of the royal rituals (*rajkarma*) in medieval India – a custom by which kings were created. "As a *samskara*, the *rajyabhishek* was thus not considered simply an act of confirmation or affirmation, a symbolic display of royal pomp and power. It was, to the contrary, held to be an 'effective' or 'constitutive' ritual, the universally performed act by which men were transformed into kings."[9] The fact that the Bhils were assigned a prominent and highly visible role in the ceremony not only provides valuable insights into Bhil-Rajput relationship but it is also a statement on the ritual, political and military status of the Bhils in the Rajput polity. Scholars associated with tribal studies, especially the Bhils, have reflected upon the significance of Bhil participation in this ceremony. According to Robert Deliege, it was the heart of the Bhil-Rajput relationship that was inscribed in this ceremony.[10] According to him, it is a testimony to the political capabilities of the Bhils and the fact that they constituted a real force and power to contend with and were not a community to be despised by the Rajputs. It is a historical fact that for a long time the successors of Bappa Rawal were not able to subdue the Bhil chiefs in the hilly tracts of Mewar on the borders of Dungarpur and Banswara. Ultimately, in the 14th century, Maharana Kshetra Singh was able to extend his kingdom over this area. As B.R. Chauhan has concluded that although the Bhils were defeated, their military strength and power had to be reckoned with and "given the status of at least junior partners in the political settlements". According to him, the rulers tried to make their tenure secure by introducing in the ritual of coronation a ceremony on the part of Bhils as an essential ingredient of the process of legitimation of authority.[11] K.S. Singh contends that tribal participation in the coronation ceremony was symbolic of their partnership in the establishment and continuation of the state.[12] At another level, Bhil participation in the *rajyabhishek* ceremony signifies the high ritual status conferred upon the Bhils by the Rajput rulers. Commonly, the Brahmins, who were at the top of the caste hierarchy, constituted the only group that was believed to be imbued with ritual purity – an essential requirement for performance of sacerdotal duties.

The Bhils themselves were conscious of the significance of their participation in this particular rite and keen to continue the practice despite the widely held belief that the man from whose veins the blood flowed died within a year.[13] The Rajputs, however, developed disdain for the practice after they had firmly established themselves on the seat of power. They started viewing the practice as a quasi-acknowledgement it conveyed of their need for investiture by an older and conquered race. They, perhaps, interpreted it as a sign of allegiance to the erstwhile Bhil power. It would be more apt to define it as a relic of Bhil power. It was continued in Udaipur till the time of Rana Hammir Singh.[14] The Rajputs offered the explanation that they had started shrinking because of impure Bhil blood. But, the true ground of dislike was that the "ceremony reminded them of the shortness of their rule and of the need of sanction by their lowest subjects".

In the sphere of state formation, the historic role of the Bhils went far beyond the *tika* ceremony. There are innumerable instances of military collaboration between the Sisodiyas and the Bhils, when the latter put up a gallant fight for the preservation of the Rajput kingdom. In the 14th century, the Bhils of Oguna and Panora provided 5,000 bowmen to Hammir during the wars. During Maharana Kumbha's reign, the Bhils remained faithful to the Rajput sovereign.[15] The Persian chronicles have many details of the battles fought by them along with Rajput armies against the Sultans of Malwa and Gujarat. It was during the bitter resistance of Maharana Pratap against the Mughal emperors that Bhils put forward an unparalleled example of tribal fidelity, spirit of sacrifice and patriotism. During the war, when Pratap lost Chittor, these were the Bhils who provided succour and shelter to the family. It has been often asserted that it was due to the active cooperation of the Bhils that Pratap was able to prolong his struggle against Mughal imperialism. The Bhils played a decisive role during the war, e.g., provision and transportation of food supplies, spying, tiring the enemy through guerilla tactics, plundering their supplies etc. Overwhelmed and surprised by the service and valour of the Bhil chief Punja, Maharana Pratap honoured him by conferring upon him a prestigious assignment in the army and the title of Rana.[16] Under his able leadership, the Bhils with their traditional weapons created havoc amongst the Mughal warriors. The Bhils provided major support system in the wars fought by Pratap. As a grateful acknowledgement, the Bhils were represented in the state emblem. It contains the figure of Maharana Pratap on one side and the Bhil chief on the other, with the fort of Chittor in the centre, thus depicting the high status of the Bhils in the polity of Mewar.[17]

Genealogies and ballads, panegyrics and bardic poems have preserved the image of the Rajput as a 'Kshatriya par excellence' with a distinctive and acute sense of honour and pride. While the Rajput has been eulogized in the bardic literature, one observes a systematic, consistent and a conscious process to underplay the role of the Bhils in Mewar polity. However, despite adverse historiographical trends that tend to marginalize the subalterns coupled with the negative perception of the tribal population by the outsiders, the Bhils of Mewar region have survived in collective memory of the people as a group which not only has chivalrous history to its credit but also a distinctive code of conduct that guarded its social and political behaviour. It is true that none of the elements that have been used in the construction of Rajput code of honour define the tribal concept of honour, i.e., a divine and illustrious ancestry carefully fabricated by genealogists and legitimized by the Brahmins, a well-developed ethic of submission, a clear-cut hierarchical stratification of clans, and elaborate rituals for projection of authority, status and honour. Nevertheless, a wide cross-section of people, from Kaviraj Shyamaldas, court historian and author of the voluminous history of Mewar, *Vir Vinod* to Col. James Tod as well as the colonial anthropologists and foreign travellers have appreciated the Bhils for their adherence to a value structure even at the cost of their lives.

The peculiarity of the Bhil code of honour was partly due to their view of life that was strikingly different from the other Hindu communities. Carstairs has defined Bhil life as an "antithesis of Brahmanical values".[18] The Bhils were as uninhibited as Hindus were restrained. Morris, during his tour of Deoli village in Udaipur division, observed that the quality that most forcibly distinguishes Bhils from the Hindus, by and large, is the latter's jest and enjoyment of life accepting pleasures and dangers in the same spirit.[19] They come across as simple, cheerful, fun-loving and emotional people who were not ashamed to show their feelings. Singing and dancing formed an important feature of the Bhil life. Men and women often sang and danced the whole night. Their social gatherings were free from restrictions and taboos. This distinctive outlook of the Bhils towards life was reflected in the values that governed their code of conduct. The principles that inspired their religious beliefs, political structure and social institutions were inclined towards egalitarianism with little accent on gradation and hierarchy.

The Bhils cherished a fierce sense of pride in their independence, identity and way of life. In fact, Bhil history is a saga of perpetual resistance against encroachment on their geographical, political and social spaces. They feared loss of independence more than the fear of death. They fought against Rajput ascendancy in the region. It was due to their stiff resistance that respect for tribal spaces formed one of the key aspects of the policy of Mewar sovereigns towards the Bhils. Throughout Rajput period one can observe Bhils' love for freedom and resistance to any encroachment in their near autonomous situation. The Rajputs could buy peace and stability only after they had left Bhil power structure undisturbed. In fact, they continued to be the real proprietors of the hills. In addition to their significant role in the ritual of *rajyabhishek*, they were allowed to collect two taxes – *bolai*, levied on the passage of merchandise and travellers for whose safe transit the Bhils became thereby responsible; and *rakhwali*, a tax which the colonial administrators dubbed as blackmail, was paid by the villagers to the neighbouring Bhil communities as a protection against plunder. In the areas where the knowledge of the Bhils about the topography and paths in the interior was useful, the Rajputs accepted the claims of the Bhil chiefs over their traditional rights.[20] Till 19th century, the Bhil chiefs continued to be the masters of valleys, forts, villages and passes and the passersby had to pay a tax to pass through the area. Tod had to virtually negotiate with them to get access to their area. According to him, in certain areas, they acknowledged no paramount authority and paid no tribute.[21] Despite the political supremacy of the Rajputs, the Bhils continued to enjoy their freedom in semi-autonomous localities of their own. The Bhils' urge for freedom, autonomy and identity continued to manifest itself even after the Britishers had assumed paramountcy in the Rajputana states.

In fact, encroachment on the geographical, cultural, political and economic spaces of the Bhils by the British was the primary cause of tribal uprisings against the latter. In addition to retention of Bhil socio-political institutions, Rajput rulers had given usufruct rights that provided all the produce they required for domestic and agricultural purposes from the forests. Their control on forest produce was so complete that one who mustered courage to cut a tree in their valley had to pay with his life.[22] The colonial period, however, witnessed an aggressive monetization of the economy of the tribal region for revenue generation and as the forests were taken over by the government agencies and commercial interests, tribal autonomy received a setback. Attempts to prevent the Bhils from cutting of wood for domestic consumption, prohibition on gathering of mangoes and leaves of mahua tree, stopping of distillation of liquor and manufacturing of salt and exaction of *begar* (forced labour) were viewed by Bhils as a violation of their traditional economic rights.

The Bhils by nature looked upon the outsiders with anxiety and apprehension. They branded the British as *vilayatis*, *firanghees* and also as *bhurias*. Unlike the Rajputs, the British, partly due to ignorance and also due to the exigencies of the colonial state, neglected tribal rights and customs. The Bhils, since the beginning, expressed resentment against the British for encroaching upon their traditional political and administrative structure and hence viewed all the policy initiatives of the British with utmost suspicion. They abhorred the establishment of *thanas* in their areas, surrendering of weapons, paying of land revenue, prohibition on collection of *rakhwali* and even the compulsion to obey the laws of the state.[23] Similarly, the Bhils regarded the extension of British jurisdiction to the civil and criminal disputes of the Bhils as a violation of tribal customs. The Bhils even resisted the census operations of 1881. So deep was their distrust and contempt for the alien that census was misconstrued as a prelude to additional taxation and a device to recruit able-bodied Bhils for the Afghan war which would result in the Bhil women being taken away by the non-Bhils. It was also feared that after the compilation of the census data there would be mal-exchange of women.[24] While the British had been able to subjugate the illustrious Mewar sovereign without firing a single shot, the Bhil love for freedom was so intense that not only did they relentlessly struggle against the *firanghees* but the dream of a Bhil Raj remained the root cause of all tribal movements till the achievement of independence.

The Bhils had revolted against the British and the state of Mewar in 1881 at Padona and after a few skirmishes were able to force the Mewar Maharana to sign a 21-point agreement. The main terms of the agreement were recognition of Bhils as protector of roads, withdrawal of custom outposts, restoration of rights over forest produce and right to collect *bolai* from the pilgrims and general amnesty for all Bhils. An antipathy for the outsider was so intense that they forced the Maharana to remove the *dak-harkaras* from their *pals*.[25] The agreement of 1882 was, in fact, an attempt to restore the distinctive and autonomous nature of Bhil economy and polity.

The process of mobilization of the Bhils was always motivated by the idea of a Bhil Raj. K.S. Singh and V.K. Vashishtha seem to agree that the Bhagat movement of Govindgiri, despite being couched in religious idiom and ostensibly aimed at moral and economic betterment of Bhils, was not without political overtones. According to Vashishtha, the assemblage of Guru Govindgiri and his disciples on Mangarh hills in 1913 was more than mere traditional mode of tribal protest against oppression. He believes that the very selection of the Mangarh hills, formerly a stronghold of Bhil dominion, as the site for the uprising, was specifically made to arouse political aspirations of the Bhils to re-establish Bhil Raj by overthrowing the authority of the states of Sunth and Banswara.[26] Similarly, during the Eki (integration) movement of Motilal Tejavat, the Bhils were inspired by the dream of re-establishing Bhil Raj. According to K.S. Singh, the fierce inclination for preservation of their identity and independence continued to define tribal participation in larger political movements.[27] Even during the national struggle for freedom, while they sought integration with the regional and national streams, there was a strong urge to preserve their distinctive identity. Similarly, their penchant for protest and resistance had led them to participate in the larger struggle for freedom but subsequently, they evinced little or no interest in the sedate constitutional politics of the local and district bodies in the 1920s and 1930s. They not only remained indifferent to electoral politics but even after independence when they were nominated to these bodies, they showed no real interest in their activities and deliberations. During the national movement too, the Bhils had demanded regional autonomy for themselves.

Coupled with a strong urge for freedom was their deep faith in their traditional social and political institutions. Along with their customary political rights, they were able to retain the essential structure of tribal social and political organization, which operated through two types of institutions: (i) Gameti or Mukhi, and (ii) Panchayat. The Gameti or the headman of a village/*pal* enjoyed tremendous clout and extensive powers. The authority of the Mukhi was final in all matters relating to the *pal*. All executive powers were vested in him. During the reign of the Rajput rulers, he was responsible for getting government orders complied by the members of the *pal*. The Kanungo of the Mewar state offered a *pagri* (turban) to him as a mark of recognition. He was given a specific percentage of the land revenue of the village. He also received customary fees in cash or in the form of land on festive occasions.

The Panchayat consisted of elders of the *pal* from different families. These members were known as Bhanjgarias. Although all mundane matters were settled by the heads and Bhanjgarias but Panchayat had to be summoned for discussion of important matters. Bhanjgaria played an important part in settling the disputes between two or more than two villages. The rulers also recognized their role as counsellors and as persons useful in arranging compromises.[28]

The position of the headman was central to Bhil social and political formation. No social transaction of any importance took place unless he was present to validate it. Yet he did not enjoy the absolutism that defined the status of the Rajput sovereign. If he was not able to fulfil his function, any of his relations may be preferred and the *pancha* composed of all elderly members also prevented him from abusing his powers.[29] His presence was not marked by the regal pomp and paraphernalia, elaborate political symbolism and a clear-cut hierarchical structure of authority that had become an essential part of the Rajput sovereign and their nobility.

Tribal solidarity marked by an acute sense of group consciousness was yet another remarkable attribute of the Bhils. The ties of the *pal* bound the Bhils despite their aversion for centralized authority. Each individual was linked to the status and honour of his particular village. Personal identity of an individual was not important and in fact he was known by the name of his village.[30] The entire village hosted a guest in the village. If a theft was committed in a village, the offended village may attack the village of the guilty person. Performance of rituals and celebration of festivals used to be the collective endeavour of the village. Gauri festival was a village matter. For its celebration the village organized a drama to be performed in the neighbouring villages. For this they visited three types of villages: where their kinsmen resided, where daughters had been given in marriage, and where they had business relations. The host village or *pal* presented gifts and food to the guest villagers, which were returned when in turn it performed the

Gauri festival in that village. Villages, which joined each other in celebration of the festival, are said to be linked in *udhari-hanti* relationship (partners in loan). Gauri festival thus unites the villagers in a network of matrimonial and business relations and is an example of heightened group consciousness among the Bhils. Whenever the village or *pal* was in distress to seek revenge, they give out alarming cries of '*fiere fiere*' and thousands of Bhils with bows and arrows, irrespective of their relationship with the respective *pal*, responded to these familiar cries.[31]

Despite their uninhibited and freedom-loving nature, the Bhils had a strong sense of social morality. However, unlike the Hindus, their code of conduct was not linked to religion and their idea of morality was more in the nature of a civil law. Puritanical values and artificial constructs that were peculiar to caste Hindus did not define the tribal code of honour, which was in the form of simplistic principles inspired by humanism and righteousness. The truthfulness and sincerity of the Bhils immensely impressed Tod.[32] Foreign travellers like Bishop Heber[33], who visited the region of Rajputana in 1820, and Louis Rousselet, who had toured the Bhil region in 1865, have been eloquent about Bhil code of honour and values. The latter recollected the qualities of the Bhils in his travelogue thus: "Notwithstanding their faults, the Bheels have two qualities which are wanting in the Hindoos – that is to say, a profound gratefulness towards their benefactors and a great respect for their pledged faith...As to the point of honour, they carry it so far that they would allow to pass in perfect safety and even protect a rich caravan which had obtained the promise of safe conduct, even from one of their children."[34]

Commitment to a vow was the hallmark of Bhil character. Shyamaldas has testified to this characteristic trait of the Bhils. A person who took the vow consumed a bit of opium which was kept on a sword or consumed some saffron mixed with water after offering it to Rishabdeo. Shyamaldas has contended that vow taken after performance of these two simple rituals had so much sanctity that no power could dissuade the Bhil to violate his word.[35]

Provision of shelter to the travellers and strangers formed an integral part of the Bhil value system. Tod and Shyamaldas have contended that the Bhils not only provided hospitality to the guests but the whole family extended protection to them at the cost of their own lives. Tod defined this behaviour as "the most cherished value of humanity". He has also observed that when a pilgrim has paid the due taxes to the Bhils, they took entire responsibility of protecting him in his territory. A Bhil man or a woman accompanied the pilgrim or the traveller till he safely reached his destination. In cases where they could not escort them, an arrow was given to them as a guarantee of security in the Bhil area.

A brief perusal of the historical antecedents of the Bhils, along with a glimpse into their distinctive political and social behaviour, projects the tribals as a group that enriched and strengthened the polity and culture of Mewar. They provided valuable military cooperation to their Rajput sovereigns in the struggle for supremacy and survival. Their prominent role in the *rajyabhishek* ceremony, recognition of their customary rights and traditional institutions and, above all, their inclusion in the state emblem along with an image of Maharana Pratap testifies to their honoured place in the political culture of Mewar. They consistently strove to preserve their distinctive identity in terms of their ancestry, religious beliefs, language, values, customs and institutions.

Their adherence and deep commitment to a value structure points to a code of honour that contrasted sharply with the Rajput sense of pride. While it is the Rajput who has been immemorialized as the relentless warrior governed by a strict code of conduct, the lengthy and well-documented history of tribal resistance shows that the Bhil was no less endowed with a martial disposition. It is, indeed, regrettable that despite their significant contribution, Bhils have yet to emerge as an indispensable partner of the Rajputs in mainstream history.

II

The Charans formed a community that enjoyed enviable social status in Rajputana states. The proud claimants to epithets like 'fountain head of inspiration' (*viratva ke prernastrota*), 'immortalizer of heroes', 'voice of the desert' and 'soul of the medieval history of the Rajputs', the Charans evolved into a peculiar institution of the Rajput polity. They played a key role as builders, guardians and preservers of the Rajput code of honour and in the process earned for themselves precedence over all other castes in the customary law of the land.

Significantly, the Charans did not have any specified status in the hierarchy of the caste system. Generally, they were accorded an intermediate position between the Brahmins and the Rajputs but some historians have categorized the Charans with the Brahmins in the social hierarchy and in terms of their proximity and utility to Rajput political culture even placed them at a higher pedestal than that of the Brahmins.[36] It is believed that the Charans themselves were not keen on their placement within the stratified Hindu social system as "they disdained being classified among lesser mortals covered by *varnashram dharma*. When occasion demanded, they put themselves amongst the Heavenly Beings, the *Devtas*. Consequently, they did not claim their origin from any limb of Brahma."[37] Like the Rajputs, the Charans sought to distinguish themselves by tracing ancestry from divine figures, especially the Pauranic Charans, Sidh and Magadh who are referred to in ancient scriptures like *Ramayana* and *Mahabharata*. *Shiv Purana* gives them the exalted task of protecting Shiva's favourite bull Nandi after the Bhats had failed to fulfil the task. Some Charan scholars claim that their ancestors descended from heaven in the company of their illustrious companions, the Kshatriyas.[38]

Later historians rejected the idea of continuity of line between the Charans and their divine scriptural counterparts and have offered historically more rational theories to explain their emergence and evolution into a distinct caste. Yet, construction of a celestial origin formed a significant element in the sacralization of the community. It was one of the mechanisms through which they sought to project their distinctive status and honourable position amongst other communities.

There are said to be two groups of Charans – the aristocratic Maru Charans and the degraded Kachela Charans.[39] Maru Charans, due to their proximity to the aristocratic classes, assumed a sense of superiority and came to be known as aristocratic Maru Charans, while those who clung to their home came to be known as Kachela Charans. The latter were considered inferior since they gave up their original bardic character which involved uncertainties and adventure and instead, chose the softer option of a settled life.

Bhats also persue the bardic profession in the Rajputana states. An attempt was made to project the Bhats as an inferior group by ascribing a divine but stigmatized descent to them. Nevertheless, they were revered as the sacred order all through Rajputana. Unlike the Charans, the Bhats could not guarantee protection but it was considered an ill omen and a disgrace to kill or beat a Bhat.[40] Charans and Bhats, due to their professional affinity, enjoyed a sacral status and were entitled to certain immunities. While both were hereditary guardians of history and pedigree of clans and families and dependent on the bounty of the *yajman* (patron) for their livelihood, certain developments distanced them from one another. The Charans acquired pre-eminence due to their association with the ruling elite while Bhats were the bards of the commoners. Moreover, Charans, due to their creative excellence and educational qualifications, wrote literary compositions of a high order and of a wide genre, whereas Bhats documented *pidhinamas* (family histories), *kursinamas*, (chronology of people who were in high position) and genealogies. It is alleged that Bhats took undue advantage of their privileged status to extort money from their patrons either by promises of spreading their fame or by threats of infamy and ignominy through their compositions. Moreover, their standard of obtaining *neg* (customary or ritual offerings in the form of cash or kind) from their patrons had descended to a very low level and virtually amounted to begging or extortion. The Charans, therefore, started claiming a higher status than their caste brethren – the Bhats.[41] Shyamaldas, the author of the celebrated history of Mewar, *Vir Vinod* and a Charan himself, is astutely silent on the identity of the Bhats as a separate caste as well as their relationship with the Charans. The Bhat rebellion during Rana Amar Singh II's reign, perhaps, led Shyamaldas to do so. After this rebellion a large number of Bhats committed suicide or became Banjaras (wandering community).[42]

In addition to these variations amongst the Charans and Bhats, some septs of Maru Charans acquired more social prestige and political clout on account of their distinguished services to the rulers and the nobles. The Charans who occupied significant positions in the courts of the rulers were known as Barhats. In Mewar, the descendants of Baru Charan, who came to be known as Sauda Barhats, acquired prominence on account of Baru's timely military assistance to Hammir in regaining his lost throne. Baru was appointed as Barhat in the Mewar court. Henceforward, the Sauda Barhats continued to occupy a coveted position at Mewar court.[43]

The Charans acquired unparalleled importance in the Rajput political system. They were conferred upon with norms of respect, marks of honour and special privileges, which at times surpassed those of Brahmins. Occasionally, notable individuals belonging to Brahmin, Kayastha, Vaishya, etc., were endowed with royal insignia and protocol of a first grade chief for their outstanding services to the ruler and the state. These privileges and distinctions were, however, personal to them and did not pass on to the subsequent generations. But, in the case of Charans, these honours and privileges were granted in perpetuity. They superseded the Brahmins in receiving *neg* (customary ritual gifts) during weddings and other such occasions. The post of honour at the main gate of the palace belonged to the Charan who demanded *neg* from the bridegroom's party. The special honour of the community was also projected through the spatial arrangement, rituals and etiquette of the court. They were given an honourable seat in the *durbars* and the chief himself offered the first palm of opium to the Charan as a mark of respect.

At the social level too, Charans enjoyed a special relationship with the Rajputs who looked upon them as brothers and sisters. No Rajput could marry a Charan girl nor keep her as his concubine. Certain distinctive behaviourial norms and taboos pertaining to social and political morality were formulated in the context of Charans too. They were classed with the Brahmin and the cow whose slaughter was forbidden by the Rajputs. Charan was said to be '*avadhya*' (one who cannot be killed).[44] In times of war, the home of the Charan was considered as a 'demilitarized zone' or a 'haven of refuge' which was not attacked or ravaged by rival armies. Such was the sanctity of the Charan's home that rival sides could send their women and children to the houses of Charans to secure guarantee of their protection. The inviolability of the Charans was so highly respected that, according to Bishop Heber, it was usual for travellers and merchants during their journeys to hire one of them as guardians to protect them from plunderers.[45] It was the Charan who enjoyed the privilege of giving *sharan* (protection) under his roof. The spilling of the blood of Charan was said to be fraught with dreadful consequences wreaked by divine wrath. At times, a single Charan could avoid bloodshed between groups of rival warriors. In case, they did not heed his exhortation, he killed himself with a *katar* (dagger) and no Rajput ever dared to violate the ban imposed by a Charan's blood. According to Qanungo, "this was no fiction but a long established institution in the code of honour and morality backed by a religious awe in that land of eternal vendetta."[46]

In popular perception, the honourable position of the Charan was due to the might of his tongue that could cut deeper than the *katar* and cut both ways. It was the dread of ignominy through Charan's satire that forced the Rajputs to keep them in good humour. Nevertheless, it is also a fact that in later phases, the Charans through their oppressive demands in the form of *tyag* (customary gift) during the weddings and birth of a child etc. had created acute financial problems for the Rajputs. The problems assumed such gigantic proportions that due to these demands the rulers were induced to resort to prohibitory measures.[47] In Mewar, the earliest initiatives for restricting the inordinate and, at times, extortionate demands in the form of *tyag* were undertaken by the Maharanas. Maharana Sajjan Singh initiated the formation of Desh Hiteshini Sabha in 1877 that aimed at regulation of marriage expenses, restriction on polygamy and unequal marriages.

The widespread unpopularity that the Charans received stimulated amongst them a keen desire to reform the community. Through Charan Sammelans, which were organized at regular intervals since 1911, they sought to consolidate themselves as a group by bridging the hierarchy that had kept them divided and to purge the community of the evils that had crept into it. The major emphasis in these conferences was on the elimination of the practice of using pressure tactics to extort inordinate sums as *tyag*. The Charan leadership exhorted their caste brethren to give up the practice, which had become a *jatiya kalank* (stigma attached to the entire caste). An attempt was made to strengthen and reaffirm the close bonds between the Charans and the Rajputs. These conferences sought to coordinate their reformative efforts with the Walterkrit Rajputra Hitkarini Sabha. A quarterly journal *Charan* was also brought out by Akhil Bhartiya Charan Sammelan (All India Charan Conference).[48]

It would be travesty of historical facts and highly unfair to the contribution of the Charans to brand them as "singers of praises" and "psychophants of Rajput princes". Significantly,

Charans had constituted an indispensable institution in the martial culture of the Rajputs. Importance of the Charans in the history of Rajputana lies in their contribution to the spheres of literature, history, war and politics. They played a key role in Rajput polity as builders of a heroic ethos. The emergence of Rajputs and their processes of state formation were marked by incessant warfare. Rajput polity during this phase was all about war and pride. Such a martial culture necessitated a distinctive value system that was in accordance with their military needs and principles. They needed a special category of persons to evolve a code of conduct that could strengthen and uphold their political systems. Thus, like all martial races, the Rajputs too required bards who could, through their spirited recitals of ballads and songs, inspire the clan on the battlefield to live upto its chivalric traditions.

The Charans played a significant role in the construction of Rajput heroism through their highly effective composition and delivery of court poetry. The literature composed by Charans can be divided into five categories.[49] *Khyats* give a systematic presentation and description of contemporary events. They were in the form of clan histories. These were retained by the Charans as records and were referred to by the ruler in the case of disputes and disagreements.

Another genre of Charan composition comprises of *vanshavalis* (descriptive genealogies) of the ruling families through which they sought to reinforce the legitimacy of the ruler by highlighting their illustrious and divine ancestry. *Vartas* or *Vat* (stories) were historical anecdotes about one or more rulers and nobles of Rajasthan. *Raso* or *veer kavya* were written to eulogize old heroes and popular contemporary rulers. Exaggerated expressions and supernatural elements were used as metaphors and similes for describing wars and battles in order to render their compositions more thrilling and effective.[50] *Geet* (songs) composed in the form of *duhas* (small verses) was a distinctive form of the Charans' literary compositions. When the rulers were engaged in continuous warfare, they did not have time to hear the lengthy epic poems and court poets were thus obligated to adopt a format that was brief but effective. This led to the poetic style called *duhas*. One *duha* consisted of two lines. The songs by Charans were not for vocal music but were meant for declamation and spirited recital in assemblies, battlefields and in the *zenani deorhi* (female quarters). It is said that the 'poetic fire' of his songs gave a Rajput the strength of ten on the field of carnage. They used their poetic talent to inspire Rajput men and women to make necessary sacrifices for preservation of religion, land and honour.

The Charans have also received applause and appreciation for their contribution as historians of medieval Rajasthan. The *khyats* (court histories and chronicles) and *vanshavalis* (genealogies) have proved to be of immense historical worth as there is scarce archival material to rely upon. Tod's trendsetting work *Annals and Antiquities of Rajasthan* was written partly on the basis of information gathered from these local histories. However, one has to exercise tremendous caution and discretion while using these compositions for construction of historical events. It has to be kept in mind that Charans were court historians who survived and flourished on the bounty of the powerful patrons. The inherent biases of the Charans and the precarious circumstances they were placed in led them to indulge in exaggerated glorification which has impaired the historical value of their poetic works and biographical eulogies. Nevertheless, their contribution towards preservation of historical details has been seminal leading Tod to hail them as "chief, though not the sole historians of western India" and by others as the "soul of the medieval history of Rajputana".

While reflecting upon the objectivity of the Charans' compositions and their utility as a source of history, it would be perhaps relevant to touch upon yet another category of literature composed by them, the *bhadda* (satire, lampoon or invective poem). The Charans were not just panegyrists and, at times, they used their immunity to criticize and censure their patrons whenever they deviated from the path of rectitude. Their satirical verses known as *Chhand Bhujang* or 'serpentine stanza' acted as checks on wanton behaviour of the rulers. These stanzas carried tremendous moral force and were effective in preventing feuds and getting justice rendered.

As poets who composed such a wide genre of literary writings, the Charans acted as important agents in the construction of a cultural ethos congenial to the Rajput political system. They were not merely preservers of legends, singers of praises and historians but guardians of Rajput code of honour and *kulreeti*, i.e., cherished ideals and traditions of clans. They transmitted ideas of valour, honour, sacrifice and heroism to Rajput men and women. Their narrations exuded 'laconic fire' and 'martial air' that captivated the minds and hearts of listeners. They interspersed their narrations with sounds of battle drums, beat of the horses and marching of the armies due to which their recitals had a hypnotic quality which spellbound their audience and had the effect of transporting them to the arena of war. The rendition of Charan poetry formed an integral part of the socialization of the Rajput boys and girls. Their recitals were held in the *zenana* for inculcating the ideas of chivalry, fortitude and sacrifice amongst Rajput girls and women. Rajput women were taught Charan verses so that they could be moulded in accordance with the demands of a warrior culture. In addition, the Charans were invited on all important ceremonies and festivals to regale, inspire and enthuse Rajput men and women with their narrations.[51]

In addition to their role as builders of heroic atmosphere, the Charans were known for their patriotism, courage and devotion to their patrons. As Qanungo has observed, "The Charan was not the proverbial strife monger between rival clans adding fuel to fire of fray on a point of honour.... The typical Charan of Rajputana was fearless of speech, true to his word unto death, kindly and charitable to all and genuinely devoted to his country's good and welfare of the Kshatriyas particularly."[52] At times, the Charans even excelled their patrons in their conformity and adherence to human virtues of moral courage and political morality. There are numerous anecdotes about Charans, when they not merely accompanied the Rajput warriors to the thickest of battle to enthuse them through fiery recitals but they actually fought side by side. Despite their meagre numbers, Charans were known for their exemplary courage on the battlefield in Mewar. During Maharana Sanga's and Maharana Pratap's reigns, the roll of honour has names of prominent Charans. In his homage to Haldi Ghati heroes, the great poet Rathore Puthar Raj has mentioned four Charan warriors - Ramsha Tanwar of Gwalior, Mansha Jhala of Sadri, Ram Rathore of Badnore and Sandu Ram.[53]

It is believed that when Aurangzeb had sent his army to destroy Maharana Raj Singh, the latter had to seek shelter of the inaccessible hills. At this time, descendants of Baru Charans, Charan Naru of Sauda Barhat used to carry information and supplies from the palace of Udaipur to the hiding place of the Maharana. Later on, when Mughal generals came to destroy temples and idols, Naru rushed to Jagdish temple situated outside the palace gate and died there for protection of *dharma* and honour.[54]

It is believed that on one occasion Maharana of Udaipur got annoyed with the Rawat of Devgarh and ordered that he should be divested of his jagir. Rawat of Devgarh was an influential jagirdar whose deposition could have flared up an armed conflict. A Charan is said to have used his persuasive skills forcing the Maharana to change his decision and avert the unseemly repercussions. Similarly, Charan Poorja severely indicted Maharana Ari Singh for objectionable and inhuman behaviour in getting his refractory nobles killed by deceit.[55]

It is the voice of the Charan that has immortalized Rajput heroism. The rulers were keenly conscious of this role of the Charan in articulating their glories and exploits. In addition to the rewards, honours and jagirs that were showered upon them, the rulers acknowledged their debt by writing adulating verses for the Charans. Maharana Raj Singh wrote a *chhand* to the effect that whosoever seeks immortality must worship the feet of the bards.[56]

The exemplary role of the Charans in character building and in perpetuating Rajput glory certainly entitled them to the status and importance that they received in Rajput polity. The Charans, in fact, fulfilled the most pressing need in the martial polity of the Rajputs, i.e., to inspire and enthuse generations after generations to make sacrifices for the protection of *dharma*, land and clan honour. They achieved the purpose through literary skills, narration, exhortation and valour.

III

Social differentiation involving demarcation of individuals into distinctive groups and statuses is a very widespread feature of human societies. In India, differences were accommodated through division of society into four occupational groups known as *varnas*, which later took the form of castes, with a further classification into numerous sub-castes. The caste system emerged as the basic organizing principle of Hindu society by 2nd century AD. A distinctive feature of the caste system was a definite scheme of social precedence amongst the castes with the Brahmin at the head of the hierarchy, followed by Kshatriyas, Vaishyas and Sudras. The four *varnas*, representing dimensions of knowledge, power, wealth and manual work, and the castes and sub-castes were entitled to varying degrees of respectability, privileges and circle of social intercourse. According to G.S. Ghurye, by the third period of Indian history, i.e., the period of *Dharmashastras* from 2nd century AD to 8th century AD, the Brahmins had emerged as the senior-most group. The *Smriti* writers – Manu, Narada, Yajnavalkya and Vishnu – exhort all three lower *varnas* to serve the Brahmins. Manu and Narada, both insist upon the kings to show honour to the Brahmins, "for a field furnished with Brahmins is the root of the prosperity of the world". The king must show himself first in the morning to the Brahmins and offer obeisance to them. Brahmins came to enjoy monopoly over the sources of legitimization and authority. Kingship as an institution had no authority of its own. Ultimate authority was the exclusive preserve of the Brahmins. The king, therefore, desperately needed the Brahmin to sanction his power. As the texts have put it, "The Brahmin can stand on its own, the Kshatriya, however, cannot and depends on the Brahmin."[57]

In the context of the Rajputana states, wherein different Rajput clans emerged as the ruling classes, it has been argued by some scholars that the Brahmins had to concede their supreme position to the Rajputs. The Rajput period has been described as a process of Rajputization or Kshatriyization wherein other classes, instead of emulating the social customs and values of the Brahmins, upheld the Rajputs and Rajput *dharma* as symbols of excellence and as role models. Significantly, it has been contended that apart from the ruling classes, i.e., the Rajputs, the Brahmins had to share, in some cases even concede their supreme position to the Charans. Scholars have argued that Rajputs were a military people engaged in continuous warfare till the conclusion of a treaty with the British. In a martial culture, concepts like victory honour, valour and sacrifice acquired utmost significance. The warrior caste required a distinctive value system, cultural ethos and a code of conduct that was different from Brahmanic Hinduism. The Rajput concept of death and salvation was different. They were not guided by Brahmanical notions of auspiciousness or by astrological position of stars. In keeping with their military nature, they even required different deities that were of martial temperament (*kroor svabhava*). They needed a new *dharma* and a new class of *Pandits* to legitimize their military actions.[58] It was in such a situation that the Charans emerged as "teacher, preacher, exponent of religion and that of guardian of moral conduct of the ruling classes". It is believed that they replaced and superseded the Brahmins as "men of literature, historians and genealogists". In the process, they became entitled to numerous privileges which were, hitherto, the preserve of the Brahmins.

Another reason for the supposed denigration of the Brahmins was the Rajput proximity to lower castes. The followers of Rajput *pirs* like Pabuji, Gogaji etc. were from backward classes. The Rajputs preferred these classes and Charans, since they could accompany them to the battlefield and live upto the Rajput ideals of chivalry and sacrifice.[59] Shyamaldas, the court historian of Mewar, has sought to enhance the importance of Charans and the Rajputs at the expense of the Brahmins. While extolling the exalted status of the Charans, the eminent historian has ridiculed and shown contempt for the Brahmins in his *magnum opus*, *Vir Vinod – Mewar Ka Itihas*. He has projected the Brahmins as an illiterate caste which survived on alms and grants. Commenting on the deterioration of the Brahmins, Shyamaldas wrote: "Almost all rural Brahmins of Rajputana and particularly in Mewar who have received land grants (*udah*) have become peasants and they are so illiterate that they can't even recite a word of *Gayatri Mantra*. To project their caste identity they wear the sacred thread and that forms their sole claim to be called Brahmins. While those living in cities and towns are either engaged in jobs and trade or survive on alms and grants. Only a few amongst them are literate and earn their livelihoods by reading out *Panchanga* or prepare horoscopes, yearly forecast etc. If any amongst them is very ambitious, then he becomes a Kathabhatt who recites stories from *Puranas*. Only one amongst thousands of Brahmins is proficient in *Vedas* or *Shastras*; they too like their caste brethren are not devoted to the welfare of their nation."[60] Shyamaldas' tirade against the Brahmins was probably due to the fact that he belonged to the Charan community and wished to project the pre-eminence of his caste. Moreover, his writings coincided with a marked decline in the social prestige of the Charans. The Charans, along with Polpats, Bhats and Damamis, demanded *neg* and *tyag* from the Rajputs on the occasions of marriage, festival and other ceremonies related to the court. These demands adversely affected the treasuries of the Rajput rulers, who could ignore these demands only at the pain of social opprobrium, ignominy and disgrace. The British officials, too, had come to the conclusion that *neg* and *tyag* were responsible for worsening economic situation of rulers and for incidence of evils like infanticide.[61] Shyamaldas, keen to bolster the prestige of his caste, coupled with a genuine desire to reform the evils besetting his fellow Charans, sought to restore and raise the honour of his group by painstakingly corroborating their divine and ancient antecedents in the epics and the *Shastras*. However, it is regrettable that in doing so he cast aspersions on the Brahmins as a whole. While it is true that Charans had acquired proximity to the ruling class and carved a niche for themselves as generators and constructors of Rajput *dharma* but their special status did not impinge adversely upon the traditional importance of the Brahmins in the spiritual, literary, religious and social realms. Noted historian G.N. Sharma has observed that it is undeniable that the number of Brahmin scholars was many times more than the Charans. Particularly, in Mewar, one comes across innumerable *Prashasti*s or rock edicts dated from 10th to 18th century which were composed by the Brahmins.[62] They continued to enjoy their pre-eminent status as spiritual guides, managers of shrines, creative genius, ritual specialists and teachers. With a view to underscore their distinguished position in the native state of Mewar, the following section enumerates the numerous areas and ways in which they continued to enrich and strengthen the polity.

The Brahmins constituted a substantial section of the population of Mewar; in 1901, their number slightly exceeded that of the Rajputs.[63] The Maharanas of Mewar venerated them as defenders of Hindu culture and religion and bestowed upon them numerous honours and privileges, in addition to substantial grants in the form of landed estates, villages and wells. At the ritual and symbolic level, the Maharanas accepted the supremacy of the Brahmins. In the ceremonies of the court, the Brahmins were not expected to offer *nazrana* to the ruler. Amongst the numerous kinds of land grants, the Brahmins were entitled to the privileged and sacred category of inalienable grants (*sahsun*) and privileges and, in lieu, they were not expected to offer any services to the state or rulers.[64] Since the grants were perpetual, they were inscribed on indestructible or long lasting material like stone slabs or copper plates popularly known as *tamrapatras* (copper plates). Along with Brahmins, Charans and Bhats were also *Shatdarshanis* (entitled to inalienable grants).[65] Although these grants were endowed upon an individual and were not meant to be hereditary, these sacred charities were seldom infringed upon. Vanity, fear of disgrace and infliction of curse prevented resumption of these lands. However, these lands could be sold, exchanged or mortgaged only with the permission of the ruler. The king revered the Brahmins and other *Shatdarshanis* as exalted and pure castes and their code of conduct required that they should not molest or perpetrate atrocities on them, even if they belonged to the other states. The Brahmins, in turn, addressed and respected the king as *Go-Brahmin-Pratipalak* (protector of cows and Brahmins).[66]

The Brahmins who worked as priests or ritual specialists could be divided into two categories – those who were attached to different social classes including the Maharana, jagirdars and the commoners; and the priests who were attached to the well-known shrines of Hinduism as managers and heads of these holy places. The first category of Brahmins was divided into three hierarchical grades. The *purohits* or ritual specialists formed the most honourable social category amongst them. These were further graded in accordance with the status and position of the class to which they were attached. At the top of the ladder were those who performed the rituals and ceremonies of the uppermost sections of the society, i.e., the Maharanas, jagirdars and the affluent sections. This was the privilege of the Bade Paliwal sub-caste of the Brahmins ever since their appointment as Rajpurohit by Rana Hammir. The *purohits* of the Maharana were known as *Bade Purohit* and they performed the daily worship and other important rituals on behalf of the Maharana. They were conferred upon with the honours and privileges of the first class jagirdar. Next to them were the *purohits* of the commoners. They received *jajmani* (offerings) in the form of gifts. The gifts consisted of *jins petiya* (grains or raw material for cooking food and clothes). These were in the form of fixed offerings given during harvest or on various social and festive occasions. Since cash endowments were not so common, the state had also fixed a share from the royal granary known as *nama* for the priests. Still lower among the *purohits* were *karmantris* who performed the funeral ceremonies and *kriya kashtha*.[67]

The second grade of Brahmins comprised of *katha vachaks* (narrators of stories from *Puranas, Bhagwad Gita, Manusmriti* and other religious texts). The Brahmin sub-castes of Bhatt Mewara, Audichya, Dashora and Ameta specialized in these Brahmannical functions. They received charities and gifts from their patron families and the state. The state conferred upon them land, cash and honorific like *Rajya Jyotish*, *Katha Bhatt* and *Vyasa.* During the narration of the *katha*, the Maharana instead of sitting on his *gaddi* sat on a lower seat. When the recital got over, the Kathabhatt was seated on an elephant with numerous gifts and personally seen off by the Maharana. There were similar other sub-castes which were patronized by the state for their proficiency in different spheres, e.g., Vediya (proficient in four *Vedas*) who belonged to the Nagar Brahmin sub-caste; Kushandi who helped the Rajpurohit by making preparations for the rituals – this position was held by Goriwal Brahmins since Maharana Bhim Singh's reign; Dharmshastri (who were conversant with the *Dharmasutras* and *Smriti* literature); Shilpshastri, who supervised the construction of buildings and lakes in accordance with the rules of *shilpshastra*; Raj Jyotisha (astrologer), who were appointed from among Brahmin sub-castes of Audumbar, Nagar, Bhatt Mewara and Gurjar Gaur and they used to determine the auspicious dates and also prepare the *Panchanga* (annual forecast); and Raj Vaidya (royal physician), a post was held by Dadhicha Brahmin in Mewar. The third category comprised of priests who were attached to local and village temples for performance of rituals. It also included those who specialized in the reading of *Panchanga*.

The royal family of Mewar gave high priority to the establishment and maintenance of ritual performance and worship in *Devsthanas* or shrines. The tutelary deity of the Mewar sovereigns was Mahadeva or Ishwara. He was worshipped under the epithet of Eklingji and his shrine, known as Eklingeshwar, was, consequently, the most venerated and richly endowed by the Maharanas. Nevertheless, they cherished highest respect for shrines belonging to other sects of Hinduism as well as other religions. There was not a single village in Mewar, which did not receive land endowments for maintenance of its religious establishments, shrines and temples.[68] In Mewar, lands in *sahsun* (perpetual charity) or religious grants amounted in value to one-fifth of the revenue of the state and the rulers believed that any attempt to reclaim these grants could invite the curse of "sixty thousand years' residence in hell". As managers and ritual specialists of these *Devsthanas*, Brahmins were entitled to superior category of temple honours, grants and privileges.

The shrines or religious establishments were broadly classified into three hierarchical categories or grades, which formed the basis of their endowments and other prerogatives. The shrines of the highest grade were Eklingeshwar, Kankroli, Savinakheda and Nathadwara. The important shrines belonging to the second grade, were the Vaishnav shrines of Charbhuja and Rupanarayan. The third grade comprised of numerous other smaller shrines spread throughout Mewar.[69] This classification was undertaken in accordance with their religious significance and the extent of devotion they commanded from the people.

The shrines of the highest order were entitled to generous endowments. The shrine of Eklingji, also known as Kailashpuri, situated 14 miles to the north of Udaipur, was endowed with 24 large villages, besides land grants from the chieftains. The other shrine that competed with Eklingji for royal favours was Nathdwara situated about 30 miles north-east of Udaipur city on the right bank of river Banas. It owes its celebrity status entirely to the image of Krishna that is said to be the original idol that has been worshipped at Mathura, ever since his deification.[70] During the reign of Aurangzeb, a royal decree had been issued for desecration of idols and shrines of Hinduism. To escape vandalism at the hands of infidels, the shrines of Krishna had to be installed elsewhere.[71] At this critical juncture, Maharana Raj Singh "offered the heads of one hundred thousand Rajputs for his service" and the deity was installed near the village at Siarh in the fief of Dilwara, one of the sixteen nobles of Mewar. Siarh, henceforward, came to be known as Nathdwara, i.e., "portal (*dwara*) of the God (*Nath*)".[72] Maharana conferred on the deity several villages situated in different parts of Mewar, yielding a revenue of several thousands of rupees. Other rulers of Rajasthan and jagirdars also gave liberal endowments for the maintenance of the shrine, deity and the head priest (*Tilkayat*). The annual income of the temple collected as revenue and offerings amounted to several crores of rupees.[73] The other revered shrine of Krishna, which received liberal grants from the Maharana and his nobility, was Dwarkadheesh. The deity in the shrine was earlier installed in Asotiya village and later shifted to Kankroli.[74] The privileges and prerogatives of these shrines were well defined in the charter that was inscribed on *tamrapatras* to distinguish it from feudal grants that were commonly documented on paper.

These religious establishments apart from generous land endowments were conferred upon the privilege of *sirna* or *sharan* (rights of sanctuary or protection) within the vicinity of the shrine and at times this may be extended to include a much larger area around the shrine. This privilege implied that no offender or criminal could be apprehended or searched by the forces of the Maharana or the jagirdars, within the extent of *sirna* or sanctuary defined by the charter. Tod believed that these places of refuge were multiplied by the numerous grants. He noted that there were occasions when Gosain of Eklingji misused the power of *sirna*. Once he had murdered somebody within the precincts of the shrine. While he was deprived of the high office, his personal expenses continued to be looked after by the state.[75]

The *Devsthanas* were also entitled to collect transit duties within the area of the shrine and nearby villages. All the products imported in the town intended for consumption at the shrine were exempted from duties. Each chief was ordered to ensure free passage of goods to the shrines. The shrine was also entitled to the revenues (*hasils*) and cesses (*burrar*) within its area. In addition, the shrine also controlled the flora that lay within its jurisdiction.

The Brahmin priests as managers of these shrines also formed a hierarchical order entitled to varying grades of honours, privileges and authority in the locality around the shrine. Apart from fiscal and land grants, the Maharana treated the priests, especially the head priests, of these shrines with utmost respect. There was a code of conduct that regulated the ruler's behaviour towards the head priest. It laid down meticulous rules of etiquette to be followed during the interaction of the rulers with the head priest. The head priests of the shrines of Eklingji, Nathdwara, Kankroli and Savinakheda were bestowed with the privileges and honours of the first order.[76] The head priests were known as Gosain or Goswami which signifies "control over the senses". The head priest of Eklingji was the Suryaguru of the Maharanas and was the descendant of sage Harita – a Nath Sadhu of Lakulish sect. He remains a celibate and adopted disciples who continued his office. Till 1818, there had been 64 such spiritual heirs since sage Harita. The head priests of Nathdwara and Kankroli, also addressed as Gosainji, were allowed to marry one wife. The Gosains of these two Vaishnava shrines belong to Vallbhacharya sect, descendants of Vallabh who had collected the seven images of Krishna, now installed in different parts of Rajasthan. The status of Gosain of Nathdwara amongst the Vaishnavites has been compared to that of Pope amongst the Roman Catholics.[77]

Although Nathdwara formed the senior-most and highly revered shrine of Krishna, it was the Gosain or head priest of Dwarkadheesh at Kankroli who was the Vaishnava Guru of the Maharanas. The devotion of Maharanas to Dwarkadeesh dates back to Maharana Jagat Singh's visit to the shrine in Mathura as early as 1636 to 1640 AD. On this particular visit, Maharana was overwhelmed by the catholicity, spiritualism and vast knowledge of Gosain Girdharilalji and accepted him as his Guru. The subsequent Maharanas later carried on the preceptor-disciple tradition. Maharana Jagat Singh had bestowed Asotiya village for the shrine on this occasion. Thus, long before the actual arrival of the image around 1670 AD, the shrine had been provided a sanctuary in Mewar.[78]

Another revered spiritual figure was the Gosain of Savinakheda, who was the Suryaguru of the Maharana and belonged to Naga sect. Maharana Jai Singh had chosen to become the disciple of the Gosain Harnathgiri, after he was impressed by his immense spiritual prowess. The Gosains of Savinakheda observed celibacy. The Maharanas, as the disciples of Gosain, visited the shrine on three occasions in a year – Guru Purnima, Raksha Bandhan and during Navratri. They received his blessings on their nomination as Yuvraj.[79] Gosain visited the palaces on auspicious occasions like marriages, birthdays, etc.

On various occasions priests were invited for consultations to a third place so that their own honour and dignity did not get diminished and subdued by the glamour and authority of the Maharana within his palace.[80] During their meetings with the rulers,. observances regarding greeting, reception and seating arrangements were framed with a view to project superior ritual status of the priests. On such occasions, the rulers used to occupy a humble lower seat called *dowitia* and the priests sat on the *gaddi*. The nature of seating has been a significant barometer of the differential status and position of individuals in the royal court and palace. When the head priests visited the palace, an additional cushion was placed on the throne for them to make it higher and by implication, more honourable. The Maharana paid obeisance by lying down on the ground, placing his head on their feet, i.e., *dandvat pranam*. Maharana used to receive the priest at some distance from the palace. The priests of the first order could visit the palaces in their *baggies* till the Surya Gokhra along with a *lavazma* (insignia and protocol) of 12 persons.[81] These priests were entitled to the honours and privileges of a first grade jagirdar and endowed with insignia like *chanwar* (flywhisk), *chhatri* (umbrella), *takhat* (throne) etc. These head priests emerged as significant judicial and executive authority within their shrines' area. The charter of grants and privileges to these shrines clearly laid down their judicial powers. All complaints had to be addressed to the Gosains.

Like the priests of these large religious establishments, priests attached to local or village shrines were also venerated. The village priesthood, like their superior counterparts, had definite claims over agricultural produce in addition to other privileges. They were entitled to a *seer* in every maund that being a 40th part of the grain in the summer harvest, *kripa* or a bundle from every sheaf of the autumn crop, i.e., *makai* (maize), *bajra* (millet) or *joar* (barley). They also received a tithe or a fixed due from oil mill and sugar mill. They were offered a platter of food on all rejoicings as birth, marriage etc. They also had the privilege of *churaie* or right of pasturage on the village pasture. When priests had landed property, they had right to *hulmoh* or unpaid labour.[82]

The Brahmins of Mewar were not necessarily engaged in priestly functions. They were entitled to hold political and administrative appointments and in that capacity too, they received territorial assignments. According to Tod, the Brahmins even took up military vocations and were not found wanting in energy or courage, "the sword was as familiar to them as the *mala* (chaplet)". As *Gurus* and *Purohits*, they supervised the education of princes and princesses, on whom they "acquired immense influence".[83] A leading family of Paliwal Brahmins had served the Maharanas for centuries as their hereditary Rajpurohits. Rajpurohit Garibdas was the key advisor of Maharana Raj Singh I. He was consulted on various issues related to administration. On the completion of Rajsamand, Maharana endowed upon Garibdas a jagir of 12 villages. He was also conferred upon with the rare privilege of *tuladan*(offerings equal to body weight) in gold.[84] The Brahmin of the Paneri sub-caste looked after royal treasures, kitchen and the section of clothes (*angiya-ri-ovary*). The Chaubisa Brahmins were *dyoridars* of *zenana* chambers and Amera Brahmins worked as *kamdars* (clerks).[85]

As men of letters, the Brahmins enriched the entire genre of literary writings – epics, *prashastis*, *vanshavalis*, poetry etc. As far as scholarship is concerned, the Brahmins greatly outnumbered the Charan composers. Sanskrit language was popular with the Brahmins who composed religious, devotional, ceremonial and laudatory works. Amongst Brahamanic literature, *prashastis* written by them have survived upto the present times. These were composed as inscriptions to be fixed on private or state constructions, viz., temples, embankments etc. They also prepared *vanshavalis* (genealogies) and wrote treatises on architecture, medicine history etc. In the reign of Maharana Amar Singh II (1698-1710) Baikunth Vyas composed *Amarsingh Abhishek Kavyam* and *Amarkavya Vanshavali*. Pandit Mangal wrote *Amarnrip Kavyaratna*. A Sanskrit stone inscription of Vaidyanath temple near Udaipur was composed in 1707. Bhatt Someshwar's *Raj Singh Rajyabhishek Kavya* describes the coronation of Maharana Raj Singh II (1754-1761). In Ari Singh's reign (1761-1773) Someshwar Bhatt prepared a *prashasti* for the Raj Rajeshwar temple at Deobari, which unfortunately could not be inscribed. The Brahmins wrote hundreds of such *prashastis* from 10th to the 18th centuries. Ironically, even Shyamaldas, who had demeaned Brahmin scholarship, had as his colleagues and contemporaries many eminent Brahmin scholars.

Occasionally, royal letters were drafted in Sanskrit by Bhatt Mewaras.[86] They were also appointed as ambassadors or sent on diplomatic missions.

In the political culture of the region, the status of Brahmins was well recognized. Significant to the pre-eminence of the Brahmins was the devotion and faith commanded by the shrine of Eklingji, both from the royalty as well as the commoners. While there were other Rajputana states who considered themselves as appointees and descendants of divine figures from the Hindu pantheon, the manner in which Mewar is identified with the reverence for the image of Eklingji was unique to the state. This naturally led to the predominance and veneration of Brahmins as managers of the shrines. The afore-mentioned discourse confirms the religious significance and spiritual aura with which the Brahmin priests were associated with in the erstwhile state of Mewar. As preceptors, spiritual guides and ritual specialists, they had access not only to a superior ritual status but were bestowed upon with special privileges and numerous material advantages. Patronization of the shrines and their priests was largely motivated by a desire for political legitimacy and social prestige, but the element of genuine and selfless devotion to the presiding deity Eklingji, other shrines and their Gosains (head priests) was definitely present. It is true that as far as political and administrative affairs are concerned, Brahmins were not so closely associated as the Oswals, Rajputs and the Charans but this dichotomy between the spiritual and the political has remained the hallmark of Indian political culture. The spiritual domain and the political domain, despite their close interlinkages, sought to operate as separate and independent spheres.

IV

Oswals were one of the important communities that played a seminal role in the sustenance and strengthening of the erstwhile state of Mewar. In popular perception, Oswals' claim to fame have been their commercial and entrepreneurial skills.

Significantly, they also formed one of the key communities from amongst whom the Maharanas of Mewar and also rulers of other Rajputana states recruited most of their officers and employees at various positions of responsibility. Various generations of many Oswal families occupied powerful administrative posts such as that of Pradhan, Diwan, Bakshi, Nagar Seth and so on. Gaurishankar Hirachand Ojha has listed the contribution of 11 famous non-Rajput families who had played a vital role in the strengthening of Mewar polity. Pertinently, seven out of the eleven families were of the Oswals who served the Maharanas in different capacities for several generations. These included Bhamashah, Sanghvi Dayaldas, Mehta Agarchand, Mehta Ram Singh, Seth Jorawarmal Bapna, Kothari Kesari Singh, Mehta Bhopal Singh and their descendants. Oswals had emerged as one of the most empowered and honoured groups in the erstwhile Mewar state.

The Oswals in Rajasthan trace their origin to different clans of Kshatriyas. Muhnot Nainsi in his *Khyat* has laid down 10th century as the possible time period when Utpaldev, a scion of the Parmar ruler of Bhinmal or Kiradu in Abu, was converted to Jainism. Agarchand and Amarchand Mehta, Sukhsampatrai Bhandari and D.R. Bhandarkar have also endorsed a later date for the origin and emergence of Oswals on the basis of archaeological and literary evidence. It has been argued that the earliest date for conversion of Rajput clans to Jainism could be 8th or 9th century as prior to that these clans were non-existent. It is believed that Rajputs, being the warrior caste, were targeted by Muslim invaders. To escape persecution and harassment, the Rajputs converted to Jainism in large numbers and in the course of time emerged as the premier merchant community.[87]

The Oswals, too, over the period of time, evolved certain norms of hierarchization within the caste and in relation to the total social stratification. Within the caste, some of the well-known distinctions were referred to as *Dassa-Bisa* (Ten and Twenty) and *Chote Sajan-Bade Sajan*: *Dassa* or *Chote Sajan* being the inferior group whereas *Bisa* or *Bade Sajan* being the so-called purer and higher category.[88] The exact basis of the emergence of this social differentiation is not clear. There are numerous caste tales that seek to explain the origin of these status-differentiating categories.

In the course of time, Oswals merged with the premier merchant community of Vaishyas or Mahajans. They claimed the status of a ritually clean caste. On the basis of their professional roles too, the Oswals were broadly divided into two groups: those who were in the service of the Maharanas/ jagirdars and the business groups. In fact, this classificatory pattern based on proximity to the royalty emerged as a significant norm of hierarchy amongst the Oswals, i.e., those who were in royal service on account of their political clout and privileges acquired a higher placement as compared to the latter group. Significantly, despite their lower placement in the caste hierarchy, the Oswals due to their political ascendancy enjoyed a higher position than the Brahmins, especially in areas where they held political power, e.g., in Mandalgarh, the Bachchawat Mehta clan members had virtually become the hereditary Kiledars and had an edge over the Brahmins in the social hierarchy.[89]

In the erstwhile state of Mewar, the Oswals had become veritable pillars of administration and polity on whom depended the stability and prosperity of the region. Their crucial role in the administrative sphere can be inferred from the *virud* (title and achievements of the courtier which were pronounced by the Charan on his entry in the court) announced on their arrival, i.e., '*Rajbhar Samarth*' (capable of wielding the burden of administration). The non-Rajput groups such as Oswals, Mahajans, Kayastha and Brahimins, who were appointed as Diwan, Pradhan, Bakshi or heads of other departments, were treated as a distinct class of officers called 'Muttsadi'. The highest post that a Muttsadi could occupy in Rajputana states was that of a Pradhan (Prime Minister). Traditionally, the post of Pradhan was held ex-officio by the principal Rajput noble of the state. In Marwar, the Kumpawat chiefs of Ahuwa and Asop had been hereditary Pradhans. The defiance and assertiveness of these chiefs, however, led to the increasing control of non-Rajputs on civil administration. In the course of time, Rajput rulers drew a distinction between the civil and military wings of the administration. The posts of Pradhan, Bakshi (commander of forces), Susatanama (the auditor and recorder of all the household expenditure and establishment) and the Sahai (secretary for both home and foreign correspondence) were held by non-Rajput castes.[90] According to A.C. Banerjee, the tendency to exclude the Rajputs from administrative posts seems to have been universal in the Rajput kingdoms. Nainsi has summed up Rajput mindset thus: "Make your brother a Pradhan and you may as well loose your kingdom."[91] A Rajput chief did not repose trust in a fellow Rajput as far as political and revenue matters were concerned. It has also been pointed out that Rajputs did not have administrative ability, thrift and industry required for efficient handling of these affairs. Qanungo has further added another reason for this preference given to a tactful and trustworthy non-Rajput for the post of a Pradhan in a Rajput principality. "On an expedition not commanded in person by the Chief or his heir apparent, different septs of the same clan would rather submit to the command of a non Rajput Pradhan than agree to have the head of one of a rival family as their commander-in-chief."[92]

The Oswals played a dominant role in the political system of Mewar. Many Oswal families had formed an intrinsic element in the feudal aristocratic order of Mewar. The Bachchavat Mehta clan was one of the most prominent families whose members were associated with administration for generations. There were as many as five Pradhans and nine Diwans of the Jodhpur, Bikaner and Mewar states from amongst direct ancestors. Eight members were appointed as Kiledars and more than 25 members served as Hakims in various *parganas*. They were all administrators of a high calibre and served as many as 15 rulers. Despite continuous intrigues against them, they rose to high positions. Bhan, Mehta Agarchand, Mehta Sher Singh, Mehta Pannalal were some of the well-known figures of the Bachchawat Mehta clan.[93]

A legendary figure from the Oswal community was Bhama Shah whose family served the Maharana with fullest devotion, commitment and a spirit of sacrifice for many generations. Bhama Shah, due to his exemplary services during the battle of Haldighati, was considered capable enough to be the Pradhan of Mewar by Rana Pratap. Bhama Shah procured resources and funds for the Maharana during military expeditions. One of the better known instances was his campaign against Malwa from where he extorted twenty-five lakhs rupees and also twenty thousand gold coins and presented them to the Maharana. His son Jeevashah succeeded him as Pradhan, who was in turn followed by his son Ahhayraj. Bhama Shah's brother Tara Chand served as the Hakim of Godwad.[94] Mehta Ram Singh's was yet another illustrious family who served the Maharanas in various administrative capacities. The first person of his clan who got associated with the illustrious Sisodiya rulers was Jal Mehta who had come to Mewar along with daughter of Maldev Songara, who was married to Rana Hammir. The Rana was able to retrieve, consolidate and expand his dominion with the invaluable advice and assistance given by Jal Mehta. Mehta Ram Singh was born in the same family line and rose to the position of a Pradhan. British Political Agent Captain Cobbe held him in high estimation due to his administrative acumen. Like other prominent Oswal administrators Mehta Ram Singh's career was replete with court intrigues and petty jealousies of his colleagues. Some of the direct descendants of Ram Singh served as Hakims in various districts.[95]

It was as financiers and managers of finances that the Oswals exercised tremendous influence, at times even a tight grip over the royalty. Bhama Shah had proved himself to be adept at financial matters. Not only did he donate his own assets liberally to the Mewar state but also conserved the resources and wealth of the state in a manner that enabled the Maharanas to lead expensive military campaigns and preserve the independence of the state. He had buried the treasure of the state in the hilly areas and therefore, when Akbar attacked Mewar, he was not able to lay his hands on the same. He kept meticulous details of the hidden treasure which he had passed on to his wife to be handed over to the Maharana and later his son continued to use these resources to finance the administrative and military affairs of the state.[96] Bhama Shah's name has acquired proverbial and iconic dimensions in the region for his generosity, sense of duty towards the state and commitment to social causes. His name has become synonymous with entrepreneurs who are known for their liberal endowments to the state and for social upliftment. Bhama Shah awards have been instituted for such distinguished persons by the state government and Maharana Mewar Charitable Foundation.

Jorawarmal Bapna was another Oswal who was adept at management and consolidation of financial resources. Col. James Tod, Political Agent in Mewar, called him from Indore to resolve the financial crisis in Mewar. In his capacity as the banker of the state of Mewar, the entire income and assets of the state were deposited with him. He extended loans to farmers and took stringent action against lawless elements to establish peace and order in the province. Because of his exemplary services, he was endowed upon with various marks of honour and the title of Seth. The fact that Maharana Swaroop Singh had visited his *haveli*, signifies his high stature in the polity of Mewar.[97]

Commonly, it were the Oswals who, as business magnates and financiers, exercised monopoly over the office of Nagar Seth. Nagar Seth was appointed in important towns and considered the highly honourable office of that particular area. According to Tod, Nagar Seth was the chief magistrate of the town under whom the junior judicial officials dispensed their functions. Because of his high status, on the 6th day of *Navratri* festival, the Nagar Seth could grant amnesty to criminals according to his own discretion.[98]

The exemplary and selfless services of the Oswals were duly acknowledged by the Maharanas not only through conferment of high offices and enormous powers but even at the level of symbolism and rituals, they were granted exclusive privileges and marks of honour. In accordance with Maharanas' order, the legendary administrator, military commander and financier of Mewar, Bhama Shah and his descendants were to be treated as guest of honour on the occasion of caste get-togethers of the Mahajans. The senior-most member of the family was honoured by a *tilak* (red powdered mark on the forehead) before the commencement of caste dinners. Subsequently, when the family was in a decadent position, with no illustrious individual, the Mahajan community retracted this exclusive privilege. On two occasions, the Maharanas promptly restored this special honour to Bhama Shah's family.

Almost all elite Oswal families in royal service were conferred upon with the privilege of *langar*, i.e., wearing gold in the feet. Many times they were honoured by Maharanas' *padhravni* (visit) at their *havelis*, especially on occasions like birth, marriage, illness or death. On the death of Mehta Agrchand, Maharana Bheema Singh himself came to express bereavement and participate in the *pindha samaroh*. On one of his visits to Mandalgarh, Maharana Swaroop Singh had visited the *haveli* of Mehta Swaroop Singh, the Kiledar of Mandalgarh fort, and partook of dinner there. When Mehta Ram Singh's son Bakhtavarsingh fell ill, Maharana Sardarsingh went to his *haveli* to enquire about his health. On yet another occasion Maharana visited his *haveli* and conferred upon him the title of *Kakaji* and the privilege of *Tazim* (this was a form of greeting in which the Maharana stood up and received the dignitary; this was the privilege that was conferred upon the highest class of nobles and officials).[99] Visits by Maharanas outside their palaces were rare occasions undertaken only to the *havelis* of selective individuals. It was a matter of conferring honour on them. In addition, the Oswal individuals who were appointed as Pradhans enjoyed all the marks of honour and privileges of first-grade jagirdars.

Amongst all the communities who served and sustained Mewar royalty, Oswals of Mewar were one distinctive group that had a remarkable affinity with the ruling classes as far as emulation of royal lifestyle and norms was concerned. The comprehensive replication of the features of royalty was perhaps motivated by a keenness to derive certain exclusivity and distancing from other social groups. Certain features that they borrowed were clearly markers of distinctive status. Some of the Oswal administrators had started adding the suffix 'Singh' to their names, which had predominantly been a Rajput surname. Even their mansions called *havelis* were a miniature replica of the Maharana's palaces. The *haveli* of the top Oswal official used to be located at the highest point in the fort and embellished with carvings, *gokhdas, baris* etc. *Havelis* were designed keeping in view the social norms that governed inter-personal relationships and status of women. Living quarters of men and women were segregated, which ensured enough space and privacy to women in the *zenana* who were forbidden to enter the men's quarters. These *havelis* were at times gifted by the Maharanas. *Haveli* had become such a distinctive status symbol of the affluent Oswal families, that they earned the epithet of *Haveliwalas*.[100] Similarly, the attire of the elite Oswal families reflected the dress norms of the royalty. Men and women conformed to the court and state customs regarding dress. Emulation of the Rajput model must have been an inevitable consequence of their closeness to the power structures, and perhaps, also the fact that they had the resources and political sanction to do so.

Not only the lifestyle was patterned on that of the elite Rajputs but the Oswals also imbibed the feudal mindset as far as social customs and behavioural norms were concerned. Like the royal families, considerable restraint and decorum governed interpersonal relationships. There was an elaborate formality as far as terms of address and mode of submission amongst family members was concerned. "They shrouded their emotions in an elaborate exchange of formal gestures and words.... (Everyone) talked to his parents as if they were dignitaries with whom he could take no liberties. The form and courtesy which the young maintained before the old lacked spontaneity... Everyone moved cautiously; every word was weighed before it was spoken. Even with the servants no one lost their temper."[101] The discipline expected from married women within the family was much more rigorous and harsh. Women had to keep their faces covered, not only from men, but also the elder women of the family and community. The code of conduct laid down with whom she could directly interact and with whom through an intermediary.

The Oswals who enjoyed proximity with the ruling classes also adopted various regressive traditions and customs of the Rajputs, especially those related to women. Widow remarriage was a taboo and injunctions that regulated widow's life were stringent. There are even stray examples of *jauhar* and *sati* amongst Oswal families who were motivated by Rajput concepts of honour and status. Observance of strict *purdah* by women was also a consequence of their desire to replicate royal etiquette. Women of the upper and middle classes could not step out without the permission of the elders and without adequate covering and an escort. Even men had to observe norms regarding clothing, which were prescribed by the state and the court. They could not venture out without covering their heads or without wearing *achkans* (special long coats) over *dhotis* (lower garment in the form of long piece of cloth tied around the waist) or *churidar pyjamas* (tight trousers). Rama Mehta writes: "The primary reason for accepting the tradition bound etiquette by the Oswals was that they were assured of economic security within the state. If one wanted the protection and economic advantage that flowed from the

'*Durbar*' then it was virtually obligatory to follow its customs. Once accepted as a loyal member of the state establishment and orthodoxy, then the family could count on having the same socio-economic security for members of the next generation."[102]

In addition to lifestyle, attire and social customs, some Oswal clans even shifted their religious devotion from Jainism to Vaishanavism. This was partly due to the influence of the royal classes and probably also to facilitate their participation in military campaigns, which necessarily involved violence and therefore went against the fundamental tenets of Jainism. Bachchawat Mehta was one such clan that experienced this transition from Jainism to Vaishnavism. In fact, every *haveli* of Bachchavat Mehta had a temple of Thakurji (Lord Krishna). Some Oswal clans even celebrated festivals that were connected to the martial traditions of the Rajputs. *Khadag Sthapana* (formal placement of sword) that took place during the *Navratri* was one such festival.

Royalty replication at various levels - social, religious, cultural and political - among the Oswals in royal services emerged as one of their distinctive traits. While it is difficult to ascertain the exact reasons for such large-scale imitation of the Rajput model, it definitely endowed them with a special position, prestige and status in the society and polity of the Rajputana states. While Oswals developed close affinity with the royal classes, they did not cherish certain martial concepts and characteristics that had become integral to Rajput identity. Barring a few exceptions, the Oswals seldom idealized the typical Rajput notions of *vair*, valour and their code of honour.

Apart from Oswals who served the royalty in various capacities, there were substantial sections of the community, who contributed to the realms of trade and commerce. These groups adhered to the puritanical values and austere lifestyle devoid of glamour and ostentation. They strengthened the state economically through their commercial activities in various spheres. Moreover, by their simple ways of living, defined by restraint and austere habits, transmitted to the society at large a distinctive value structure and social ethics.

V

The historians of Mewar have been unequivocal in their admiration for the policy of religious tolerance and respect for other religions that defined the polity of Mewar. Shyamaldas has recorded with pride that despite being devout Hindus the rulers of Mewar gave liberal endowments to the shrines and mosques of the Muslims. G.H. Ojha contends that, in addition to other factors, the magnanimity of its rulers towards all the religions has formed the basis of Mewar's claim to the exalted honorific of 'Hindooa Sooraj'. It is a well-known fact that the 17th member of the August and highest category of '*Solah Umraos*' (sixteen nobles) was a Muslim from Sind Mirza Abdul Rahim Beg. During the Maratha raids, Muslims from Sind had formed a separate battalion. In the war between Mahadji Scindia and Maharana Ari Singh this battalion had put up a valiant fight and many amongst them had made the supreme sacrifice of their lives. Consequently, in 1770 AD, their chief Mirza Abdul Rahim Beg was rewarded with the highest distinction of a first-grade chiefship in the court of Mewar. He was entitled to the royal insignia and privileges that were commonly bestowed on the *Solah Umraos* and was addressed by the title of Jamadar. During the boat ride on the occasion of Gangaur, he was given a seat in the boat – a privilege not conferred on the entire first-grade nobles. This episode in the annals of Mewar is a shining example of the religious magnanimity of the Maharanas. It also underscores the supremacy of chivalric behaviour as the major determinant of honour and status of individuals in the polity of Mewar.

The Muslims had been an integral part of Mewar polity. They served in the army on responsible and trustworthy positions. The posts commonly held by them in the army were

Jamadar, Havaldar and Subedar. The Muslim warriors had fought valiantly against the Marathas. Consequently, many Muslim families had been rewarded with land grants. It is a well-known fact that in the battle of Haldighati, an Afghan Muslim Hakim Khan, who made the supreme sacrifice of his life, led the *haraval*. A *mazar* had been erected on that place in his honour. The Muslims were appointed on numerous posts in different administrative departments. They served as accountants and also as clerks and *munshis* who were proficient in Urdu and Persian languages. There were Muslim *ustads* to teach the languages.

The Maharanas gave equal respect to the religious teachers and heads of Muslim communities. While the Shankaracharya and other revered Gurus of the Maharanas were honoured by insignia like flywhisk, *chhatri* and royal paraphernalia, the religious head of the Bohra community received similar marks of honour and respect from the rulers. Like the Hindu priests, the Qazis and Maulvis of the Muslims too received grants and charter of rights from the Mewar government. They were also endowed upon with marks of honour depending on their stature within the community. Elaborate arrangements were made by the administration during the Muslim festivals, particularly on Moharram when *tazias* were carried in large processions. Not a single instance of Hindu-Muslim discord during such festivals has been recorded in the history of Mewar. Tod has also appreciated the liberal attitude of the Maharanas in religious matters. The Maharanas had not only offered *sharan* to Mughal prince Khurram (later, emperor Shah Jehan) but even allowed him to erect a shrine of Muslim saint Madar in his palace in Udaipur. Tod has observed that it was indeed an affecting proof of religious tolerance that even after the passage of two centuries the shrine and its establishment had been maintained and even the turban that Shah Jehan had exchanged with the Maharana had been preserved in the palace. The Muslim community had complete freedom to impart education through religious institutions like maktabs and mosques.

Muslims were engaged in many occupations like dying, bangle making, weaving, weapon making etc. The traders belonging to the Bohra sect formed a flourishing trading community in Mewar. They had received special trading privileges from Maharana Sajjan Singh in 1878 when they had not supported a strike by the merchants in Udaipur.

The Muslims were thus not only not discriminated against but were given equal opportunities to participate in the political, cultural and social life of the region. They strengthened the polity and enriched the cultural fabric of the region by their contribution in various spheres.

The above discussion on various social groups focuses upon their significant role in the erstwhile polity of Mewar. It seeks to refute the myth of the predominance of the Rajputs in the sustenance and survival of the native states of Rajputana. It, instead, projects a social and political fabric which was based on close interrelationship, interaction and interdependence between the diverse groups. While preserving their distinctive cultural identities and traits, they sought to collaborate with each other and, thereby enrich and strengthen the state in different realms. The contours of mainstream history needs to be recast and redefined with a fresh and broader perspective in order to redress the historical neglect to which these classes and groups have been subjected to. In fact, history of Rajputana states would acquire totality and depth only when it goes beyond the Rajput centric construction and focuses upon the different ways in which these classes aligned with the ruling classes to strengthen the state.

A brief perusal of these social groups also delineates the norms of hierarchization and stratification that they cherished within the group as also within the total social structure. Significantly, despite being placed lower in the social hierarchy, they had their own notion of honour amongst themselves and in relation to the ruling classes. The ruling elite, i.e., the Maharana and his jagirdars were conscious of the exemplary contribution of these social groups to the polity of Mewar. It was, perhaps, this realization that led them to bestow each group and their prominent families with marks of honour, exclusive privileges and substantial power. In fact, the royals, rather than adopting an exclusivist attitude, sought to integrate the different groups with an assimilative and accommodative approach. Not just Rajputs but each group, howsoever lower in the status hierarchy, was made to feel as an integral part of the political culture.

Nevertheless, within Rajasthan, it is the protector image of the Rajputs that has remained more pervasive as compared to the spiritual aura of the Brahmins. The Kingly model and martial characteristics enjoyed greater pre-eminence than the Brahmanical values. In most of the regions in India, the model of sanskritization[103] commonly observed is the Brahmanical model in which the low caste and tribal groups emulate the rituals, customs, ideology and way of life of the Brahmins in order to claim a higher position in the caste hierarchy. In the region of Rajputana, however, the Rajput model has been quite predominant, i.e., the groups in these areas who wish to improve their status do so by adopting the values, code of honour and lifestyle of the Rajputs. The model of Rajputization had been a predominant feature for not only certain castes within the Rajputana states but also the ruling clans outside the region including the Marathas who traced their origin to the Sisodiyas of Mewar. Even in the present times, the stereotypical image of the Rajputs as defenders of *dharma*, land and honour continues to fascinate and captivate the imagination of the people, both within and outside the region.

Notes

1. K.R. Qanungo, *Studies in Rajput History*, p.48.
2. L.P. Mathur, *Resistance Movements of Tribals in India*, p.7.

3. For myths regarding origin of the Bhils refer Robert Deliege, *The Bhils of Western India*; L.P. Mathur, *op.cit.*; N.D. Chauhary, N.N. Vyas, R.S. Mann (eds.), special issue of *Tribe* on Rajasthan Bhils, Vol.78 (1975).
4. L.P. Mathur, *op.cit.*, p.7.
5. For views regarding projection of Bhils as a tribe in anthropological and historical writings refer Deliege, *op.cit.*, pp.16-21; K.S. Singh, *Tribal Society in India*, pp.1-4.
6. Cited in Shyam Sharma & Bhagwan Lal Kachchawa, 'Rajasthan ki Bhil Janjati: Bhartiya Itihas ke Pannon Pe,' *Tribe*, Rajat Jayanti Visheshank, Vol.25, Nos.1-2, p.86.
7. M.L.Verma 'Nikunj', *Bhilon ki Samajik Vyavastha*, pp.35-37; R.S. Mann, 'Bhils in Historical Perspective', *Tribe* (special issue on Rajasthan Bhils) Vol.78, p.20.
8. James Tod, *Annals and Antiquities of Rajasthan* (henceforth, *Annals*) Vol. I, p.181.
9. Ronald Iden, 'Ritual, Authority and Cyclic Time in Hindu Kingship', in J.F. Richards(ed.), *Kingship and Authority in South Asia*, p.54.
10. Deliege, *op.cit.*, p.51.
11. B.R. Chauhan, 'Tribalisation', *Tribe* (special issue on Rajasthan Bhils), Vol.X, p.38.
12. K.S. Singh, *op.cit.*, p.92. Such instances of tribal participation in coronation ceremonies are not uncommon. In Banswara, the ruler received the coronation *tika* from a Bhil. Similarly, in Dungarpur, the Balwalia sept of Bhils enjoyed this privilege of anointing the Maharawal (ruler) till quite recent times. In Jaipur state, every Kachchawa ruler of the state, on his installation, received the *tika* of blood obtained by incision of toe of a Kalikoh Mina. Minas are another old tribe who had ruled the region till the 16th century. Even outside Rajputana, such examples are found in Garjhat (Orissa), Chhota Nagpur (Malwa) and Rajpipla (Gujrat). The Halbas of Bastar, Bhuiyas of Gangpur and Khonds of Kalahandi were endowed with similar privileges of participation in coronation ceremonies of Rajput chiefs in their respective states.
13. *Ibid.*, p.92.
14. Scholars differ over the name of the ruler during whose reign the practice of Bhil participation in coronation ceremony was discontinued in the state of Mewar. Some records mention Maharana Amar Singh II while others have recorded Maharana Jagat Singh as the last ruler who was anointed by the Bhil chiefs of Oguna and Undari. Refer G.H. Ojha, *Udaipur Rajya ka Itihas*, Vol.II, p.114; R.S. Mann, 'Bhils in Historical Perspective', *Tribe*, Vol.X, 1978, p.13; R.S. Sharma & Bhagwan Lal Kachchawa, 'Rajasthan ki Bhil Janjati...', *Tribe,* Vol.25, Nos. 1-2, 1993, p.88; R.P. Kathuria, *Life in the Courts of Rajasthan*, p.55.
15. *Annals*, p.218.

16. R.S. Sharma & Bhagwan Lal Kachhawa, 'Rajasthan ki Bhil Janjati...' in *Tribe*, Vol.25, Nos.1-2, 1993, p.88; G.H. Ojha, *op. cit.*, p.113.
17. K.S. Singh, *op.cit.*, p.91; B.R. Chauhan, 'Tribalisation', *Tribe*, Vol.X, 1978, p.32.
18. Morris Carstairs, *The Twice Born*, cited in Deliege, *op.cit.*, p.110.
19. For details on Bhils' attitude to life, refer, Deliege, *op.cit.*, pp.83-115; R.S. Mann, 'Bhils in Historical Perspective', *Tribe*, Vol.X, 1978, pp.17-18.
20. L.P. Mathur, *op.cit.*, p.22.
21. Robert Deliege, *op.cit.*, p.45.
22. James Tod, *Travels in Western India* (henceforth, *Travels*), p.52.
23. L.P. Mathur, *op.cit.*, p.33.
24. K.S. Singh, *op.cit.*, p.139.
25. *Ibid.*, p.139; L.P. Mathur, *op.cit.*, pp.73-92.
26. V.K. Vashishtha, *Bhagat Movement*, p.38.
27. K.S. Singh, *op.cit.*, pp.140, 141, 151.
28. L.P. Mathur, *op.cit.*, p.18.
29. Bhil headman was known by several names such as Patel, Naik, Gameti, Rawat, Vasavo and Mukhi. For details regarding his status and functions, refer Deliege, *op.cit.*, pp.90-92.
30. S.L. Doshi, *Bhils: Between Societal Self Awareness and Cultural Synthesis*, p.53.
31. Shyamaldas, *Vir Vinod* (henceforth, *Vir Vinod*), Vol.I, pp.191-193.
32. *Travels*, pp.53-54.
33. M.A. Laird (ed.), *Bishop Heber in Northern India: Selections from Heber's Journal*, (henceforth, *Bishop Heber in Northern India*) p.271, 279, 280.
34. Louis Rousselet, *India and its Native Princes (Travels in Central India and in the Presidencies of Bombay and Bengal)*, p.137. Also refer chapters nos. XI & XIII titled 'The Country of the Bhils.'
35. *Vir Vinod*, pp.191-193.
36. *Annals*, p.34. Charans were numerous in Marwar where their influence and number was quite pervasive. Tod has contended that in Mewar after Maharana Hammir's reign their influence had far exceeded those of the Brahmins. Nonetheless, it is true that as compared to Marwar and other Rajputana states, their importance and number had started waning in Mewar. Significantly, there are many instances when the Maharanas punished them. Tod has recorded one such incident that occurred during the reign of Maharana Kumbha. A Brahmin astrologer had predicted that Kumbha would meet his end at the hands of a Charan. As a result, the latter banished them from his dominion, resuming all their lands. Tod believed that given the powerful position of the Charans in the erstwhile political culture of the Rajputana states, "this was a strong measure in those days and which few could have the nerve to attempt or firmness to

executc". The order was later repealed by heir-apparent Raimal. Similarly, during Amar Singh II's reign serious differences had erupted between him and the *Mangta* class (those who extend their palm for alms), i.e., Brahmins, Charans, Bhats, etc., who refused to contribute to the military funds of the state. Later, a settlement was reached with the Brahmins and the Charans but the Bhats were left out of the same. They got infuriated and rebelled against Amar Singh's order. It is believed that their rebellion was crushed brutally. Elephants were let loose on them and they were expelled from the state. As a result, 2,000 Bhats committed suicide outside the city and 84 villages assigned to them were confiscated. Instances of such harsh treatment to these classes who were otherwise held sacred and also an integral part of the polity were, perhaps, peculiar to Mewar. See *Annals*, p.234; Ojha, *op.cit.*, p.608.

37. Rajendra Joshi, 'The Contextual Dynamics of Caste in the Rajput System (14th to 16th century)' in N.K. Singhi & Rajendra Joshi (eds.), *Religion, Ritual and Royalty*, pp.304-313.
38. *Vir Vinod*, Vol.I, pp.191-193; Gulabdan, *Charan Charjain aur Unka Adhyayan*, pp.7-9; K.S. Ujjwal, 'Charans: Their Origin, Status and Importance', paper read in the II International Conference on Rajasthan, Udaipur, 17-21 December 1991; *Bishop Heber in Northern India*, pp.268-269.
39. K.R. Qanungo, *op.cit.*, p.51.
40. *Bishop Heber in Northern India*, p.5; G.V. Vyas, *Mewar ka Samajik aur Arthik Itihas*, p.16.
41. G.V. Vyas, *op.cit.*, pp.116-117.
42. *Ibid.* For details, refer G.H. Ojha, *Udaipur Rajya ka Itihas*, Vol.II, p.608.
43. K.R. Qanungo, *op.cit.*, pp.51-52.
44. Joshi, 'Charans: The Contextual Dynamics of Caste' in N.K. Singhi & Rajendra Joshi (eds.), *op.cit.*, pp.368-369.
45. *Bishop Heber in Northern India*, pp.368-369.
46. K.R. Qanungo, *op.cit.*, p.52.
47. Shipra Vyas, 'Social Legislation in Rajasthan Related to the Problems of Women' (unpublished Ph.D. thesis, Department of History and Indian Culture, University of Rajasthan, 2000), pp.101-120.
48. For details, refer *Report of Akhil Bhartiya Charan Sammelan*, 1911 and 1927.
49. For details regarding the different categories of court literature composed by the Charans, refer R.P. Kathuria, *op.cit.*, pp.206-217.
50. Some of the expressions are as follows: when the armies move the earth shakes; the dust storm hides the sun; when the battle begins the fairies garland the brave heroes; when the blood is shed *yoginis* drink it from the

skulls; when warriors lay dead, Lord Shiva prepares a garland with their severed heads.

51. Interview with Laxmi Kumari Chundavat. Also, Varsha Joshi, 'Charan Sahitya Mein Rajput Nari', in Pratibha Jain & Sangeeta Sharma (eds.), *Bhartiya Stree*, pp.167-179.
52. K.R. Qanungo, *op.cit.*, p.51.
53. K.S. Ujjwal, 'Charans...', p.9.
54. K.R. Qanungo, *op.cit.*, pp.51-52.
55. R.P. Kathuria, *op.cit.*, pp.211-214.
56. *Vir Vinod*, Vol. I, pp.175-179; K.S. Ujjwal, 'Charans', p.17.
57. G.S. Ghurye, *Caste and Race in India*, pp. 42, 43, 82, 83.
58. Rajendra Joshi, 'Charans...' in Singhi & Joshi (eds.), *op.cit.*, pp.304-313.
59. *Ibid.*, p.312.
60. *Vir Vinod*, Vol.I, pp.185-186.
61. G.N. Sharma, Shyamal Das aur unka Vir Vinod, in *Parampara*, No. 82-83, 1987, pp.54-55.
62. *Ibid.*, p.55.
63. A.C. Banerjee, *The Rajput States and the British Paramountcy*, p.44.
64. *Vir Vinod*, Vol.I, p.137.
65. *Ibid.*; G.V. Vyas, *op.cit.*, pp.51-52.
66. R.P. Kathuria, *op.cit.*, p.72.
67. For these gradations among ritual specialists, refer Dharmpal Sharma, *Mewar: Sankriti Evam Parampara*, pp.65-73; G.V.Vyas, *op.cit.*, pp.99-100.
68. *Vir Vinod*, Vol.I, p.137.
69. Interview with Mewar Mahamandaleshwar Mahant Murli Manohar Sharan Shastri. He shared invaluable information with us regarding the Devsthanas in Mewar and their heirarchisation which formed basis of their endowments and privileges.
70. *Annals*, p.412.
71. There are seven major shrines of Lord Krishna apart from Shrinathji-Navneetpriyaji, Dwarkanathji, Mathuranathji, Vithalnathji, Yadunathji, Gokulnathji or Gokulchandraji & Manmohanji.Out of these the three shrines of Shrinathji, Dwarkadeesh and Vithalnathji were installed at different places in Mewar.
72. *Annals*, p.416; Ojha, *op.cit.*, p.547.
73. G.N. Sharma, *Glories of Mewar*, p.59.
74. Interview with Mewar Mahamandaleshwar Mahant Murli Manohar Sharan Shastri; *Vir Vinod* Vol.I, p.142.
75. Interview with Mahantji; *Annals*, pp.419-420.
76. *Vir Vinod*, Vol.I, p.142; Dharmpal Singh, *op.cit.*, p.13; Interview with Mahantji.

77. *Annals,* p.438; Dharmpal Singh, *op.cit.*, pp.16-17;
78. *Ibid.*, p.17.
79. *Ibid.*, p.16.
80. Interview with Mahantji.
81. The Gosain of Eklingji enjoyed special privileges. He performed the *Talwar Bandhai* (investiture) of the new Maharana. When he visited the palace in Udaipur, the Maharana received him at some distance at Nani Bai ki Rehant. He had a personal jagir comprising a few villages. He was the chief of Kailashpuri Nagari.
82. *Annals*, Appendices X & XI. These are official documents confirming the privileges and grants to the shrines, pp.442-444.
83. *Ibid.*, pp.406-407; Ojha, *op.cit.*, pp.1110-1111.
84. B.L. Panagarhiya & N.C. Pahariya, *Political, Socio-Economic and Cultural History of Rajasthan*, pp.140-142.
85. G.V. Vyas, *op.cit.*, pp.100-101.
86. R.P. Kathuria, *op.cit.*, pp.197-201.
87. To underscore the antiquity of the group the Charans and Bhats have traced the origin of the Oswals as far back as 400BC to Utpaldev who, alongwith 1 lakh 80 thousand Kshatriyas, was converted to Jainism by Ratna Prabha Suri. Modern scholars, however disagree with this version of origin. Mangilal Bhutodiya, *Itihas ki Amar Bel: Oswal*, Vol.II, pp.113-149.
88. *Ibid.*, pp.323-328.
89. Lalit K. Mehta, *Caste, Clan and Ethnicity: A Study of the Mehtas in Rajasthan,* p.152.
90. A.C. Banerjee, *op.cit.*, pp.27-28.
91. *Nainsi's Khyat*, vol.II, p.69.
92. K.R. Qanungo, *op.cit.*, p.52.
93. Lalit K. Mehta, *op.cit.*, p.176.
94. Ojha, *op.cit.*, pp.992-994.
95. *Ibid.*, pp.1013-1021; Mangilal Bhutodiya, *op.cit.*, pp.398-399.
96. Ojha, *op.cit.*, pp.992-994.
97. *Ibid.*; Mangilal Bhutodiya, *op.cit.*, pp398-399.
98. *Annals,* pp.119 & 466.
99. Ojha, *op.cit.*, p.994; Lalit K. Mehta, *op.cit.*, p.197.
100. For details regarding the life-style and social norms of the Oswals, refer, Lalit K. Mehta, *op.cit*; Rama Mehta, *Inside the Haveli;* Rama Mehta, 'From Purdah to Modernity', in B.R. Nanda, *Indian Women: From Purdah to Modernity.*
101. Rama Mehta, *Inside the Haveli*, p.28.
102. Rama Mehta 'From Purdah to Modernity', in B.R. Nanda, *op. cit.*, p.114.

103. The concept of sanskritization as a theory of social mobility was formulated by noted sociologist M.N. Srinivas. For details, refer M.N. Srinivas, *Social Change in Modern India*, pp.1-45. For a more comprehensive understanding of social stratification and mobility in India, refer K.L. Sharma, *Social Stratification in India: Issues and Themes.*

III

Transition in Polity and Shift in Paradigm of Honour

III

Transition in Polity and Shift in Paradigm of Honour

7

Nationalism, Peasant Protests and Freedom Struggle in Mewar

In different cultural traditions there is construction of historical, imaginative, Pauranic and mythical heroes who reflect certain values. Changes in socio-political and philosophical thought processes have influenced construction of new values and ideals. The emergence of the idea of nationalism in the 18th century signified the birth of a new concept with distinctive emotions and values. Evolution of nationalism resulted in identification of an individual with a broad level of cultural identity.[1] People belonging to different native states or British-administered territories related to regional and national identities simultaneously. Dissemination and acceptance of new concepts became a challenge for the exponents and leaders of the nascent nationalism.

With the emergence of nationalism, an effort is made to construct the concept of motherland. Notable among thinkers who have contributed to the concept of motherland in modern India were Bankim Chandra Chatterjee, Aurobindo Ghose and Subramaniam Bharti.[2] For them, India is not a mere geographical expression but it is a living and vibrant entity with certain unique features. The distinctive conceptualization of motherland is articulated in several creative writings, e.g.,

Anandmath, Bharat Durdasha, Bang Darshan, Durgesh Nandini, Andher Nagari etc. Bankim Chandra's song '*Bande Mataram*' became the national song of the freedom movement. In this composition, Bankim has put forth Indian nation in a personified form; for him, it is a "real living spiritual entity".

In Indian cultural tradition Mother Goddess is conceptualized as a symbol of universal power. In Pauranic tradition, Mother Goddess symbolizes creativity, fertility, power as well as destruction. One can trace several such versions in folk and Pauranic tales. In Indian mythology powerful kings have meditated for years to have blessing of Mother Goddess. In colonial India, this metaphor is constructed both for strength and sacrifice. Revolutionaries have considered it a matter of pride to make sacrifices for the motherland.

Aurobindo has given graphic description of Mother Goddess and motherland. According to him, motherland is 'Bhavani Bharti' which symbolizes infinite power. In contemporary times, its degenerated situation is because its millions of people have become timid due to a curtain of darkness that has covered their minds and souls. In his article entitled '*Bhavani Mandir*' Aurobindo writes: "For what is a nation? What is our mother country?' It is not figure of speech, nor a fiction of the mind it is a mighty *shakti* composed of *shaktis* of all millions of units that make the living unity of the *shaktis* of three hundred million people."[3]

In the course of the freedom struggle it was important that the idea of nationalism was communicated to the millions of people. While addressing rallies in villages, Jawahar Lal Nehru articulated the concept of *Bharat Mata* or Indian motherland to the villagers. While the people shouted the bold slogan of *"Bharat Mata ki Jai"* (victory to Mother India), Nehru would, at times, amuse and surprise the people by asking them unexpectedly, "Who was this *Bharat Mata*?" After some hesitation, a peasant replied that it was *dharati*, the good earth is India that they meant. Nehru explained: "India was all this that they had thought but it was much more. The mountains and the rivers of India, and the forests and the broad fields which gave us food were all dear to us, but what counted ultimately were the people of India, people like them and me, who were spread out all over this vast land, *Bharat Mata* (Mother India) was essentially these millions of people and victory to her meant victory to these people." Nehru saw an identity of interests among Indians, which bound them as a nation despite the fact that each region differed from the other: "To the peasant, I spoke of this great country for whose freedom we were struggling, of how each part differed from the other and yet was India, of common problems of peasants from north to south, east to west, of the *Swaraj* that could be for all and every part not for some... from Khyber Pass... from the north west to Kanya Kumari or Cape Comorin in the distant south."

About the dissemination of the concept of Indian nation as a whole, Nehru said: "The task was not easy, yet it was not so difficult as I had imagined, for our ancient epics and myths and legends, which they knew so well, had made them familiar with the conception of their country, and some there were always who had travelled far and wide to the great places of pilgrimage situated at the four corners of India."[4] Thus, in extremely comprehensible and simple style, Nehru communicated the concept of nation to the millions of people who were not educated and not familiar with the emergence of nationalism in other parts of the world. Awareness of common features like geographical areas and common culture created a feeling of unity which again got strengthened by attaching to the present a common purpose and the dream of a common future.

I

Cultural dimension is extremely significant, both to the establishment of colonial empire and for the subsequent struggle for freedom. For an imperialist power, colonies are only 'blank spaces' and this attitude results in insensitivity to the cultural identity of the colonized people. Not only this, to seek legitimacy and justification for administrative intervention, the imperialists condemn the colonized subjects as orthodox, backward and uncivilized. Subsequently, they reject the subject people's demand for responsible government under the plea that the people lack the requisite ability to govern themselves. The aforesaid condemnation and rejection is a painful experience for the colonized people.

African and Asian people's struggle against imperialism had significant cultural dimensions. Edward Said writes: "In the process of freedom struggle, colonial people discover their own history, cultural unity and harmony. They also seek to restore characteristic feature of their national identity." Similarly, they also discover and seek pride in their own language. Colonial struggle against imperialism, thus, is not merely an attempt to win political freedom but also an endeavour to discover different aspects of human and cultural history. Inspired by this idea, some of the writers have constructed their society differently from the writings of imperialist writers. Salman Rushdie's *Midnight's Children* is an important example of this category. Several critics and creative writers have sought to present a different picture of their own society, which has been described by Edward Said as an effort towards the "voyage in".[5]

In the Indian context a discussion of the views of Ravindra Nath Tagore and Mahatma Gandhi regarding the concept of nationalism is significant. Tagore considered the contemporary concept of nationalism as a "crisis of civilization". According to him, Indians should have constructive attitude towards nationalism rather than imbibe its narrow and competitive characteristics. He is critical of aggressive nationalism.[6] In his opinion, there is a limit to one's dedication towards the nation. In fact, the nation should not be the object of devotion but something beyond that. D. Boyce, in *The Soul of the Black*, has expressed similar views. Pertinently, Gandhi too has laid emphasis on co-existence rather than aggressive nationalism. Gandhi's quest for self led him to make significant contribution to Indian nationalism.[7] He is known the world over for his unique method of protest based on non-violence. At a deeper level essence of non-violence relates to inner self of an individual. In the course of non-violent struggle, the *satyagrahi* goes through a cleaning process and expects change of heart in the so-called adversaries. In this struggle, there is no room for idea of victory or defeat. According to Ramashray Roy, "*Satyagraha* is not only a non-violent technique to resolve conflict, it's a method of self-development specially that of adversaries as well."[8]

In the process of journey within, Gandhi discovered various characteristics of the society at large. The Orientalists and exponents of Indian renaissance have constructed glorious past in the form of golden age based on the infallibility of *Rig-Veda* and classical cultural tradition. Gandhi, however, adopted concepts rooted in popular consciousness. Thus, in the course of the national movement, he refers to *Ram Rajya* as ideal state, *ashram* as training centre, *yatra* as mobilizing campaign and *Panchayat Raj* for decentralized polity; these were concepts with which even the common man was familiar with.

In political culture, the process of struggle has often resulted in construction of new symbols, myths and paradigms for creating political awareness and inspiring mobilization. Every society has its own understanding of its historical past and based on that is the popular memory of their cultural tradition. Gandhi's selection of symbols and lifestyle exemplify his understanding of the contemporary cultural tradition. *Khadi* was one of the important symbols Gandhi adopted during the process of mass mobilization. *Khadi* was not only a symbol of self-reliance and self-respect but through it he could identify with millions of villagers of this country. Similarly, to disseminate the concept of welfare state based on truth and justice, he refers to *Ram Rajya*. In his *ashrams,* several dedicated *satyagrahis* were trained and through the lifestyle of the ashramites Gandhi exemplified his ideas. Similarly, Dandi Yatra and Harijan Yatra were techniques of establishing mass contacts. It is interesting that people were familiar with

Gandhian symbols even in distant parts of the country where he could not go personally. Gandhi succeeded in establishing communication because of his powerful vibrant dialogue style. In his effort to make freedom struggle broadbased, Gandhi popularized and gave new meaning to traditional symbology. Lloyd and Susanne Rudolph have rightly observed that Gandhi gave creative interpretation to popular symbols and his charismatic impact is due to evolution of a unique style of protest based on purity of means and concept of love and justice. Gandhi cannot be placed in the strict Weberian sense of classification of charismatic personalities. His emphasis was on conservation of traditional institutions rather than revolutionary changes.[9] Yet, in the 20th century, Gandhi emerges as one of the unique charismatic heroes who inspired moral values in politics of struggle and devised new symbols. Gandhi's personality, lifestyle and symbology digressed sharply from the aura that surrounded the rulers and monarchs. Nevertheless, Gandhian phenomenon proved that charisma in political culture was not the preserve of the monarchical polities.

II

It is crucial to examine how Rajasthan, a region divided into 19 states and two chiefships, which had different rulers, history and somewhat different administrative settings, were linked with mainstream struggle for freedom of the country. How was Gandhi's unique technique of protest communicated to the people in remote corners of the state? Significantly, the key aspects of the paradigm of national struggle and well-known symbols associated with non-violent protest were adopted and popularized by local and regional leaderships. Similarly, at the national level, certain aspects of the symbolism of Mewar were also constructed and projected to arouse nationalistic feelings.

In Indian history, the region of Rajputana occupies a distinctive place in the tradition of struggle and protest. Rajputana states have been divided into four regions – Mewar, Marwar, Matsya and Dhundhar. Amongst these, the erstwhile state of Mewar is particularly associated in popular memory with a glorious tradition of struggle and sacrifice. The heroes, monuments and anecdotes of the erstwhile state have remained a source of inspiration not only for the people of Rajasthan but also millions of people all over India, particularly during the freedom struggle. The history of struggle is embedded with chivalrous images from Mewar, the most prominent being the heroic picture of Rana Pratap, the impregnable fort of Chittor stretching over several kilometres, and the battlefield of Haldighati exemplifying the maxim of death rather than dishonour. It needs to be notified that during the period of renaissance and freedom struggle creative writers highlighted the inspirational historical symbols of Mewar. Creative works of the renaissance period such as Bankim's *Raj Singh*, Dwijendra Lal's dramas like *Mewar Patan* and *Rana Pratap*, W.K. Kulkarni's *Pratapi Pratap Singh*, K.P. Khadilkar's *Premdhwaj* and R.C. Dutt's *Mewar ek Kahani* highlighted the importance of the code of honour and tradition of struggle of Mewar. It is interesting how there were repeated references to Haldighati as battlefield, which testifies virtues like courage and sacrifice.

The emergence and growth of struggle in Rajasthan can be traced in three phases. The first stirrings of popular agitation against the opposition of the ruling class surfaced in the rural areas. The agony and deprivation of the tenants provided pathos, content and motivation to the peasant protests that took place in different Rajputana states. The second phase was marked by a shift from local and land issues to various national level issues and movements including various activities organized under the aegis of constructive programme. These issues were propagated through Praja Mandals and other regional organizations. Lastly, the Praja Mandal movement resulting in the replacement of royalty by a responsible form of government that was marked by a simultaneous process of merger of princely states, leading to the formation of a unified state of Rajasthan.

In the earliest stage it was the peasantry in the jagir of Bijoliya *thikana* (feudal estate) which pioneered the series of peasant agitations that rocked the different Rajputana states in the 20th century. Bijoliya was the first-grade *thikana* of the erstwhile Mewar state; in colloquial language, it was known as 'uparmal'. The *jagir* shared its boundaries with Bundi in the east, Gwalior in the south and *khalsa* land of Mewar on the north-west. This geographical situation facilitated relations and contacts with the peasantry of the bordering areas. This proved to be a favourable factor in the course of the struggle as the peasants often migrated to these neighbouring areas as a method of protest against the Rao or the jagirdar. These areas offered them means of subsistence when they fled from their own lands. The intense suffering and deprivation of the peasantry caused by the three factors fuelled the movement: *begar* (forced labour), *lagats* (extra cesses) also known as *lag-bags*, and an uncertain share of the jagirdar in the crop yield. *Lagats* were extra cesses, which were imposed under some extraordinary circumstances for a short period. However, with the course of time, these *lagats* were being retained for longer periods and in some cases even became permanent. In Bijoliya, the number of these *lagats* had reached 74.

The movement drew strength and publicity from the effective leadership who projected the agitation on a national scale. The timing of the movement too proved to be a positive factor since its effective phase coincided with the non-cooperation movement launched by Gandhi. In addition to this favourable factor, the *thikana* had a predominant peasant group belonging to Dhakad caste. It is largely believed that movement was generated and sustained because of their large numbers, predominance and social solidarity. Quite pertinently, the movement lasted for a period of 44 years; beginning in 1897 and finally came to an end in 1941.[10]

The course of the movement can be divided into two distinct phases, the first lasting till 1916. During the earliest phase, the leadership was predominantly rural and the peasants despite resorting to different methods of protest could not seek redressal of their grievances. The second phase begins with the assumption of leadership by urban leaders like Vijay Singh Pathik, Manikya Lal Verma and Ram Narain Choudhary. The first stirrings of the movement began in 1897 when the leaders of the Dhakad caste met on the occasion of a death feast in the community. It was decided to send Nanji Patel of Berisal village and Jhakri Patel of Gopal Niwas to Maharana Fateh Singh in Udaipur to enlighten him about the problems of the peasantry in Bijoliya. It was only after waiting and pleading for six months in the city that they were able to seek an interview with the Maharana. However, these preliminary efforts failed to yield results. No measures were taken to relieve the peasantry. To add to their woes the two complainants were punished and ex-communicated from the jagir by the jagirdar Rao Krishnasingh Panwar. The harsh treatment meted out to the two peasant leaders generated fear and terror in the entire area and for some years the peasantry remained subdued.

The agitation revived in 1904 when a new tax called *chanwari* was imposed. On the occasion of the daughter's marriage, the father was required to deposit Rs. 13 at the *thikana*'s office. The imposition of the new tax came as a rude shock for the already impoverished peasantry. The new tax meant additional financial burden for them, particularly in view of the fact that the extravagance involved in the celebration of daughters' marriages was as it is a nightmarish experience for them. To protest against the new levy not a single girl was married in the *thikana* for a period of two years. When this failed to have any impact on the Rao, they went to meet him with 200 marriageable girls. The Rao ignored their plea and asked them to sell their daughters in order to pay *chanwari* tax. The insensitivity, coupled with the derogatory remarks about their daughters, provoked the peasantry beyond measure. They resorted to their traditional and perhaps the most effective method of protest, i.e., migration and desertion of fields. Overnight, innumerable villages were vacated by the peasants, who went to Gwalior. On hearing this Rao realized his folly and himself went to meet the peasants. He apologized for his rude behaviour and through his ardent pleas was able to invite the peasants to his palace and conceded some of their demands such as reduction in the land revenue demand. *Chanwari* tax was reduced by 50 percent. In times to come, liberal land revenue assessment was also promised.

In 1906, Rao Kishan Singh died childless and was succeeded by a close collateral Prithvi Singh. He withdrew the concessions granted by his predecessor in 1904. In March 1913, one thousand peasants met the jagirdar but failed to elicit a favourable response from him. Yet again, they decided to migrate *en masse* to neighbouring Gwalior. Many peasant leaders including Sadhu Sitaram, Fatehlal Charan and Brahmadev were exiled. In 1914, when the agitation was still continuing, Prithvi Singh died. Since the new incumbent was a minor, the *jagir* was placed under court of ward management. The peasants were promised several concessions, which were never granted.

The second phase of the movement could be said to begin with the entry of Vijay Singh Pathik, Manikya Lal Verma, Ram Narain Chaudhary and also the rural leadership. Under Pathik the movement was strengthened in two significant ways. Firstly, he provided a strong organizational backing to the movement by setting up Uparmal Panchayat Board, which emerged as the chief negotiator on behalf of the peasantry with concerned authorities. In addition to this apex body, Kisan Sabha was formed in every village. The panchayat emerged as an influential body that resolved civil and revenue cases. The peasant reposed full faith in the panchayat throughout the movement. Even in difficult situations, particularly when the state in order to weaken the panchayat, issued notification to the effect that it would not receive any petition or complaint through the panchayat or its officials, the peasants showed remarkable commitment towards the body by refusing to submit either individually or collectively any application to the thikana without the mediation of the panchayat. Moreover, the Kiṣan Panchayat was not dependent on any outside agency for financial backing. The panchayat emerged as a symbol of the solidarity, strength and self-confidence of the peasants and even created ripples in the British officialdom.

Efforts were also made, at the behest of Pathik, to bring about reformation in the lifestyle and habits of the peasantry, which included prohibition of alcohol. Pathik also demonstrated his ability as a shrewd negotiator who cleverly used his contacts in the *thikana* to know about the correspondence between the jagirdar and the Maharana regarding Bijoliya. He made incessant tours to innumerable villages calling upon peasants to remain firm and united. During his visits, he also distributed his handwritten Mewari newspaper '*Uparmal ka Danka*' to the peasants.

Pathik also made strenuous efforts to give widespread publicity to the movement on a national level. He sent Manikya Lal Verma to attend the Congress session in 1918. The latter succeeded in projecting the movement and its leader on this national platform. Pathik himself attended the Congress sessions in Amritsar and Nagpur in 1919 and 1920 respectively. This proved to be a wise tactic as the travails of the Bijoliya peasantry gained national prominence. This, in turn, increased the pressure on the Maharana of Mewar and the British officials to address the peasants' demands. The leadership and the movement of Bijoliya peasantry occupied prominent spaces in national level newspapers like *Pratap, Maratha, Navyug Sandesh, Tarun Rajasthan, Bombay Chronicle,* etc. Prominent national leaders like Tilak, Gandhi and Madan Mohan Malviya showed personal interest in the progress and programmes of the movement. Tilak published the atrocities of the jagirdar in Bijoliya in his newspaper *Maratha.* He reminded the Maharana of his illustrious ancestors and their honourable status and antecedents. Gandhi too sent his private secretary Mahadev

Desai to collect complete details about the agitation. In order to strengthen and broadbase the movement, Pathik even encouraged and succeeded in his endeavours to enrol women in the movement. They attended the meetings of the Kisan Sabhas and sang songs composed by Manikya Lal Verma and Pathik.

In view of these factors, the movement gained considerable momentum and strength. The peasants were charged by a new-found assertiveness and refused to pay *lags*. Consequently, the *thikana* officials resorted to repression of the movement by all possible methods - imprisonment of leaders, torturing woman and children, burning standing crops, etc. Meanwhile, Indian National Congress, under the leadership of Gandhi, launched non-cooperation movement in 1920. As the movement gained momentum in 1921, the British government realized the urgency of resolving the crisis in Bijoliya lest it should become a part of the non-cooperation movement. The British also feared that the peasant agitation might spread to other areas as well.

Ultimately, in 1922, Agent to Governor General (AGG) Holland invited the panchayat for talks. The panchayat leaders had put forward the condition that during the negotiations their representatives would share the same seating arrangement as the officials. It was indeed a unique spectacle and a victory for the hitherto oppressed peasantry when they held parleys with the Maharana's officials on an equal basis. As a result of the negotiations, 34 *lagats* were removed; *begar* was by and large abolished; cases against the peasants withdrawn; and a revenue settlement was promised within a period of three years. This agreement was indeed a remarkable achievement for the peasantry who had been able to secure success after years of agitation, persecution and deprivation.

The movement however revived in 1931 when the Bijoliya jagirdar refused to honour the agreement of 1922 in spirit. This wave of the agitation lasted till 1944. The major issue in the movement was the refusal of the thikana to return *mal* (unirrigated) land to those peasants who had surrendered the same in protest against excessive land revenue demand. Inspired by the agitation at Bijoliya peasant unrest began in Begun thikana for the same set of problems, e.g., there was resentment against *lag-bags.* Influenced by the leaders of Rajasthan Seva Sangh, peasants at the Kalkhand and Chandkheri decided to boycott the practice of *begar* and also refused to pay land revenue. In 1922, at Mandavari, local zamindar ordered firing when peasants were holding a meeting to decide the strategy of their agitation. The suppression by zamindar continued unabated. In 1923, in a peasant meeting, there was firing leading to loss of life. At this juncture, the Mewar government intervened. The government opined that Hari Bhai Kinkar, Manikya Lal Verma and Pathik were responsible for peasant unrest. Eventually, in 1925, there was a settlement between the peasants and the *thikana*. The repercussions of the movements in Bijoliya and Begun could be traced in other areas. Some of the significant ones were Bhinder, Parsoli, Jamoli and Dhariawad where the peasants came in conflict with the jagirdars.[11]

In 1923-24 peasants of Bansur and Thanaghazi raised voice against excessive land revenue. In May 1925, a commission was constituted to explore possibilities of settlement between the jagirdars and the peasants. Meanwhile, about 800 Rajput peasants organized a meeting at Nimuchana. At this juncture, Commander Chhaju Singh ordered firing using machine guns resulting in the death of 95 peasants. A large number of them were wounded and there was loss of cattle too. In this tragic incident nearly 145 huts were burnt to ashes. There are different versions about loss of life in this incident. According to some, 50 people died in the firing. The incident was widely reported as 'second Jallianwala'. Gandhi described the event as 'Dyerism Double Distilled'. The event was also widely covered in *Tarun Rajasthan* and *Pratap* and even in the national newspapers. Eventually, an Inquiry Commission was set up, concessions were granted and fixation of land revenue ordered as demanded by peasants.[12]

Similar tragic events took place in Dabra village (Didwana) in state of Marwar where a large gathering of peasants was to be held on 13th March, 1944 under the auspices of Lok Parishad and the Kisan Sabha. Leaders like Mathura Das Mathur, Dwarkadas Purohit, Chhaganraj from Chaupasani, Radhakrishna Bohra, Kishan Lal Shah and Chaudhary Harindar Kumar, along with 500-600 Jats, were participating. The peasants marched in procession to reach the conference venue. On their way armed men of the jargirdars surrounded them. Both the sides attacked each other with spears, guns and swords. Two peasants died while legs of the wife of one Pannaram were decapitated and face of another woman was deformed. The leaders were mercilessly beaten. Choudhary Ramuram of Ladnun, who was coming to participate in the conference, was shot down in the way. The Dabra incident received widespread publicity in the national newspapers. Due to the furore caused over these atrocities, the state government instituted an inquiry against the perpetrators of the violence.[13] Such acts of violence and repression had become quite common in the various *thikanas*.

The above discussion focuses upon the distinctive features of the peasant protests that surfaced in the beginning of the 20th century. Widespread unrest and sporadic agitational activities leading to serious disturbances characterized them. Significantly, despite the official policy of the Indian National Congress of non-intervention in the princely states, the peasant agitation in Bijoliya and other places attracted the attention of the national level leadership. The movement drew appreciation from many leaders including Gandhi. He assured Pathik that if the Mewar state immediately did not address the grievances of the peasantry, he would himself lead a *satyagraha* in Bijoliya. Eventually, however, there was no redefining of the jagirdar-peasant relationship. Yet, the movement was an eye-opener in two senses. Firstly, in addition to *begar* and an uncertain land revenue demand, it exposed the tremendous burden of *lag-bags* on the impoverished peasantry. Secondly, it also revealed the complexities that emerged in the *jagirs* as a result of the agitation. While the jagirdars had been in virtual control of these areas, the widespread peasant protests led to the involvement of the Maharana and the British as far as issues relating to land settlement were concerned.

The political developments in the Indian states in the 1920s were reflected in the formation of two organizations. The Chamber of Princes, constituted in 1921 at the behest and initiative of the native rulers for consolidation of their interests *vis-a-vis* the British Government and also to strengthen their hold upon the states' people, was an attempt at collaborative action on the part of the princes. The other organization founded in 1927 – the All India States' People Conference – represented the political aspirations of the people in the native states and was an effort to bring them on a common platform. Its objective was defined as attainment of responsible government for the people in the Indian states through representative institutions under the aegis of their rulers. Significantly, both the bodies claimed to be the real representatives of the people of the Indian states.

Another subaltern and marginalized group in the region, which resorted to agitation in the 20th century, was of tribals – the Girasias and the Bhils. They were subjected to similar woes as the peasants, e.g., exaction of *begar*, absence of revenue settlement and imposition of *lag-bags*. The new agrarian excise and forest policies adopted after the establishment of British paramountcy had deprived the tribals of their ancient rights. They were deprived of their control over forest produce and were not allowed to indulge in shifting cultivation. The Bhils were mobilized and organized by committed and eminent leaders like Govindgiri, Molital Tejavat, A.V. Thakker and Manilal Kothari. The efforts of these leaders achieved tremendous success due to a tradition of group solidarity and fierce concern for freedom among the Bhils and the Girasias.[14]

Govindgiri mobilized the Bhils aiming at their upliftment in moral, social and political spheres. He belonged to the Banjara caste and early in his life exposed to ritual purity and austere lifestyle of the Brahmins. Later, he came under the influence of Swami Dayanand Saraswati. It is believed that largely due to his influence Govindgiri set up Samp Sabha which aimed at promoting unity, organization and brotherhood amongst the Bhils. Through this organization he also aimed at socio-religious and moral reformation of the tribals. The members of the Samp Sabha were called Bhagats. Govindgiri prescribed certain simple behavioural rules for his followers: give up faith in *bhopas* (enchanters), *vantaras* (witches), and as a safeguard against them establish *dhunis* (firepits) and *nishans* (flags). He advised them to take regular bath, observe temperance, take vegetarian diet, remain obedient to parents, and forsake murder, theft, adultery, deception and hunting. He sought to address certain practices to which stigma was attached and had tended to project the Bhils as uncultured and uncouth *vis-à-vis* the caste Hindus. Govindgiri also endeavoured to inculcate amongst the Bhils a sense of superiority over the Brahmins, Banias and Rajputs by propagating that the latter kept their women in degrading position. The steady mobilization of the Bhils under the leadership of Govindgiri generated confidence among them who now became less amenable to the autocratic behaviour and orders of Rajput Thakurs. Their increasing confidence and assertiveness was reflected in their refusal to perform *begar* for officials.

In 1913, Govindgiri organized an assemblage of the Bhils on Mangarh hills where he lit a large *dhuni* (spiritual flame). It has been suggested that choice of Mangarh hills, which had earlier been a stronghold of Bhil dominion, was specifically made "to arouse political aspirations of the Bhils to re-establish Bhil Raj". According to some writers, Govindgiri used to organize an annual *mela* (fair) on Mangarh hills since 1903 where he used to lit a large *dhuni.* Each year, thousands of Bhils from neighbouring states reached there with coconut and *ghee* (purified butter). Thus, the fair was actually an annual conference to mobilize, unite and arouse the Bhils. Punja Dhirji, a young Bhil disciple of Govindgiri, propagated the idea of a Bhil Raj. He also led the militant section of the movement. It is not clear whether the assemblage at Mangarh was only a conventional tribal mode of protest against feudal oppression or was motivated by definite political ambitions. Nevertheless, it generated widespread fear in the neighbouring states of Banswara and Dungarpur and even amongst the British government. From the hills, Govindgiri sent a charter of demands to Lt.Col. J.C. Kaye, Resident of Mewar. He implored the state for greater social and religious freedom for his disciples, abolition of *begar,* reduction in land revenue, right to use forest produce, permission to employ a battalion of 2,000 Bhils with rifles for his protection and withdrawal of police warrants issued against his followers. The Political Agent did not pay heed to the charter of demands and ordered dispersal, which was refused by the agitated Bhils. Consequently, on 17th November, 1913, the Mewar Bhil Corps accompanied by troops of Rajput rulers attacked the Bhils on Mangarh hills. In the military operation, 25 Bhils were killed and 900 were captured. Later, all the Bhils were released except Govindgiri, Punja, 30 Gametis and other leaders belonging to Banswara and Sunth states that were retained by the police. Govindgiri took the entire blame upon himself. He was sentenced to 10 years' imprisonment and Punja was deported for life.

Despite its apparent failure against the military might of the British, Govindgiri's movement impacted the Bhils in many positive ways. At one level, the reformation process followed by protest had a salutary effect on their mindset and psychology. It enhanced their social aspirations, removed a sense of inferiority in relation to other castes and alleviated their fear of Rajput aristocracy. The Bhagat movement also led to moral upliftment of the Bhils who had forsaken old habits of crime, plunder and strife in large numbers. It also involved structural changes as remedial measures were introduced to bring about changes in their situation. States of Sunth, Banswara and Dungarpur abolished *begar* and commenced the procedure for land revenue settlement. Forest regulations, which were considered the most irksome by the Bhils, were liberalized. Significantly, the Bhil uprising induced the Rajput states to deal more tactfully and sympathetically with the Bhils. Maharawal of Banswara impressed upon his jagirdars the necessity of a more humane and liberal treatment towards the Bhils and were even asked to desist from interference in their socio-religious life.

Another leader, who was deeply committed to the cause of the Bhils, was Motilal Tejavat. He was born in an Oswal family in Mewar. While working as Kamdar with the jagirdar of Jhadol and later as an accountant in a shop, Motilal was moved by the heart rending atrocities perpetrated on the Bhils by the jagirdars, their officials and the moneylenders. To generate consciousness among the Bhils, he addressed them when they assembled in large numbers in the annual fair at Matrkundiya, near Chittor. His speeches had a magical effect and under his influence the Bhils took an oath in the name of Eklingji to maintain solidarity and decided on non-payment of *lag-bags* and performance of *begar*. These endeavours for promoting unity and consolidation amongst Bhils are known as *Aki* movement. In addition to Jhadol, the movement spread to Sarada, Palasia and even to the *khalsa* villages of Mewar and became firmly entrenched. The popularity of the movement led to its repression by the jagirdars as well as British authorities. On 7th March, 1922, when Tejawat along with 2,000 Bhils assembled in Idar, a British force under Major Sutton started firing. A total of 22 people died on the spot and numerous others injured. Tejavat acquired tremendous hold on the Bhil psyche and on one occasion in August 1924 when he was arrested by the jagirdar of Jhadol, 7,000 Bhils from 65 villages gathered and secured his release. Tejavat went to Udaipur with thousands of Bhils with a charter of 21 demands to be submitted to the Maharana. It was called *Mewar Pukar* (Mewar Call). Quite significantly, the Maharana conceded 18 of the 21 demands. Acceptance of the majority of the demands amply proves the strength and solidarity that the Bhils had acquired in this region under the leadership of Motilal Tejawat.[15]

Tejawat's commitment to tribal welfare led him to shift his movement to Sirohi where he mobilized the Girasias as well as the Bhils. The tribals in this region too were reeling under the oppressive policies of the native rulers and the jagirdars. The British authorities were deeply distressed by his entry into the region and were willing to offer terms of surrender if he desisted from taking part in the protests of the tribals. Despite stiff opposition of the British and the jagirdars, Tejawat administered the oath of '*Aki*' to Girasias of numerous villages in Sirohi. The refusal of the Girasias to pay land revenue till exaction of *begar* and *lag-bag* was stopped led to military action by the state in Siyawa village near Abu Road. In the action six tribals were killed, 100 huts were burned and there was loss of cattle too. The repression by the state further intensified the fury of the Girasias. At this juncture, Tejawat reached Bhula village where 5,000 Girasias from Idar, Danta, Mewar and Sirohi had assembled. It was decided that each peasant would pay Rs. 1.25 and about 17 kg maize per plough as land revenue to the state. They even established Panchayat Raj (local self-governing institutions) and raised a parallel government by nominating from among themselves a king, tehsildar and a faujdar. Whenever the *durbar* officials came to collect land revenue, the Girasias declared that they would remain as firm as *bakhad* (hills) and refused to pay the revenue. In another meeting at Valoria, a village adjoining Bhula, the Girasias reaffirmed their resolve to continue the struggle and remained adamant on their demands. When all efforts to persuade them failed, a British force under Major Prichards besieged Valoria and Bhula villages. Firing continued for seven to eight hours, stored grain was burnt and villages put on fire. The encounter left 50 dead, 640 huts were reduced to ashes, about 25,000 kg grains were destroyed and a sizeable number of cattle lost. This outrageous act of brutality received widespread publicity throughout India. Rajasthan Seva Sangh conducted an independent inquiry in which extensive losses were reported. After this grisly episode, through the mediation of AGG, negotiations were arranged between the ruler of Sirohi and the Girasias. The latter succeeded in extracting numerous political and economic privileges. The state promised lenient treatment towards Girasias, reduction in land revenue, limited rights over forest produce, especially timber for construction of huts, and exaction of *begar* only for the state and not for the officials for their personal work. Significantly, the caste panchayats were empowered to resolve civil and revenue cases.

In summation, one would like to examine the far-reaching consequences of the widespread tribal and peasant agitation in the princely states of Rajputana. It was indeed an admirable achievement for these hitherto suppressed sections that their formidable adversaries – the Rajput rulers, jagirdars and even the British authorities – were forced to adopt a conciliatory attitude. At times, they had to virtually plead for peace negotiations, which were conducted on an equal basis. They successfully challenged the erstwhile political elite, which in the past had seemed larger than life and indomitable. The sustained struggle definitely corroded the power of the entrenched power structures. The growing assertiveness and strength of the people's movement must indeed have been a revelation for the ruling classes.

During this phase, the local and regional protest movements – both peasant and tribal – despite their rural character, acquired national prominence. They attracted the attention of the national leadership, particularly Gandhi, who was highly impressed by the role of leadership and the peasantry in the Bijoliya agitation. In the course of the struggle the tribals and the peasantry demonstrated exemplary solidarity, grim determination and indomitable courage. Their struggle occupied wide spaces in the national press. These movements also popularized a variety of mobilization techniques like illegal handwritten news sheets, picketing, use of traditional *melas* (fairs), passive resistance in the form of non-payment of taxes. Significantly, while in other states, freedom movement paved the way for peasant agitation, in Rajputana states, the peasant and tribal agitations were a precursor to the national movement The leaders of these agitations later used their experience and charisma to lead the larger struggle for freedom from aristocratic rule and integration of princely states in the Indian Union.

Moreover, these widespread efforts at mobilization created consciousness amongst the oppressed peasantry for their subsequent agitation for land rights. While their immediate gains may not be very spectacular, their show of strength and undaunted courage created a favourable climate for post-independence agrarian reform.

III

In the second phase, the linkages between the regional and the national issues and their subsequent merger began. Many aspects of the constructive programmes of Gandhi started permeating the native states – long before Congress had officially associated itself with the freedom struggle of the princely states. Some of the issues that were tenaciously and vigorously espoused and propagated were *khadi*, upliftment of Harijans (low-caste people), prohibition of liquor, spread of education, social reform, tribal welfare, etc. In the region of Rajputana, in addition to the typical Gandhian issues, admirable reformation work was undertaken amongst the tribals who were concentrated in large numbers in certain pockets of Rajasthan, particularly in Mewar and Bagad (Banswara and Dungarpur).

This phase witnessed the formation of numerous organizations, which were committed to both reform activities and

Gandhian constructive programme. Committed individuals, with a sense of social service and spirit of sacrifice, initiated a process of social resurgence, especially among tribals and Harijans. Efforts were made to eradicate social malpractices like child marriage, *purdah*, untouchability and other rigid social norms, which hindered the process of education. Amongst the Bhils, they particularly strove to remove alcoholism, animal sacrifice as also the customs of elopement with unmarried girls, abduction of women and *dapa* (brideprice). Attempts were also made to improve their lifestyle and change their habits. Another major focus of their endeavours was to facilitate access to education among the deprived and backward sections.

The leaders in Rajputana were deeply influenced by Gandhi's commitment to Harijan upliftment and welfare activities. Ram Narain Chaudhary, who had joined Gandhi's Harijan Yatra, took upon himself the responsibility of Harijan welfare in Rajputana. It was on his initiative that Rajputana Harijan Sewak Sangh and its numerous branches were set up in different states. In 1934, Manikya Lal Verma along with Shobha Lal Gupta had set up Sevashram in Nareli, about seven miles from Ajmer. The chief objective of the organization was to prepare a committed cadre of workers for constructive activities, particularly in the sphere of Harijan welfare. Each trainee was required to stay in the *ashram* for two months during which he was expected to wear *khadi*, undertake spinning work and read Gandhian literature. The *ashramites* were involved in Harijan upliftment work. The inmates visited the Harijan colonies to create awareness for education and cleaning of the residential areas.[16]

A year later, Verma wished to extend the scope of his constructive activities. He keenly felt that in this region, apart from Harijans, other deprived and oppressed social categories were in greater need of such interventions. With this objective in mind, he shifted to Bagad region where Bhils constituted approximately 75 percent of the total population. He sought to ameliorate their condition from the scourge of illiteracy, poverty, alcoholism, superstitions and social evils. He selected Khadlai *pal* as centre of his numerous activities. Khadlai *ashram,* as it was popularly called, started with a boys' school. It was an uphill task to convince people to send their children to school. It was Verma's persuasive skills that succeeded in winning over the confidence of the Bhils. Later, he set up 12 schools in other Bhil *pals* of the region. To generate consciousness among the Bhils, Verma composed a long poem that vividly described their oppression by the state and the moneylenders. It also highlighted the harmful effects of social practices like sale of daughters, death feasts and alcoholism. Bhil students of his school recited the poem before large gatherings of tribals. Such renditions had a magical effect on the Bhils who started thronging the *ashram* in large numbers. As the scope of his activities extended, he set up Bagad Sewa Mandir. Under its auspices wide-ranging constructive activities were taken up for the social and economic upliftment of the tribals. It comprised of a library, dispensary, carpentry unit, *khadi* centre, dying unit, spinning and weaving unit, well-digging unit, seeds unit and a cow shed. There was also a *chowk* (open courtyard) for deliberations amongst tribals and farmers. The tribals were taught cattle rearing, breeding, preparation of manure and also encouraged to grow new crops like oilseeds, wheat, cotton, etc. Credit facilities were also arranged to protect the tribals from the clutches of the moneylenders. He also tried to dissuade them from their addiction to alcohol as also certain malpractices like animal sacrifice.[17]

Verma's campaign for ameliorating the plight of the tribals was undertaken against all odds. Rough terrain, lack of funds, and strong hostility of the state were further compounded by the extremely suspicious mindset of the tribals. However, in all his endeavours, Verma's wife Narayani Devi and family shared his enthusiasm and concern, his travails and adversities. It was during these difficult days that Verma lost his son for want of proper medical care and nutrition. Even this momentous loss did not dissuade Verma from his crusade.

Bhogilal Pandya was another prominent leader who strove incessantly for the betterment of the deprived and the underprivileged sections, particularly the tribals and the Harijans. Spread of education remained central to the programme of social reformation and economic betterment of these subaltern groups. He was a teacher in a government school where he taught till 1942. However, while engaged in job, he made incredible efforts at the individual level for the upliftment of the deprived sections of society. At the young age of fifteen, he had set up a hostel in Dungarpur for facilitating access to education for the poor boys living in remote villages. Later, his wife Maniben lovingly addressed as 'Ba' took over the responsibility of food and other arrangements of the hostel inmates. Pandya raised funds and other resources for the hostel by appealing to the affluent sections of society.[18]

Despite being a Brahmin Pandya strove tirelessly for the Harijans. Every evening, he visited their colonies, where through his exhortations he sought to dissuade them from their bad habits like eating the meat of dead animals, collecting leftovers of food and alcoholism. He also tried to impress upon them the benefits of education for their children. Influenced by Gandhi's epic fast in 1932, he set up Harijan Sewak Samiti in Dungarpur. As its secretary, he set up schools in Harijan colonies. In these endeavours, he received full cooperation from his wife who was always keen to live up to the social ideals cherished by her husband. The untouchables and other low-caste people had easy access to her kitchen. Although Pandya had to suffer humiliation and threats of ostracism from the caste Hindus, these did not deter him from his commitment to the betterment of depressed classes.

In 1933, with the cooperation of Rajguru Mahant Suryadas, Bhogilal Pandya took out a procession of Harijans in Dungarpur that later proceeded to the temple located in Rajaji ki Chhatri. This was the first instance of temple entry of Harijans in Dungarpur. Another significant instance of temple entry took place in the city of Udaipur. During the 1950s

Harijan Sewak Sangh workers led the movement under the leadership of Kesarilal Bordia, popularly known as 'Dadabhai'. He and veteran leader Bhurelal Baya had organized temple entry of the Harijans at the historic Jagdish temple of Udaipur. It is interesting that in the conservative atmosphere of Rajasthan, courageous women activists like Shanta Trivedi and Sushila Dashottar participated in the procession. The temple, situated in the heart of the city, held iconic status in the cultural and religious life of the people of Mewar. Dadabhai and the workers of the Harijan Sewak Sangh had to face severe opposition from the Brahmins and other high-caste groups, at times, even suffer from social ostracization. The temple entry of the Harijans had been a highly sensitive issue in the conservative environs of the region. In 1947, Mewar Praja Mandal had to encounter public uproar when there were rumours that it was planning temple entry for the untouchables in the shrine of Nathadwara. The Praja Mandal leaders went out of their way to assuage popular sentiments. Thereafter, they desisted from approaching the issue of entry to the Nathadwara temple that was imbued with strong and deep-rooted emotions.

In 1938, after Manikya Lal Verma's departure from Bagad who had successfully mobilized and conscientized the Bhils, particularly in the realms of education, social reform and economic activities, Pandya felt the urgency of filling the gap. Consequently, Sewa Sangh was established to continue the constructive and reformative work amongst the tribals of the region. Sewa Sangh, in addition to education and improvement in agricultural skills, sought to eradicate certain practices among the Bhils, e.g., *dapa*, abduction of women, elopement with unmarried girls, animal sacrifice and alcoholism. Sewa Sangh also tried to enlighten the Bhils about their civic rights. Many schools and colleges were opened under its auspices. It also offered invaluable services during calamities like famines and floods. Other veteran leaders, who made significant contribution to the activities of the Sangh, were Hari Deo Joshi, Chandu Lal Gupta, Govardhan Lal Gupta, Shiv Lal Kotadiya,

Bhairav Lal Verma, Krishna Gopal Bhil etc. National level leaders like Ramehwari Nehru and Thakker Bapa, who on their visit to Dungarpur had closely observed the activities of the Sangh, were highly impressed by the dedication, simplicity and zeal of its workers.

Sewa Sangh played a commendable role in transforming the mindset of the tribals, particularly towards the spread of education. The state authorities resented the widespread impact of the Sangh in the region. The Maharawal of Dungarpur felt threatened by its activities, particularly the increasing awakening among the Bhils. Consequently, the state resorted to repressive measures and banned the schools managed by the Sangh. The activists of the Sangh, including the tribals, displayed tremendous resolve and courage when they took a vow that they would rather die than see the closure of their schools. The grit, determination and sacrifice of the tribals during this difficult phase are a testimony to the incredible work done by the Sangh. Many tribals made the supreme sacrifice of their lives to fulfil their vow. The names of Nana Bhai Khant and a 13-year old tribal girl Kali Bai of Punawara village who lost their lives to the atrocities of the state have become legendary for their commitment to the cause of education.[19]

Later, the tribals who were actively associated with the activities of the Sangh emerged as significant participants in Quit India movement of 1942. Thus, the Sangh was not only an organization committed to constructive programme but as political agitation gained ground the members of the organization became involved in the freedom struggle. In this context, Pandya had unequivocally remarked: "The Sangh believes that our (native states) fate is linked to our brethren in British India and demands immediate freedom. If the Sangh does not participate in this struggle (for freedom) then it is not fulfilling its commitment towards its motherland and united India."[20] Although Praja Mandal was set up in Dungarpur as late as 1944 but Sewa Sangh under the able leadership of Pandya had already achieved admirable success as far as mobilization and political awakening of the people was concerned.

Many innovative schemes were adopted in the region for spreading education in the region. Hari Bhai Kinkar and his wife Mahima Devi emerged as exemplars in this field. He established Vidya Pracharini Sabha in 1916-17 along with some of his colleagues which marked his initiation into public life. His deep commitment to education can be seen in his innovative scheme called the 'Muththi Fund'. Under this scheme, a handful of grains were collected from each household and the funds thus accumulated were used for the spread of education. He also started a small library called '*Giten ki Gashti*' in which low-priced small books were available. He toured numerous villages to create consciousness and spread awakening on progressive issues, particularly education. Interestingly, in rural areas, he used songs instead of speeches to mobilize the illiterate villagers.[21]

Rajasthan Sewa Sangh was yet another organization, which did pioneering work during this phase in many spheres like amelioration of peasants, propagation of *khadi* and various other types of reformation work. It was set up in Wardha in 1920 by Vijay Singh Pathik, Ram Narain Chaudhary and Hariji Brahmchari. The members of the Sangh were required to observe certain vows, which included life-long commitment to national service and non-involvement in religious or communal dispute. The Sangh had evolved a unique and effective method of resolving local issues and problems. In a disturbed area, the Sangh deputed its members to look into the grievances and make necessary recommendations. Consequent upon this, a panchayat elected by the people was authorized to resolve disputes. Thus, the initiative and leadership remained in the hands of the local people who took remedial measures. People offered written commitment to follow the leadership of the panchayat. The method of protest included a petition on behalf of the panchayat to the jagirdar, and on failure to get a favourable response *satyagraha* was launched. The *satyagraha* was led and guided by one of the members of the Sangh. The Rajasthan Sewa Sangh, with its team of selfless and dedicated workers, played a laudatory role in generating political consciousness in Rajasthan, especially in rural areas.[22] The activities of the Sangh had contributed in preparing the social base for the subsequent freedom struggle in the Rajputana states.

Another Gandhian cause that was widely propagated in the native states since the 1920s was *khadi*. An important organization involved with *khadi* work was Gandhi Ashram at Hatundi. Many prominent leaders like Hari Bhau Upadhyaya were associated with it. Khadi Mandal and Charkha Sangh were also set up in different parts of Rajasthan as early as 1926. Motilal Tejawat and Jamna Lal Bajaj were other leaders who popularized *khadi* in this region. Even Maharana Fateh Singh bought two bales of *khadi* from Jamna Lal Bajaj in 1926. Other organizations which aimed at the multiple objectives of popularization of *khadi*, removal of untouchability, prohibition of liquor and national integration were Harijan Sewak Sangh set up in 1932; Rajasthan Sewak Sangh instituted by Ram Narain Chaudhary and Shobha Lal Gupta; Jiwan Kutir began by Hiralal Shastri in 1929 in Vanasthali; and Khadi Prachar Sabha founded in 1932. Other prominent leaders who were involved in *khadi* work and constructive activities were Siddhraj Dhaddha in Jaipur, Mukta Prasad Vakil from Bikaner and Master Bholanath in Alwar.[23] Evidently, multiple activities like advocating the cause of *khadi*, upliftment of Harijans, tribals and women created a broad socio-economic base for the emergence of more active political movement.

It was during this phase that *khadi* emerged as a symbol of protest, solidarity and self-reliance. It is indeed surprising that seemingly innocuous looking and extremely humble clothing could challenge the overwhelming supremacy and power of the native rulers. *Khadi* cap, popularly known as Gandhi *topi*, was viewed as a symbol of sedition and wearing the same was in itself a veritable crime.[24] In Mewar, a person who donned a *khadi* cap was seen as a potential threat and immediately put under police surveillance. Maharaja Jai Singh of Alwar state used to get deeply disturbed at sight of Gandhi *topis* and *khadi* attire. He sent warning to prominent leaders of the freedom struggle Kunj Behari Lal Modi and Hari Narayan Sharma through his Prime Minister Shri Alakhdhari. He reportedly told them that according to local customs white cap signified mourning, and hence they should desist from wearing the same. However, the two leaders continued to carry on their propaganda for popularization of *khadi* and also the tri-colour flag. In Sirohi too, the display of national flag was banned by the state. Similarly, in Banswara, people were scared to talk to Bhupendra Nath Trivedi, a local leader, because of his *khadi* attire.[25] According to some erstwhile leaders of the freedom struggle, the slogans and symbols like *khadi, charkha, Gandhiji ki Jai, Vande Mataram, Jawahar* jacket, etc., generated widespread fear amongst the royalty.[26] Use or display of these symbols invited harsh punishment from the state authorities. Nevertheless, these symbols gave visibility to the Gandhian ideals that inspired the national movement.[27] These also generated an impression of the continuation of the movement even during its passive phases. The potency of *khadi* as a unifying symbol was tremendous. It cut across ideological barriers to earn respect from opposing viewpoints. Arjun Lal Sethi, despite his commitment to extremist and revolutionary trends within the movement and his differences with the Gandhian group, used to wear a *khadi* cap. On one occasion, his cap was auctioned for Rs. 1,100.

In the personal lives of the leaders switchover to *khadi* attire was seen as a significant ideological shift. It demonstrated, on the one hand, their commitment to new political values and loyalty to the national movement, while on the other, it also implied quite categorically revulsion for the venerated symbols of the royalty and the British rulers. The following song conveys this implication quite forcefully:

> *"Ek do pili pagdi phenk do,*
> *Khoob pehna sona, khoob pehni chandi,*
> *Ab pehnenge khadi, raj karega Gandhi,*
> *Gandhi ki andhi, Swarajya ka jhanda,*
> *Government ki topi mein bambool ka danda".*[28]

Khadi, thus, signified a shift from the glamour and ostentation of the royal symbology and the authoritarianism of the imperialist symbolism of the British. Hence, it appealed to a wide cross section of people.

The numerous kinds of constructive activities undertaken during this period form a crucial stage in the growth of nationalism in the region of Rajputana. Although these were non-political activities, but they definitely led to mobilization and political awakening of the tribals, peasants, Harijans and also women. They testify to the fact that Gandhian influence was seen not merely as far as style of protest is concerned but other aspects of his constructive programmes were also adopted and popularized by the local and regional leadership. Significantly, these programmes aroused public consciousness to a level that when active political movements were launched people were politically mature to participate in them. The volunteers who were trained in *khadi* programme, educational activities, *ashram* discipline, and tribal and Harijan welfare eventually emerged as active participants in political processes. Narendra Pal Singh Chaudhary, a prominent leader of the freedom struggle in Mewar, underscored the seminal role of these constructive programmes in providing strength and stimulus to later political movements. According to him, the earlier scattered and diffused endeavours in numerous spheres merged to render Praja Mandal into a widespread and powerful movement.[29]

IV

> *"Mharo Veero Shiromani Desh, Mhane Pyaro Lage Re."*
>
> (I love my *des* (region) which is like a high jewel amongst the brave).[30]

Till date, this popular song in the region of Mewar reflects unique sense of history and regional pride. One can recollect various songs, slogans and proverbs that reflect people's love for their region - Mewar. They articulate characteristics of the region or their own identification with their region. It is interesting to analyze how despite their intense attachment and abiding love for their region and its distinctive history, people belonging to erstwhile princely states transcended their regional identity to establish emotional ties with the larger concept of nationhood. To inculcate among these people attachment to the concept of a united nation was indeed a formidable task as regional identities have been close to people's hearts. In fact, conscious efforts were made to reconcile regional identity with national aspirations. In this context, the exemplary role of regional organizations like Praja Mandal, Lok Parishad, etc., and also the seminal contribution of the regional leadership needs to be examined.

The activities of Praja Mandals and similar organizations received an impetus after the historic Haripura session during February 19-21, 1938 when the Indian National Congress passed a long resolution wherein native states were considered integral parts of India which cannot be separated. It advocated 'full responsible government' and 'guarantee of civil liberty in the states'. In Marwar, Praja Mandal had been set up in 1934, which was later reorganized in May 1938 as Marwar Lok Parishad. Jaipur Praja Mandal had been founded in 1931 but its sphere of activities was confined to social reform and promotion of *khadi*. It even kept away from peasant agitation in Sikar and Shekhavati region. It was after the Haripura resolution that Praja Mandal was organized under the leadership of Jamna Lal Bajaj and its objective was defined as establishment of responsible government and ensuring elementary rights for the citizens of the state.[31]

In April 1938, Mewar Praja Mandal started functioning with Balwant Singh Mehta as its President and Manikya Lal Verma as Secretary. The fact that 2,000 people enrolled as members of the Praja Mandal within three days of its formation is a proof of the growing political consciousness in Mewar. The state immediately declared Praja Mandal as an unlawful association and exiled Manikya Lal Verma. The ban was removed on February 22, 1941 only after an agitation was conducted by Manikya Lal Verma from Ajmer.[32] Praja Mandal leaders were faced with multiple objectives. Firstly, they had to familiarize people with the concept of a united nation. Secondly, the people in Mewar had to be mobilized in support of the Praja Mandal movement, which aimed at setting up of responsible form of government. It was an uphill task as people were emotionally attached to the Maharana. The Mewar Maharana had a distinctive status on account of his sacral antecedents – as the descendant of Lord Rama and as the appointee of Lord Shiva. Moreover, the rulers were still imaged as *'Mai Baap'* (mother and father), *'Annadata'* (provider of food) and *'Pratipalak'* (sustainer).

The Praja Mandal acted cautiously as far as its objectives and programmes were concerned. The aim of Praja Mandal was declared as "achievement of responsible government under the aegis of Maharana". Quite pertinently, the leaders' statements continued to reflect loyalty and respect towards royal houses and rulers while agitating for responsible government. Veteran leader of Mewar, Manikya Lal Verma said: "Mewar Praja Mandal respects Maharana Sahib and his throne, he should be respected and there should be no difference in his style of living but people should have their say in the administration of the state."[33] In their pamphlets and speeches, the bureaucracy was blamed for misleading the Maharana and for the dismal state of affairs in the region.[34] While later historians continue to view this ambivalence in political attitude as a paradox, it was necessitated on account of popular sentiment for kingship.

The Praja Mandal movement proved to be a veritable link between the national and the local as well as urban with the rural. The movement had adopted nationalist symbols, issues and programmes but it consistently kept itself involved with the local problems of the Mewaris. It did not agitate merely for political issues but socio-economic problems of the masses, peasants and the tribals also remained a persistent concern of the Praja Mandal leaders. This involvement remained pertinent to the creation of public opinion in favour of the organization. In order to broaden the social base of the movement, Praja Mandal devoted attention to public welfare activities. In 1943, floods in Khari river caused enormous loss of human life and cattle and also extensive destruction of property. These floods have been recorded as one of the most devastating in the history of Mewar. Praja Mandal workers were the first to reach the affected areas and a joint relief committee of the state and the public was constituted with Bhawani Shankar Vaidya, a member of the working committee of the Praja Mandal as its Chief Secretary. Bhure Lal Baya, Vice President of the Praja Mandal was the chief organizer of relief measures.[35]

Praja Mandal also associated itself with the problems of the peasants. It seriously addressed the menace that the peasants faced in the form of pigs. In Mewar, the killing of wild animals like lions and pigs was banned. When Maharana began his hunting expedition, killing of pig was considered an auspicious beginning. It was called *'Mahurat ka Shikar'* (auspicious beginning). The peasants had to suffer enormous damages on account of royal prohibition on killing of pigs as these beasts fed on the crops and other agricultural produce. The extent of damage can be gauged from the popular saying that meant that a fully fed pig can destroy or eat upto one-fourth acre of crops. The number of pigs that were killed by Maharana Fateh Singh gives an idea about the large number of pigs that must have been there in the region – 1,500 killed by gunfire and another

300 trampled by horses. In 1942, the Mewar government issued fresh legislation re-imposing the earlier ban on killing of pigs. In addition to a prison term, a fine of Rs. 50 (an enormous amount in those times) was levied on those who violated the law. Praja Mandal leaders started the movement for lifting up this ban on killing of wild animals.

It needs to be mentioned that peasant issues were taken up by Praja Mandal to win their confidence and support. It was essential to mobilize peasantry, as it was their participation that could have created broad social base for the political agitation. It was not an objective that could be easily accomplished, particularly in the background of deep distrust that the peasantry had developed in urban leadership in the post-1922 phase of the Bijoliya movement. When Praja Mandal was formed in April 1938, the Bijoliya Kisan Panchayat passed a resolution on November 24, 1938 that they would not participate in the agitation launched by the Mewar Praja Mandal.

The Praja Mandal leadership began the popularly called 'pig movement' in Nahar Magra for lifting the ban on killing of pigs. They organized many meetings to mobilize the peasantry on the issue and involve them in the agitation. However, the peasantry was too terrified of government repression and showed least enthusiasm for the cause. In the first two meetings organized in Khairali, there was no participation of peasants. The meeting organized on the occasion of Dhuni Mata Fair on 28th July, 1946 in Nahar Magra was able to attract large crowds. A year-long movement, under the leadership of Manikya Lal Verma, Balwant Singh Mehta, Bhure Lal Baya, Mohan Lal Sukhadia and other local leaders, ultimately secured the desired results in February 1947.[36]

The Praja Mandal projected itself as a people's organization while highlighting and expressing deep concern for the specific grievances that afflicted different classes and social groups – peasantry, traders, educated middle classes. The problems of the peasantry were given primacy in its programmes, e.g., *begar* (forced labour), oppressive taxation, police atrocities on farmers, lack of education, particularly military training for their children, transportation facilities for foodgrains and medical treatment for their cattle. There was also a demand for Kisan Panchayats with authority to resolve civil cases. The aspirations of the middle classes found expression in specific demands like access to educational institutions and representation in municipal bodies. The concern for public welfare was also conveyed quite explicitly when they incorporated programmes such as education, health, eradication of corruption in administration and issues such as increased burden of taxation, extravagance in administration and royal expenses and demand for people's representatives in the local bodies. The Praja Mandal appointed a Foodgrains Committee to deal with acute scarcity of food grains.[37] Through such programmes an attempt was made to broaden the social base of the movement and to make Praja Mandal movement popular amongst different social categories whose cooperation remained vital for the success of its activities.

The primacy given to local and regional issues was accompanied by equally vigorous endeavours for popularization and permeation of the ideals of nationalist freedom struggle, particularly the Gandhian technique of resistance. It may be mentioned that while Gandhi and Nehru adopted an attitude of neutrality in the princely states, leaders in the native states constantly desired adoption of direct action programmes and greater participation of Congress leaders in their states. Prominent leaders from Rajputana states – Manikya Lal Verma, Hiralal Shastri, Ratan Devi Shastri, Jai Narain Vyas, Ranchhoddas Gattani, Narendrapal Singh Choudhary, Bhure Lal Baya used to be keen to remain in contact with significant national leaders.[38] Although Congress had officially adopted a policy of non-intervention in the agitation of the princely states, yet even before 1938 the national leaders continued to evince interest in the protest movements in Mewar. During the Bijoliya peasant agitation, Tilak, Madan Mohan Malviya and Gandhi had intervened on different occasions. Tilak put forward a resolution on Bijoliya agitation in the Congress session. On Gandhi's insistence, Madan Mohan Malviya met Maharana and later sent his private secretary Mahadev Desai on a fact-finding mission to Bijoliya. On the basis of Desai's report, Gandhi wrote to the Maharana to take steps for the amelioration of the peasants. When Praja Mandal was banned in 1938, Manikya Lal Verma met Gandhi. Thereafter, Jamna Lal Bajaj requested Mewar's Prime Minister to lift the ban on the organization. On hearing about the inhuman treatment meted out to Manikya Lal Verma by the Mewar police, Gandhi advised the Praja Mandal leaders to institute legal proceedings against the police and act fearlessly. Other leaders who took keen interest in the princely states of Rajputana were Acharya Narendra Dev and Jai Prakash Narain.[39]

The regional leaders tried to communicate the distinctive nature of the Gandhian style of protest to the people in the colloquial language. Manikya Lal Verma articulated the same very effectively in the local dialect. He reminded the people that the inhabitants of Mewar had never surrendered before exploitation. Therefore, the exploitative laws should be challenged. His interpretation of the non-violent struggle and the way he articulated it before the masses is fascinating: "In this war one doesn't kill anyone nor does one raise hand, not even use abusive language. In case government servant abuses, at that time you remain quiet, [if] he beats, just laugh. If he handcuffs you, consider it as a golden chain... You must be recollecting Prahlad's instance who wanted to dissuade his father from inflicting atrocities and to do so he himself suffered but he did not raise his hand and he did not grudge... This struggle is based on this policy."[40] It is evident that to prepare a broad base for Civil Disobedience Movement and non-violent freedom struggle, local tradition and mythological icons were extensively used. The adaptation and innovation by local leaders in propagating Gandhian ideology of purity of means and end as also exemplification of the spirit of non-violence was unique.

In order to disseminate the concept of nation, beyond the confines of Mewar, the regional leaders tried to propagate and project the charisma of the national level leadership. Tilak Jayanti and Gandhi Jayanti were celebrated. 26th January was commemorated as Independence Day.[41] During such celebrations, the rituals and symbology of the nationalist freedom struggle were employed extensively, e.g., organization of *prabhat pheris*, unfurling of the tri-colour flag, reciting national songs etc. Through the staging of such rituals, the nationalist leaders succeeded in arousing feelings of nationalism among the people who were now able to identify with the ideal of a united nation. In addition to these rituals, numerous newspapers and journals were published for dissemination of concept of nationalism. Jai Narain Vyas edited a journal entitled *'Akhand Bharat'*, meaning undivided India; the title itself suggesting how deeply entrenched the concept of nationalism had become in regional states.[42]

Significantly, at no stage of the struggle there existed conflict between the two identities – regional and national. In fact, regional pride and love for nation co-existed during the period of freedom struggle and strengthened each other. No effort was made by the regional leadership to obliterate or dilute regional identity in order to give precedence to national feeling. Verma, a leading Gandhian leader of Mewar, exalts his love for Mewar in his composition '*Mewar Hamara*':

> "We belong to it (Mewar)
> We love it more than our lives.
> We are Mewaris.
> Mewar is ours."

In yet another composition '*Bharat*', Verma gives vent to national pride that also became an inspiring national song of Mewar:

> "Tell me the name of land
> Where Gandhi, Gautam and Ram

are born in different ages.
That is Hindustan, Hindustan, and Hindustan."[43]

In this context, the ingenuity of local leadership in communicative skills and the manner in which they devised, designed and paraphrased subtle ideas in their own style to suit the regional requirements was indeed admirable. These leaders personified the persona, charisma and ideology of the national level leaders in their specific regions. Interestingly, Manikya Lal Verma was called '*Mewar ka Gandhi*' and Bhogilal Pandya as '*Bagad ka Gandhi*'. The efforts and initiatives of these leaders transformed and extended regional loyalties into love for the nation. Moreover, they instilled nationalism in a manner that it did not threaten or diminish the deep attachment to regional identities, symbology and history.

In the context of freedom struggle in the native states certain misconceptions continue to prevail. It is often asserted that in these regions the political agitation not only took off quite late as compared to British India, it was also not marked by the intensity and widespread character of the movement that was to be seen in the non-princely states. To illustrate the correct perspective, it would be instructive to look at some of the vital, progressive and hitherto unexplored aspects of the freedom struggle in the Rajputana states. At the outset, one needs to look at the seminal significance of the early peasant and tribal agitation. Widespread unrest and periodic disturbances that characterized these protests created ripples in the native ruling classes and also the British authorities. For the first time in the history of the region, the entrenched power structures were subdued by the strength, solidarity and resistance of the hitherto suppressed categories. Secondly, despite being localized in nature, these struggles attracted the attention of the national level leadership. Many leaders of the Congress, despite the policy of non-intervention in princely states, evinced keen interest in the progress and achievements of these movements. The Bijoliya agitation was particularly seen as one of the earliest peasant struggles in the country. These spectacular protest movements were also widely reported in the national level newspapers. Consequently, the atrocities committed on deprived sections by the rulers and the jagirdars were publicized for the first time. It is true that these protests did not lead to any fundamental change in the rural community life, agrarian relations or the pattern of landownership. The various peasant uprisings definitely raised the confidence and awareness level of the peasants and tribals. More significantly, new and effective methods of protest and mobilization were devised. These should be viewed as incredible achievements in an autocratic political culture where people could not even dream of remonstrance and resistance. The vital significance of the widespread protests lies in the fact that they definitely created grounding for the subsequent political agitation. The favourable climate for the post-independence land reforms was perhaps the result of the remarkable strength and solidarity demonstrated by the peasants during the agitation.

Another significant aspect of the struggle in the Rajputana states has been the incessant and hectic constructive and reformation work. Ironically, these activities have not been duly emphasized in the historical writings. Veteran leaders of the region like Manikya Lal Verma, Bhogi Lal Pandya, Narendra Pal Singh Chaudhary, Hari Bhai Kinkar, Hari Bhau Upadhyaya, Jai Narayan Vyas, Hiralal Shastri and others plunged headlong into activities that sought to merge regional identities into a national identity. The leaders espoused causes and symbols that reflected the trends of the Gandhian movements at the national level. *Khadi*, Harijan welfare, tribal upliftment, spread of education and social reform formed some of the most cherished causes which were popularized through numerous organizations. Involvement in these activities was an arduous task in view of the grim scenario in the region. On the one hand, the leaders and the activists were always suspects in the eyes of the state authorities, while on the other, the oppressed groups for whose betterment they were striving looked upon them with suspicion. The British government too was skeptical about their endeavours. Lack of resources, inclement weather and harsh terrain of the region further compounded this pervasive hostility. It required unbounded enthusiasm, considerable organizational skills, effective mobilizational strategies, personal charisma, indomitable courage and willingness to suffer and sacrifice to carry on such dedicated work for long periods of time amidst adverse situation. Viewed from this perspective, the constructive activities provided socio-economic background to the freedom struggle in the native states.

The exemplary role of local leaders in the process of struggle has not been adequately highlighted in history writing. While it is true that the towering leaders at the national level had carved a niche in popular imagination but it were the local leaders who had played a pivotal role in generating and sustaining the struggle. First and foremost, it were the regional and local leaders who had played a key role in disseminating the charisma, symbology and ideology of the national leaders, particularly Gandhi. In fact, it was their incessant efforts that had popularized Gandhi in the region long before 1938 when the Congress officially confirmed the princely states as integral part of India's war of independence. They took great pains to keep in touch with the national leadership and draw their attention to the plight of the people in the native states. They had created political awakening in the state and familiarized people with Gandhi's distinctive style of protest and also his constructive programmes. In fact, it was their spadework that led the Congress leadership to conclude that the environment in the princely states was ripe enough to be made a part of the nationalist struggle. They evolved mobilization strategies, created inspirational and powerful symbols and adopted effective communicative skills through which they sought to reconcile the regional identity with nationalist aspirations. To inculcate among the people of the princely states the concept of a united India was a formidable task as they were not only deeply attached to their region but also had intense emotional ties with the Maharana and the jagirdars. To wean them away from their traditional political loyalties and impress upon them the need for responsible form of government was an incredible achievement. Due to their humility, charisma, spirit of sacrifice and service, these leaders were often seen in their localities and regions as personification of the national leaders, particularly Gandhi. The seminal contribution of the leaders at the regional and local levels was indeed critical to the process of struggle and transition.

Another remarkable feature of the political struggle in the Rajputana states was the participation of women in the protest movements of the region. Women were active participants in the early peasant agitations of Bijoliya and Begun. They attended the meetings of the Kisan Panchayat and participated in the rallies organized by the leaders. In the Begun peasant agitation, when more than 500 men were arrested, women descended in large numbers to take charge of the agitation in the face of severe repression by the state and the British authorities. In the subsequent phase, wives of many prominent leaders emerged as pillars of strength who enthusiastically participated in the constructive activities like *khadi,* tribal and Harijan welfare and educational activities. Narayani Devi Verma (Manikya Lal Verma's wife), Mahima Devi Kinkar (Hari Bhai Kinkar's wife) and Mani Ben (Bhogi Lal Pandya's wife) displayed rare capacity to sacrifice and suffer for the welfare of the underprivileged. They shed their age-old social prejudices and taboos to emerge as champions of the impoverished tribals and the oppressed untouchables. Not only this, they continued to strive for their betterment even at cost of their health and proper education of their own children. In the process, they emerged as inspirational figures for women at large; stimulating them, building their confidence and bringing them out of the four walls of the house. Notwithstanding the fact that

Rajputana states were often projected as retrogressive and feudalistic, women participated in large numbers in the active phases of the freedom struggle.

The freedom struggle in the region was characterized by yet another peculiar feature. Quite interestingly, the demand for responsible government never translated into disrespect for the rulers. The erstwhile rulers were never maligned either by the leaders or the people at large. Their public image as divine representatives continued to be upheld, hailed and revered even during the active phases of the struggle. While the new leadership and new symbology inspired by the Gandhian ideology and values carved a niche for themselves, the traditional symbols and aura that surrounded the monarchy remained close to people's hearts. It led to the emergence of a political culture wherein two sets of values co-existed. The Gandhian impact led to the dissemination of values of simplicity, austerity, concern for the deprived and capacity to suffer. The monarchical paradigm, on the other hand, eulogized the glamour, ostentation, sacral status and authority associated with the ruler. In some ways symbolism associated with the earlier regimes in Mewar remained pertinent to the freedom struggle within the Rajputana states as well as at the national level.

Notes

1. For emergence of nationalism, refer J.H. Carlton, *The Historical Evolution of Modern Nationalism* p.12; Hans Kohn, *The Idea of Nationalism,* p.10, 16, 19; Pratibha Jain, *Gandhian Ideas, Social Movements and Creativity,* pp.1-27.
2. Jyoti Prasad Suda, *Main Currents of Social and Political Thought in Modern India*, Part I, p.319.
3. *Sri Aurobindo*, Vol.I, p.65; Sri Aurobindo Ghosh, *Speeches*, pp.173-174.
4. Jawaharlal Nehru, *The Discovery of India*, p.44.
5. Edward Said, *Culture and Imperialism,* pp.259-261.

6. Ravindra Nath Tagore, *Nationalism,* pp.110-111; and *Crisis of Civilization*; Amiya Chakravarti (ed.), *A Tagore Reader*, p.99.
7. Dharmpal, *Bharat ka Swadharma*, p.27.
8. Ramashray Roy, 'Vyakti, Samaj, Rajniti: Navvyakhya', in Asha Kaushik (ed.), *Gandhi: Nayi Sadi Ke Liye*, pp.34-35.Gandhi frequently wrote about the qualifications of a *satyagrahi*. See *Young India*, 8 January 1925; *Harijan*, 25 March 1939.
9. For a detailed analysis of charismatic heroes refer, T.K.Oommen, *Charisma, Stability and Change*, p.7. To understand how Gandhian charisma is distinct from the categories of charisma enumerated by Weber, refer B.N. Ganguly, *Gandhian Social Philosophy*, p.15. Gandhi's influence has been defined as magnetic power, see Horace Alexander, *Gandhi Through Western Eyes*, pp.18-29; *Romain Rolland and Gandhi Correspondence*, p.16.
10. For details regarding the movement in Bijoliyan, refer Shankar Sahai Saxena, *Jo Desh Ke Liye Jiye*, pp.16-79; Lalit Pandey, 'Svadhinta Sangram Mein Bijoliya-Begun Kisan Andolan', in Dev Kothari (ed.), *Swatantrta Andolan Mein Mewar ka Yogdan*, pp.49-66; Dushyant Ojha, *Vijay Singh Pathik*; Savitri Parmar, *Veh Agni Purusha*.
11. Mahendra Khadagawat, 'Rajasthan ke Kisan Andolan', *Sujas*, June-July 1998, pp.92-96.
12. *Ibid.*, p.20; S.S. Gehlot, *Rajasthan: Swadhinta Purva evam Pashchat* (1857-1997), pp.92-96.
13. Mahendra Khadagawat, 'Rajasthan ke Kisan Andolan', *Sujas*, June-July 1998, pp.92-96.
14. For details on tribal protests, refer L.P. Mathur, *Protest Movements of Bhils under British Raj*; V.K. Vashishtha, *Bhagat Movement*; Robert Deliege, *The Bhils of Western India*.
15. The national leaders, particularly Gandhi, kept in touch with the activities and achievements of the *Aki* movement under Motilal Tejawat. The latter had professed himself to be a follower of Gandhi and expressed his faith in the doctrine of non-violence. Manilal Kothari, another committed leader of the tribals, kept Gandhi informed about the progress of the movement. However, Gandhi was deeply disillusioned by the frequent incidents of violence that were quite common among the tribals. They often resorted to armed action against the officials of the jagirdar. In fact Gandhi had refused to accept Tejawat as his disciple. It is interesting to observe the relationship of the rural, tribal and regional leadership with the foremost national leaders. While, on the one hand, the leaders at all levels were keen to remain in touch with Gandhi, the national level leaders too continued to evince interest in the grievances of the subaltern categories in the princely states.

16. Narendra Sharma 'Kusum', *Manikyalal Verma,* pp.39-45; S.S. Saxena, *op.cit.*, p.82.
17. *Ibid.*, pp.80-99; Savitri Parmar, *op.cit.*, pp.9-11, 110-111.
18. Natwar Tripathi, *Bhogilal Pandya*, p.3.
19. Utsav Lal Sharma, 'Nana Bhai aur Kali Bai', *Sujas*, June-July 1998, pp.66-68.
20. Natwar Tripathi, *op.cit.*, p.14.
21. Sumnesh Joshi, *Rajasthan Mein Swatantrata Sangram ke Senani*, pp.238-239.
22. Nirmala Joshi, 'Kahani Swatantrata Sangram Ki,' *Sujas*, June-July1998, p.9; Pemaram, 'Rajasthan mein Ahinsak Kranti aur Congress', paper presented in the seminar on 'Bhartiya Swadhinta Sangram evam Rajasthan ki Sahbhagita', Department of Political Science, University of Rajasthan, 22-23 March, 1986.
23. Siddharaj Dhaddha's commitment to *khadi* has been indeed admirable and even till today he wears hand-spun clothes. Sumnesh Joshi, *op.cit.*; B.S. Trivedi, *Hiralal Shastri*, pp.26-29; Bhagwatilal Sacheti & Prahlad Narain Vajpayee, 'Mewar Swatantrata Andolan aur Rachnatmak Karya', in Dev Kothari (ed.), *op.cit.*, pp.189-206.
24. M.L. Sukhadia, a prominent freedom fighter, the first Revenue Minister and later the Chief Minister of the state, recalled the enormous significance attached to *khadi topi.* According to him, the donning of the *topi* was perceived as a revolutionary step or even a revolt by the state authorities. When he, along with some of his companions from school, wore Gandhi caps, people watched them with horror; see K.L. Kochar, *Mohanlal Sukhadia*, p.76. A close associate of Manikya Lal Verma, Bhanwarlal Jhanwar, while recounting his Praja Mandal days, described how wearing *khadi topi* was a crime and a symbol of sedition; see Savitri Parmar, *op.cit.*, p.615. *Khadi topi* had replaced the *pagri* as a symbol of pride. Often to hurt the emotions of the freedom fighters and to provoke them policemen of the princely state of Dungarpur used to kick the *khadi* caps with their feet; see Naresh Tripathi, *op.cit.*, p.12. Roop Narain, a participant in the Quit India Movement of 1942, recorded his nostalgic feelings about the Gandhi cap. According to him, the *topi* was a veritable symbol of pride and was called *Azadi ka Mukut* (crown of freedom). He reminisced how they refuted the orders of the jail authorities in Multan to take off their *khadi topis*. Later, the extreme provocation caused by the order of the authorities forced them to retract the rule prohibiting the wearing of Gandhi *topis* in the jail premises; see Roop Narain, 'Gandhi Topi ki Raksha', *Gandhi Marg*, September 2002, pp.62-64.
25. Gokul Bhai Bhatt sought to propagate the national flag by stitching and attaching the same on his Gandhi *topi*. Many people emulated him and used their shirts to display the national flag; see Sumnesh Joshi, *op.cit.*

Some of these incidents related to *khadi* have been reported from life-sketches of the leaders of the freedom struggle in Sumnesh Joshi, *op.cit.*

26. In the erstwhile Bikaner state allegiance to *khadi* was viewed with alarm. In some *dharmshalas* (inns) individuals wearing *khadi* cap and attire were not allowed to stay. Magharam Vaidya, President of Bikaner Praja Mandal, on his visit to Dudhwakhara village in 1946, had to suffer this kind of humiliation. He was told by the Brahmin manager of the *dharmshala* that he had strict instructions to restrict entry to people with *khadi* caps; see Man Singh Mehra, 'Dudhwakhara: Kisan Andolan Ke Jane Anjane Paksh', *Sujas*, June-July, 1998, p.24.Savitri Parmar, *op.cit.*, p.53.
27. Ranchchod Das Gattani, a veteran freedom fighter and prominent leader of the Marwar Lok Parishad, recollected how the sight of Gandhi *topis* and *charkhas* were enough to stimulate nationalist fervour. According to him, the twin symbols emerged as effective vehicles of Gandhian charisma and ideology. Interview with Ranchchod Das Gattani.
28. B.K. Sharma, 'Mewar Prajamandal ki Samajik aur Vaicharik Prishtbhumi' in Dev Kothari (ed.), *op.cit.*, p.97.
29. *Rajasthan Swadhinta Sangram ke Sakshi: Kuch Sansmaran* (Udaipur, Dungarpur, Banswara), Pratham Pushp, pp.69-70.
30. *Mewar was des*, i.e., nation and crossing Mewar implied going to *pardes* (alien lands or nation). Within the region of Rajputana too, sub-regional identities were closer to people's hearts. Similar sentiments were expressed in numerous other songs reflecting people's identification with their native states and its geographical dimensions, e.g., *Marudhar Mharo Des, Marudhar Matari Seva* and *Marudhar Mai* are some of the songs which convey people's love for their region – Marwar. For full version of the songs, see Jai Narain Vyas, *Marwari Rashtriya Geet.*
31. Due to repression of the rulers in some states people's conferences could not be formed within their territorial limits and had to be located outside the state, e.g., Sirohi Praja Mandal was formed in Bombay in 1933; Bikaner's Praja Mandal was established in Calcutta in 1936; and Jaisalmer Praja Mandal was formed in Jodhpur in 1945. See V.D. Mathur, *State's People's Conference*, pp.67-140.
32. Located in the heart of Rajasthan, Ajmer remained a centre of hectic nationalist activities during period of freedom struggle. It came under British control as a result of alliance with Daulat Rao Sindhia in 1818. Being a British territory, there were no restrictions on political activities, which were exercised in the princely states. Hence, it proved to be a favourite refuge for the freedom fighters in the native states of Rajputana. See S.S. Saxena, *op.cit.*, pp.100-129.
33. B.K.Sharma, 'Mewar Praja Mandal ki Samajik aur Vaicharik Prishtbhumi' in Dev Kothari (ed.), *op.cit.*, p.91. There are many songs of

this period, which criticize jagirdars and bureaucracy for their inhuman behaviour and corrupt practices. However, in these compositions, Maharana or the rulers of other states are eulogized and absolved of all wrong doings. For songs composed during the period of protest movements to inspire people, refer Narayan Singh Bhati & Hukam Singh Bhati, *Gora Hat Ja: Swatantrata Andolan ki Rajasthani Prerak Rachnaain.*

34. Similar trends were noticeable at the national level in the first phase of the national movement, i.e., the moderate phase of the Indian National Congress. The leaders professed loyalty to the King of England, while creating political awareness amongst the people. Noted historian B.R. Nanda has sought to explain this ambiguous phenomenon wherein early Congress leaders often reiterated their loyalty to the Crown. Firstly, according to him, such professions were useful as a political strategy for "with a hostile administration in India and an unsympathetic Tory regime in England, it would have been foolish for the Congress to alarm its enemies unduly and to invite repression which it was in no position to resist." Secondly, they had genuine faith in the sense of fairplay and justice of the British. Refer B.R. Nanda, *Gokhale: The Indian Moderates and the British Raj*, pp.481-485.
35. Lakshmikant Vyas, 'Khari Nadi ki Baad aur Praja Mandal', in Dev Kothari (ed.), *op.cit.* pp.157-166.
36. Interview with Rajendra Pal Singh Chaudhary, prominent leader of the struggle from Nathadwara. Refer Bhairulal Lohar & Bhagwatilal Sacheti, 'Suar Andolan aur Praja Mandal, in Dev Kothari, *op.cit.*, pp.167-173. In 1922, Marwar Lok Parishad had raised the problem of export of female cattle – cow, buffalo and sheep – to Bombay, Ahmedabad, Nasirabad and Ajmer. In 1924, after initial suppression, the movement succeeded when a ban was imposed on the export of female cattle. Praja Mandals and Lok Parishads raised the issues affecting the peasants in all the states of Rajputana.
37. V.D. Mathur, *op.cit.*, p.100; *Mewar Praja Mandal*, Bulletin No. 6, June 1947.
38. Most of them recount with deep emotion and nostalgia their encounters and meetings with national level leaders, particularly Gandhi, Nehru and Patel. Interviews with Balwant Singh Mehta, Ratan Devi Shastri, Ranchchod Das Gattani and Rajendra Pal Singh Chaudhary.
39. D.N. Nagda, 'Rashtriya Swatantrata Andolan Tatha Mewar: Antah Sambandh Tatha Netratva', paper presented in the seminar on 'Bhartiya Svadhinta Sangram evam Rajasthan ki Sahbhagita', Department of Political Science, University of Rajasthan, 22-23 March, 1986.
40. B.K. Sharma, 'Mewar Prajamandal ki Samajik aur Vaicharik Prishtbhumi', in Dev Kothari, *op.cit.*, p.93.

41. Ratan Lal Mishra, *Rajasthan ka Swatantrata Sangram: Durlabh Dastavej*, p.59.
42. For the role of newspapers and journals, refer L.P. Mathur, *Role of the Press in the Growth of Representative Institutions in Rajputana*; and Dwarka Lal Mathur, 'Swatantrata Andolan Mein Samachar Patron Ki Bhumika', in Dev Kothari, *op.cit.*, pp.212-217.
43. S.S. Saxena, *op.cit.*, pp. 289-291.

8

Abolition of Jagirdari in Rajasthan

The end of princely rule in Rajputana states and its subsequent merger with an independent and democratic India signified a dramatic transformation in the political environment of the region. However, at the time of the formation of Rajasthan, land, its most important economic resource, was still controlled by the ruling elite, mostly Rajputs of the previous regime. In the political culture of the Rajputana states, land not only formed a primary economic resource but was also a crucial element in the sustenance of a peculiar political and military system of the Rajputs based on clan system. There were large tracts in the state, which were controlled by assignees, grantees and sub-grantees of the erstwhile chiefs and rulers. The total extent of land was broadly divided into two categories: *khalsa* lands, which were directly under the control of the rulers; and non-*khalsa* or jagirdari lands, which lay under the authority of the jargirdars. While 66 percent of the land was *jagir* having 52 percent of the villages and 34 percent of the land was *khalsa* with 48 percent of the villages.[1] The republican revolution envisioned by the new leadership was possible only if this dominant section of the ruling class, its privileges and authority were challenged.

Quite pertinently, in Rajputana states, two factors – birth and the area of land owned – determined a man's place in the social hierarchy. These two factors were usually linked, as ownership of land was in most cases regulated by birth. "Land was sacred as its possession indicated the owner's place in his clan as well as his economic competence." According to J.N. Sarkar, "land was the only possession that can give him (Rajput gentleman and noble) a life of honour and comfort... there was no crime which a Rajput would not commit for the sake of land. Father killed son and son murdered father. Women of the noblest clan gave poison to their trusting kinsmen. Kings took the lives of royal ministers."[2] The ruling class in every Rajputana state derived its income, identity and status from land, as trade and commerce were considered repugnant to their martial traditions. In short, as Tod has observed, "the Rajput vaunts his aristocratic distinction derived from the land and opposes the title of '*Bhomia Raj*' or government of the soil, to the '*Bania Raj*' or commercial government"[3] which was seen as an 'epithet of contempt'.

I

The jagirdari system owes its origin to the ancient institution of assignment of land for revenue collection and maintaining part of armed forces. The kings often chose to pay their noblemen, chiefs of the army and other important government functionaries not in cash but by assigning tracts of land. The peculiarity of this system in the erstwhile states of Rajputana is attributed to the clan system. In the initial stages, land was assigned to the closest clan kinsmen, i.e., those who descended from a common lineage, which originally established dominance in the area. The ruling clan held the most productive and largest estates on military tenures that required them to supply horses and foot soldiers to the ruler in times of war. Brotherhood and equality, rather than submission and inferiority, defined the relationship between the ruler and his nobles since it was believed that it was the lineage and not the direct ancestors of the ruler who had conquered the state. In most of the states in Rajputana, the chiefs considered the state the patrimony of the entire clan, leading to claims of a quasi-independent status. As the nobles owed their position and property to lineage rather than the ruler' favour, they did not easily submit to his control. The peculiar and powerful position of the Rawats of Salumber raised difficult problems in Mewar. The rulers in almost all the states tried to stymie the authority of the clan as represented by the chief. One of the methods adopted by the medieval Rajput rulers to weaken the clan system was to assign land endowments to nobles who were "foreign in country and blood". The epithet '*Kala Patta*' or black grant was applied to all grants to foreign chiefs.[4] Of the 16 principal chiefs (*Solah Thikana*) of Mewar, as many as nine were "foreign in country and blood". The *Solah Thikana* families of Mewar were listed as follows: "Three Jhala, three Chauhan, and four Chundavats, two Saktavat, two Rathore, a Sarangdevot, and a Panwar."[5]

The introduction of non-clan members in the nobility however did not dilute the authority of home chieftains. In addition to immense economic power, they exercised enormous civil and judicial power over their estates, which covered over half the territory in most of the native states. The power was virtually shared by a territorial nobility and the ruler, also the clan chief. In their estates, they behaved like rulers, their establishment being a virtual replication of the ruler's court and regalia. According to Tod, "the court and household economy of a great chieftain is a miniature representation of the sovereign's: the same officers, from the *purdhan* or minister to the cupbearer (*panairie*) as well as the same domestic arrangement. He must have his *sheesh mahal* (mirror apartment), his *bari mahal* (garden on the terrace within the palace), his *mindir* (temple) like his prince. He entered the *durrisala* or carpet hall, the minstrel (*dholi*) preceding him rehearsing the praises of his family and he takes his seat on his throne while the assembled retainers, marshaled in lines on right and left, simultaneously exclaim, 'health to our chief'..." When a chief succeeded to his patrimony, his *aan* (pledge in the honour of the chief) was proclaimed within his *seema* or boundary.[6] The jagirdars commanded utmost loyalty from the subjects, which superseded their gratitude towards the Maharana. A popular saying, *Raj ka malik weh, pat ka malik yeh*,[7] i.e., he (Maharana, the ruler of Mewar state) is the sovereign of the state but this (jagirdar) is his chief testifies to the enormous influence of the chiefs. In fact, the peasants' allegiance to the Maharana was theoretical since he was a distant concept for them. Their immediate loyalty was towards the jagirdar – the representative of the Maharana.

During the pre-British period, the chaos and confusion in most of the Rajputana states has been often attributed to the growing assertion of independence by the jagirdars. The nobility faction became so dominant that Maharana of the Mewar state had to seek the help of Mahadji Scindia in 1791 to crush the Chundavats. The sovereign authority of the rulers was being challenged and restricted by powerful feudal lords. Tod believed that it was easier to make a goat and wolf drink water from the same pond but extremely difficult to persuade the Chundavats and Saktavats to labour in concert for the welfare of the prince and the country. Regarding Tod's effort to resume the illegally held lands, a jagirdar himself remarked that even the almighty cannot reform Mewar of this evil.[8]

In fact, it was not so much the menace of the Marathas but the sheer desperation and powerlessness of the rulers in bringing refractory nobles under control that drove the latter into accepting alliance with the British. Even during the period of British paramountcy, the power of the nobility remained, by and large, undiminished. The British viewed the jagirdars as a countervailing force. According to Rudolphs, the initial effect of British paramountcy in the 19th century not only sustained this diffusion of power (between the ruler and his nobility) but also undermined the effort of some rulers to centralize power at the expense of their nobility.[9]

Apart from the jagirs or land endowments granted to the nobility, the ruler provided several endowments to distinguished warriors and government functionaries. Liberal land grants were made for the support of a temple, mosque or an educational or charitable institution. These were known as *shatdarshan* (perpetual) grants. Yet another category of minor assignment was *inam* or *muafi*, which were granted to members of priestly class or other servants of the lower category for services rendered or for continuing services. The total number of tenures of jagir lands in Rajasthan was 45. The Venkatachar Committee (August 1949) had identified broadly eight categories of jagirdari tenures prevalent in Rajasthan: *Jagir, Juna Jagir, Bhom, Bakshish* and other charitable grants, *Bhomichara, Inam*, service grant and permanently quit-rented estates and lands.[10]

II

The oppression perpetrated by jagirdars on the peasants had remained a crucial element in the mobilization of popular support for the freedom struggle. The land tenure and land revenue system was characterized by preponderance of intermediaries, absence of well-defined rights of tenants as also the refusal of the jagirdars to introduce fixed money rents. In most of the jagir areas, the jagirdars realized the rent by taking share of the produce. Generally, one-half of the produce was the rule and a share less than that an exception. The Rajasthan Jagirdari Abolition Committee was right when it observed: "Wherever revenue is paid in kind the incidence is bound to be much higher as compared with khalsa rates."[11] It is a well-known fact that no where in khalsa areas would one expect such a high degree of rack renting and overexploitation. Besides, the peasants were also subjected to extra ceases, locally known as *lagats* or *lag-bags*. A perusal of lag-bags is an ample proof of the severe, at times, oppressive nature of the jagirdari exactions. There were about 75 *lagats* in Bijoliya and other areas of Mewar and more than a hundred in Marwar.[12]

The method of collecting rents and cesses was also very oppressive for the peasantry. Earlier, the *ijara* or *theka* system (the contract for collecting land revenue to the highest bidder) was fairly common. Influential moneylenders and small jagirdars who took over the *ijaras* or *thekas* adopted stringent methods for collection of land revenue. The system of *katha* was (brutal practice of stretching legs between wooden poles in an unbearable posture for long hours) used to torture peasants in jagir areas which testifies to the abject and utterly powerless condition of the peasantry in jagirdari areas.[13] The system of *begar* (forced labour) at very nominal payment was also in vogue in the feudalistic regime of the jagirdars. A large number of landless proletariat from the *Chamar* (leather workers considered ritually impure and hence untouchables) communities were hired by the jagirdars to work on compulsory basis on their fields. In addition to economic miseries and physical hardships, the cultivators occupied the lowest rung in the social hierarchy and were hence subjected to numerous indignities. The jagirdars looked down upon the cultivators except those of their own clan or belonging to the priesthood.[14]

III

With the extinction of princely regime, the most pressing concern of the government was dismantling of the political and economic institutions of feudalism. Jagirdari system prevailed over 62 percent of the total area of the new state. It was indeed a formidable challenge, in view of the historical backdrop of the state. Even Tod had felt that, as compared to the other classes, it was difficult to deal with the feudal lords. He had observed that he could conclude an agreement with them only after harassing, painful and protracted discussions according to which they agreed to surrender all khalsa fiefs illegally seized during times of trouble and commotion.[15] The British authorities found that the word 'restitution' was an anathema to the jagirdars. Yet, in the post-independent era, the jagirdari areas were resumed without a single shot being fired. This stupendous achievement can be attributed to a variety of factors.

Widespread agrarian discontentment in numerous states of Rajputana had led to peasant agitation in these areas. The Bijoliya peasant agitation, which commenced in 1897 and continued till 1942, had gained national prominence when it received considerable attention at the annual session of Indian National Congress at Ahemdabad in 1921. There were similar movements in Marwar, Sikar, Alwar, Bharatpur and Begun. The Nimuchana tragedy in Alwar, police firing at Kudar in Sikar and Dabra massacre in Marwar have been some of the prominent incidents which underscored the acute misery of the peasants and repression of jagirdars. These incidents invited the concern of the national level leaders and were widely reported in national newspapers. The prominent leaders, who mobilized and led peasants, were: Vijay Singh Pathik, Manikya Lal Verma, Sadhu Sita Ram, Prem Chand Bhil, Ram Narain Bhil (Mewar), Hari Bhau Upadhyaya, Jai Narain Vyas, Ranchhod Das Gattani, Mathura Das Mathur, Baldev Ram Mirdha (Jodhpur), Ram Narain Choudhary, Master Chandrabhan, Choudhary Hari Singh (Sikar) and Kumbha Ram Arya (Bikaner). The aforesaid leaders played a significant role in the various peasant uprisings in the state. Pertinently, many leaders associated with peasant movement in pre-independence period had become a part of the government after the formation of a democratic representative government in integrated Rajasthan. Their commitment to the peasantry led them to advocate changes in the agrarian structure. Efforts of the peasant leadership provided the necessary situation in which land reforms acquired priority in the post-independence period. Mohan Lal Sukhadia, as Revenue Minister, promptly responded to this agenda. Notwithstanding the commitment of national level leaders, especially Nehru and Pant, to the issues of land reform, the contribution and initiative of local and regional leadership was of seminal significance.

The Indian National Congress, since the inception of the freedom struggle, was ideologically committed to a change in the structure of landownership. The Congress ministries formed under the Act of 1935 in U.P., Madras, Bihar, Bombay, Central Provinces and Orissa had tried to give economic relief to the peasants through reforms in the system of land tenure and reduction of burden of rent, land revenue and debt. However, any fundamental change in agrarian relations, i.e., elimination of jagirdari system, was possible only after independence.[16] With the achievement of independence and transition to an egalitarian democratic framework, it was increasingly felt that the jagirdars had become an anachronism in a political culture which cherished values like liberty and equality as opposed to the feudalistic values of submission and hierarchy. The imperatives of new political culture also compelled the Congress to hasten the process of agrarian reform. Democracy with adult franchise had reduced the political clout of the erstwhile jagirdars and increased the urgency of meeting the long-standing demands of the peasantry, which was mobilized and conscientized to a large extent by the Congress leaders themselves. It has also been argued that Congress faced a rival source of political power and leadership in the erstwhile jagirdars. Rudolphs have observed that liquidation of a "feudal class in command not only of the incomes of the estates but also considerable staff through which they administered revenue, police and judicial functions" had become a necessity for the political fortunes of the Congress.[17] The reforms were further necessitated by the financial requirements of the new administrative set-up. It was contended that the jagirdars controlled 62 percent of the land, the state's most productive resource and their revenue income deprived the state of an important source of financial support. The aforesaid historical, political and administrative factors hastened the process of land reforms and their implementation in a state that had been often denigrated as a stronghold of feudal institutions.

In the post-independence era, the Congress government at centre and in the state of Rajasthan reaffirmed their resolve to complete the process of jagirdari abolition as quickly as possible.[18] The government's commitment to the peasantry was reiterated at timely intervals in numerous documents; in the AICC resolution in July 1954; in the conference of Chief Ministers and Presidents of Provincial Congress Committees; in the First Plan document; and in the Congress election manifestos.[19] The Congress also took necessary legislative and administrative steps such as getting the constitutional amendments of 1951 and 1955 passed by the parliament.[20] These enactments were aimed at strengthening the hands of the state legislature for implementing jagirdari abolition by keeping land reforms outside the jurisdiction of civil courts. It was laid down that the resumption of jagirs or insufficiency of compensation did not imply violation of the fundamental rights and, hence, not permissible in the courts. This was indeed a commendable measure as it plugged one of the most important loopholes that could have delayed the implementation of land reforms.

Quite evidently, these measures demonstrate the sincerity of the political will to push land reforms, which were brought about in a phased manner resulting in the most rapid and peaceful economic revolution of modern Indian history.

IV

The process of land reforms, especially pertaining to agrarian relations and landownership, can be divided into four phases. At the outset, certain protective interim laws were sanctioned pending enactment of permanent laws. In anticipation of the legislation giving statutory rights to the tenants, the jagirdars and zamindars had started ejecting tenants in an arbitrary manner. With a view to protecting the tenants from such wholesale ejection, the Rajasthan government enacted the Rajasthan Protection of Tenants Ordinance in June 1949.[21] It proved an effective check on further ejectment and provided a quick and simplified process of reinstatement of ejected tenants. While some disagree over the actual benefits of this Act, it is contended that tenants all over Rajasthan took the fullest advantage of the provision. It remained in force till 15th October, 1955 when its provisions were incorporated in the

Rajasthan Tenancy Act, 1955. Yet another interim measure was the Rajasthan Removal of Trees Regulation Ordinance, 1949 which was enacted to prevent reckless felling of trees by interested persons in view of the impending land reforms legislation. The other immediate Acts that were passed included Rajasthan Produce Rents Regulation Act, Rajasthan Agricultural Rents Control Act, and Rajasthan Summary Settlement Act.

In order to achieve a judicious and long-term solution of agrarian relationship, the central government appointed Venkatachar Committee in 1949 to inquire into the jagirdari system and to suggest remedial measures. Quite significantly, taking initiative in the matter, the Rajasthan and Madhya Bharat government had insisted upon the formation of such a committee. The Committee submitted its report in December 1949. The major recommendation of the Committee was the abolition of jagirdari system. Abolition was justified on the basis that jagirdari system had outlived its utility. Moreover, on legal grounds too, proprietary rights did not back jagirdari control of landed estates. In view of these findings, the jagirdars could have been deprived of their landholdings without being offered any compensation. However, the Committee adopted a moderate policy and suggested abolition of jagirdari system but recommended that jagirdars should be given financial assistance based on considerations of social justice.[22] Moreover, the national leaders too were in favour of adopting a lenient attitude towards the erstwhile jagirdars. Patel was for abolition of jagirdari system but he wanted to do so through payment of compensation and not through wholesale or effective expropriation, especially as he believed that jagirdars' cooperation in the freedom struggle was useful.[23] It was felt that monetary compensation was a small price to pay. In keeping with this mindset, the Committee did not recommend the wholesale abolition of all jagirs. Dool Singh has rightly observed that in formulating its recommendations, the Committee "aimed at the immediate rather than the ultimate; the practical rather than the ideal and the expedient rather than the doctrinaire;

because at every stage of its conclusion, spirit of compromise was more marked than logic."[24]

The first important step towards agrarian reform was the Rajasthan Land Reforms and Resumption of Jagirs Act, 1952. The Act rated as one of the most outstanding laws passed by the state legislature came into effect from 18th February, 1952. The actual process of resumption, however, started after two years because of the stay orders obtained by certain jagirdars from Rajasthan High Court. It was only after the land reform measures were made impermissible in law courts that the Act could be implemented. The main thrust of the legislation was to acquire jagir land leaving the jagirdars only with *khudkasht* (self-cultivated lands). The Act, apart from abolition of jagirs, vested all rights, titles and interests of the jagirdars in the state government. Henceforth, the state government was responsible for land revenue assessment of all jagir lands.

Significantly, the Act contained certain provisions, which were favourable to the jagirdars. The most important being the right to retain some jagir land as *khudkasht*, i.e., any land cultivated personally by jagirdar. In the Act, *khudkasht* was defined as:

(a) land cultivated by one's own labour;
(b) by the labour of any member of one's family; and
(c) by servants on wages payable in cash or personal supervision of any member of one's family.

Those jagirdars who did not possess adequate land for *khudkasht* could not later than 31st August, 1958 or within three months of the date of resumption apply for the same. The maximum area of land allotted as *khudkasht* under these provisions was as follows:

(a) where the area of jagir lands does not exceed 60 acres, one-half of the area;
(b) where the area of jagir lands exceeds 60 acres but does not exceed 200 acres, 25 percent of the area in excess of 60 acres, in addition to area permissible under clause (a);

(c) where the area of jagir lands exceeds 200 acres but does not exceed 500 acres, 15 percent of the area in excess of 200 acres plus the area permissible under clauses (a) & (b);

(d) where the area of jagir varies between 500 and 1,000 acres, 10 percent of the area in excess of 500 acres plus the area permissible under clauses (a), (b), (c);

(e) when the jagir area exceeds 1,000 acres, 5 percent of the area in excess of 1,000 acres plus the area permissible under all the four preceding clauses subject to an overall limit of 500 acres.

The maximum area that could be retained by the jagirdars as *khudkasht* was, thus, restricted to 500 acres of unirrigated land. However, those jagirdars who were already in possession of *khudkasht* land in excess of the maximum, before the commencement of the Act, were allowed to retain it.

Jagirdars were entitled to compensation for the resumption of their jagir lands. Compensation payable to a jagirdar was seven times his net income in the basic year. Henceforth, he would cease to pay any tribute or land revenue to the government. Moreover, he would not be debarred from recovering his past arrears of rent and other dues in respect of his jagir rights. Private lands, buildings, wells, tanks, house sites, enclosures, stores, etc., shall continue to belong to the jagirdars. Various rights of the jagirdars in respect of his jagir lands, forests, trees, minerals, bazaars stood resumed to the government. All rents and cesses accruing on the land after the date of resumption were payable to the government. It would not recognize any right or interest created by a jagir in favour of the third parties nor shall it be liable for the payment of any debt incurred by the jagirdars. All buildings used for schools, offices, hospitals and other public purposes shall be deemed to have been transferred to the government. The Jagir Commissioner could cancel all leases and contracts made in anticipation of the resumption and not in the normal course of management on or after 1st January, 1949. In addition to compensation, there were provisions for loans for development purposes, marriage and education of children, pension for retired employees of jagirs, absorption of jagir employees into state services, ex-gratia payment for improvements of wells, tanks, etc., and for loss incurred due to substantial fall in their income. Jagirdars, who were not sufficiently educated, were given assistance by jagir department staff in preparing claims.

To facilitate the whole process, office of Jagir Commissioner was created and a full-fledged Department of Jagir Resumption was set up. In June 1954, the resumption commenced when the two biggest jagirs of Sikar and Khetari were resumed. The other jagirs were taken in a phased manner. By 1st March, 1960, all non-religious jagirs, whether settled or non-settled, were resumed. Resumption of religious jagirs of over Rs. 5,000 took place from November 1959, while jagirs with income over Rs. 1,000 were taken over with effect from 1st August, 1960. By 1st July, 1963, all types of jagirs were resumed. In all, 2,98,896 jagirs were resumed and an amount of Rs. 46 crores was paid by way of compensation in cash or in the form of bonds.

The data of the state and information collected from the jagirs shows that most of the jagirdars had at least some land as *khudkasht* and were not left in the lurch. However, as there was little unoccupied land and the government seriously followed the policy of not dispossessing tenants with heritable occupancy rights, the *khudkasht* land to erstwhile jagirdars was allotted in the area commanded by the irrigation projects. On an average, Rs. 4 lakhs were advanced as loans to former jagirdars for cottage and small-scale industries whereas annual advances for development purposes averaged Rs.10.7 lakhs. The most progressive feature of the Act was the relief it brought to the tenants. After the resumption, the tenants of jagir lands became *khatedar* tenants holding lands directly from the government with transferable and heritable rights.

Even a cursory appraisal of the Act reveals the balanced approach of the government – while abolishing feudal regime it was decidedly liberal on the jagirdars. They were not only able to retain a portion of the land but also received compensation, rehabilitation grants and other privileges, facilities and assets.

Another important legislation aimed at restructuring agrarian relations was the Rajasthan Zamindari and Biswedari Abolition Act, 1959 that came into force from November 1959. It provided for the abolition of zamindari and biswedari estates. It had provisions for payment of compensation, allotment of *khudkasht* and rights of tenants, almost on the lines of the Jagir Abolition Act. The zamindari and biswedari systems existed in some 4,870 villages spread over eight districts of Rajasthan. Out of these as many as 3543 villages representing more than 70 percent of the total area were in the two districts of Alwar and Bharatpur and 1,146 villages are in Ganganagar district. Most of the area of these estates (about 80%) was in possession of estateholders themselves at the time of abolition. This was in striking contrast to the situation in jagir areas where most of the land was in the possession of the tenants. Under this Act, a total of 3,18,860 zamindari and biswedari estates were abolished through notifications in different states. This Act also brought the same relief to the tenants in these areas as in jagirdari areas on resumption of jagirs.

In Rajasthan, jagirdari and zamindari/biswedari abolition laws did not affect the villages and lands included in the inventories of private properties of the rulers of erstwhile states. In order to acquire these estates, Rajasthan Land Reforms and Acquisition of Land Owner Estates Act was passed, which received the assent of the President of India on April 6, 1964.[25] The process of acquisition was, however, delayed for 12 years as eight ex-rulers filed writ petitions in the Rajasthan High Court leading to a long legal debate. The Single Bench of the Rajasthan High Court declared ultra vires chapters 4-5 of the Act and the schedule. After certain amendments to the Act in 1975 by the state government, the order of the Single Bench was set aside by the Division Bench of the Rajasthan High Court and the process of acquisition of the estates of ex-rulers could start only thereafter.

As is evident from the above discussion, in Rajasthan, the process of jagirdari abolition was initiated and completed in stages. Significant enactments were made in 1952, 1959, 1964 and ultimately concluded in 1975. Although there were certain loopholes in the Acts, nevertheless these measures had far-reaching consequences in altering land relations and marked the beginning of a modern era. Most significantly, they ensured ownership rights for the tenants – a measure that was a big leap towards democratization of agrarian relations.

The second major plank of the envisaged land reform was concerned with tenancy legislation. Tenancy reform had three objectives: first, to guarantee security of tenure to tenants who had cultivated a piece of land continuously for a fixed number of years; second, reduction of rent paid by the tenant to a fair level; and third, to endow the tenants with ownership of land he cultivated, subject to certain restrictions. The senior Congress leadership was committed to protect the rights of the tenants. In fact, a provision in the 1952 ordinance, which enabled the jagirdars without *khudkasht* to acquire the same by evicting tenants, was dropped. In this context, Pant observed that the "cultivators are looking forward to further improvement in their conditions. If, on the contrary they are now faced with ejection, it will clearly be a retrograde step diametrically opposed to the spirit of land reforms."[26]

At the time of formation of Rajasthan, tenancy laws were conservative, ill-defined, diverse and oppressive. The need for uniform tenancy law for the state was keenly felt in view of the varied conditions existing in the former states. The most important enactment in this direction was the Rajasthan Tenancy Act, 1955, which was brought into force from 15th October, 1955.[27] This Act consolidates and amends the previously operative laws relating to tenancies of agricultural lands. It also provided for certain measures of land reform. The State Land Commission, 1959 has observed that it can safely be claimed as one of the most progressive tenancy legislations in India.

The most important feature of the Act was the conferment of higher right to tenants. The Act put an end to multiplicity of tenancies and instead, provided for two categories of tenants – *khatedar* and *ghair-khatedar*. Every person, who at the commencement of the Act, was a tenant of land otherwise than as a sub-tenant or a tenant of *khudkasht* became a *khatedar* tenant under section 15 of the Act. A *khatedar* tenant enjoyed rights of transfer, inheritance, gift and mortgage in respect of his holding and was a full owner of his land. A tenant who is not a *khatedar* is known as *ghair-khatedar*.

Another important feature of the Act was the simplified procedure by which tenants of *khudkasht* and sub-tenants, who were recorded as such in the annual registers, could also acquire *khatedari* rights. Originally, the provision was to apply for acquisition of such *khatedari* rights but later by an amendment they were automatically elevated to the class of *khatedars*. This was indeed a very favourable legislation for tenants, which facilitated their transition from sub-tenant of *khudkasht* to a *khatedari* status. Section 19 of the Act also provided for *khatedari* rights to those tenants of *khudkasht* and sub-tenants who were not recorded as such in the annual register. They had to apply for these rights.

In addition to the classes of tenants, the Act deals with numerous issues related to landholdings of the tenants, i.e., devolution, transfer and exchange of tenancies, gift and mortgage of holding, surrender, abandonment and extinction of tenancies, fixation of rent, restriction on removal of trees. The Act also specifies the primary rights of the tenants. The new legislation entitled them to a written lease of the holding, free dwelling site in the village, extraction of stone or other material for dwelling house, making improvement in the holdings, plantation and removal of trees on the holdings. The Act abolished forced labour and all payments in the form of *lag-bag* and other cesses. The fixed rent in cash to be charged from sub-tenant was not to be more than twice the cash rent payable by tenant in chief, the rent in kind was fixed at one-sixth of the gross produce. The Act provided effective check against arbitrary ejection. The tenant could be ejected in exceptional situations, e.g., non-payment of arrears of rent, illegal transfer or sub-letting and for detrimental act or breach of condition. Tenant who was ejected wrongfully was entitled to certain relief measures such as reinstatement and compensation, and he can move court for reinstatement by a simplified summary process as well. To check arbitrary eviction under the guise of voluntary surrender, it was laid down that such surrenders would be recognized only if they are accompanied by a written agreement duly attested by Tehsildar or by Chairman of the Municipal Board.

The provisions of the Act thus tried to bring relief to tenants by giving them fixity of tenure, ownership of land and above all freedom from oppressive jagirdari regime. As a result of this Act, a total number of 1,37,831 tenants got *khatedari* rights over an area of 7,91,209 acres of the state. Conferment of ownership of landholding to the tenants suffering from deprivation and powerlessness since centuries was a landmark in the socio-economic and political annals of the state of Rajasthan. It was an effective and emphatic step in the transition from feudalism to democracy. By redefining class relations, a sincere effort was made to evolve equitous social order. At the personal level, it was a great psychological triumph for the peasants who now cherished a unique sense of pride and empowerment derived from ownership of land.

V

Although the process of abolition of jagirdari was by and large fairly smooth and peaceful, the erstwhile jagirdars had offered resistance and after protracted negotiations were able, in a large measure, to protect their interests. To reduce the adverse impact of the reform measures on their status and resources, the Rajput jagirdars united under the banner of Kshatriya Mahasabha (the caste association of the Rajputs founded in 1888).[28] The Rajputs, in view of their past relationship of mutual dependence and obligation, sought to project themselves as a cohesive social group of an erstwhile consolidated feudal order. The Sabha represented the jagirdars' interests before the Venkatachar Committee and also tried to organize and mobilize Rajputs in to a political force in the new democratic set up by coordinating their participation in the first elections in 1952. It was this body which provided teams for negotiating the final terms of land reform legislation.

In the initial stages, Rajput jagirdars irrespective of their class interest had presented a united front. However, the nitty-gritty of the negotiations brought into open the latent class differentiation that separated the big jagirdars from the Bhomias (jagirdars with small landholdings). Despite their projected unity in the first phase, the Venkatachar Committee and the Home Ministry took the view that there were economic disparities in the circumstances of the large and small jagirdars. It was keenly felt that any initiative for land reform should recognize this divergence between the two groups. Thus, to protect interests of the small jagirdars, the 1952 ordinance provided that jagirs whose income fell below Rs.5,000 per annum would not be resumed. However, for the small jagirdars, the situation took an unexpected and startling turn when the leadership at the national and state levels radically changed its policy towards the issue of land reform. By 1953, the government was veering towards the view that to democratize agrarian relations, it was necessary to do away with jagirdari altogether. It was found that the earlier decision to keep jagirs with an income of less than Rs.5,000 outside the purview of the resumptive clauses would leave 50 percent of jagir lands unaffected. This was naturally viewed as a retrograde step as it would leave the procedure of abolition of jagirdari incomplete.

The last round of negotiations resulted in a split of the Rajput order. The big jagirdars were not only able to retain *khudkasht,* but also got liberal compensation and substantial privileges. On the other hand, the small jagirdars were deprived of *khudkasht* as well as income associated with their traditional status as lords of the soil. Their response was to form a new association under the name Bhooswami Sangh as they felt cheated, not so much by the Congress government, as by their own erstwhile superiors who had hitherto dominated the affairs of the Kshatriya Mahasabha. They mobilized and agitated throughout 1954 by holding meetings in which the demands of small jagirdars as distinct from the prominent jagirdars, were clearly spelt out, i.e., *khudkasht*, liberal rehabilitation grants as well compensation for wells, forts and other permanent structures. More significantly, the outbursts of the Bhooswami Sangh leaders laid open the fissures between the two groups of jagirdars when they publicly condemned the betrayal by big jagirdars.[29] It was indeed a surprising and unanticipated fallout of the process of land reforms. It subverted the historical legacy of the class solidarity, the ethic of submission and mutual dependence that had been the hallmark of medieval Rajput polity. The agitation culminated into a massive *satyagraha* in Jaipur in June 1955, followed by another one in April 1956. Bhooswami Sangh organized massive rallies against the proposed land reform measures in which the participants brandished swords.[30] The second Pant Award conceded additional rehabilitation grants that graduated according to the size of the jagir, with the smallest entitled to the highest ratios. The Act provided rehabilitation grants of five and eleven times the net income for jagirdars with gross income of Rs.5,000 and below. The scale is based on the principle that the jagirdars with less jagir incomes should be given more liberal assistance in their rehabilitation after the resumption of their jagirs. In other cases, the rehabilitation grants range between twice and four times the net income. To satisfy the demands of the smaller jagirdars or Bhooswamis, yet another award given by Prime Minister Nehru in 1958 provided for additional rehabilitation grant in the shape of additional multiples of the net income to jagirdars whose gross annual income did not exceed Rs.5,000. The scales were as follows: [31]

(1)	Where gross income of jagirdars, calculated in accordance with the provisions of the second schedule, does not exceed Rs.250	Four times the net income of the jagirdar as determined in accordance with the provisions of the second schedule.
(2)	Where such gross income exceeds Rs.250 but does not exceed Rs.2,000	Three times the net income.
(3)	Where gross income exceeds Rs.2,000 but does not exceed Rs.5,000	Twice such net income.

Although the whole process of land reforms in the post-independence era weakened the solidarity of the Rajput Thakurs, but eventually, the practical and liberal approach of the state government satisfied the former jagirdars – both big and small.

VI

The series of legislations enacted by the government was devised to abolish the oppressive political and economic structure of the feudal era. However, over a period of time, certain limitations have been identified not only in some of the clauses of the Land Reform Act but also the legal lapses and inordinate delay that marked its implementation. The critics believed that these shortcomings diluted the potential of the reforms to bring about radical changes in the agrarian structure of the region. The compassion showed to the jagirdars in the terms pertaining to retention of *khudkasht* and payment of compensation coupled with bureaucratic delays adversely impacted this progressive transaction.

First and foremost, the clauses dealing with retention of *khudkasht* land have been the most vulnerable features of the Act. The critics have focussed upon the injustice that was committed in allowing the jagirdars to retain large extent of *khudkasht* land. It is contended that not only was the area of land permitted as *khudkasht* very extensive but what constituted *khudkasht* or personal cultivation was very loosely and liberally defined. This made it possible for not only those who tilled the soil but also those who supervised it or did so through a relative or provided capital and credit to the actual cultivator could claim that tract of land as *khudkasht*. According to Bipan Chandra, this was despite the fact that Congress Agrarian Committee (Kumarappa Committee) in its report of 1949 had clearly stated that only those who pool in a minimum amount of physical labour and participation in actual agricultural operations could be said to be performing personal cultivation.[32] It never intended the tenant's holding to be reduced to below economic level. The outcome of such a liberal attitude towards *khudkasht* was that even jagirdars who were absentee landowners could retain large tracts of land.

Another pitfall in the whole scheme was the decision to give away an amount of Rs. 48 crores as compensation which has been seen as a blunder and contrary to the democratic spirit of the reforms. It has been contended that in the early years, the Congress did not have comfortable majority and it had to rely on feudal support for the formation of the government. The Congress government hoped to strengthen its position in the legislature by encouraging some of the jagirdars to cross over to their party. Moreover, Rajput support was, perhaps, helpful to some Chief Ministers who wished to counter-balance the increasing Jat influence in the party.[33] These political constraints led the government to peddle soft towards the erstwhile jagirdars and offer them enormous privileges.

Thirdly, the criticism focuses on the inordinate delay in the implementation of the numerous measures for agrarian restructuring. It has been argued that while the provisions of the Acts were well intended, the fault with post-independence reforms has been the lack of will to implement them. Jagirdars tried to obstruct the implementation by repeatedly challenging the constitutionality of the laws, involving the government of Rajasthan in dilatory tactics to gain time and in the meanwhile ejecting the tenants from choicest irrigated lands in the name of *khudkhast*. The Kshatriya Mahasabha fought for the interests of the jagirdars and the bhomias. During the negotiations, they pressurized to get more *khudkhast* land, liberal compensation, and rehabilitation of the staff of the states and jagirs. As a result, they were successful in extracting a profitable package from the state government. Moreover, the big agriculturists, who constituted the largest interest group in the legislature, used their political weight and resources to influence legislators of other parties and to maintain status quo. Most of the members of the legislative assembly later conceded that the vested interests of the big landlords and other influential persons were the biggest hurdle in the proper implementation of land reforms.[34] While it has been rightly observed that the only effective remedy to rectify these loopholes was immediate implementation of land reforms without the slightest delay, it is a widely accepted fact that lack of documents that could identify and ascertain the ownership of land proved to be yet another baffling problem for the bureaucratic machinery that was responsible for implementing the numerous Acts.

Similar fate awaited the implementation of Rajasthan Land Reforms and Acquisition of Land Owners Estate Acquisition Act, 1963, which aimed at acquiring the large tracts of land under the control of the erstwhile rulers. Before the Act was implemented eight rulers filed writ petitions in the High Court. In this context, Justice M. L. Shrimal has rightly observed that the state government kept sleeping over the Act for 16 years, thus hampering the process of agrarian reform. Even after the amendment to the Act in 1975, the authorities have not seriously endeavoured to get the cases resolved. In view of such an undue delay in the implementation of the Act of 1963, these landowners transferred the major part of their landholdings to individuals and *benami* transactions were done on a large scale.[35] Subsequently, there was insufficient land left to be distributed among landless persons, thus nullifying the basic objective of the proposed reform measure.

The rulers and the jagirdars not only obstructed land reform by using the legislative and judicial wings of the administrative system but also used the executive authority to retard the process of agrarian restructuring. It has been observed that the corrupt and inept administrative machinery, responsible for implementing land reforms, often collaborated with jagirdars and big farmers. At times, the lower level revenue staff had served as the rent collecting agents of the former jagirdars. Similarly, the erstwhile political elite also enjoyed clout in the bureaucratic circles. There are instances when some retired senior officials, especially those belonging to the Indian Civil Service and the law department, took up assignments as advisors to ex-rulers. The collusion of officials with the feudal elite definitely contributed to the inadequacy of implementation of the progressive laws.[36]

Further, the tenancy rights were flouted either overtly or covertly. Under the guise of voluntary abdication, tenants, especially the less secure ones, were evicted from their lands. The Rajasthan Tenancy Act had prohibited transfer of land by gift, sale or mortgage by people of scheduled castes and tribes. It was laid down that for 12 years such a transfer by these castes would be considered illegal. However, at times, the land allotted to these groups was grabbed by upper caste landowners either by forcible punishment or by way of mortgage. In fact, such illegal evictions had become such a common practice that the Fourth Plan had to incorporate a recommendation that all such transfers and the fictitious voluntary surrenders should only be in favour of the government that could then allot the land to eligible persons.[37]

A study sponsored by Research Programmes Committee of the Planning Commission under Dr. Dool Singh in 1964 looked into the socio-economic effects of the land reforms, their implementation as also their evasion. The findings of the study reveal the inefficacy of the tenancy rights as far as some of the primary rights of the peasants are concerned.[38] These rights have proved to be more illusory than real. It was found that many tenants did not apply for acquisition of *khatedari* rights. Quite surprisingly, the tenants did not have the knowledge of the right of acquisition of legal ownership of land while others were prevented from exercising the right due to the undue influence of the landholders. Thus, the procedure of application, inquiry and disposal could not confer *khatedari* rights upon the cultivators as intended by the legislature. According to a rough estimate, about 90 percent of the sub-tenants did not get written leases. Inquiry revealed that the main reason was the reluctance on the part of the landholder to issue leases for fear of losing their land. Moreover, even the tenants refrained from insisting on the same for they were afraid of offending the landholder lest he should refuse to let out land in future. The tenants could not avail yet another of their primary rights, i.e., obtain a site for his residential house in village *abadi*. A sample study shows that only 12 percent tenants could secure such allotments. The inefficiency of this provision has been attributed to the non-cooperative and obstructive attitude of the village Patwaris. Whereas in some villages sufficient land for allotment as house sites did not exist.

Yet another study has shown a very shocking pattern of landownership in the state. It has found that 2.91 percent of the rural families are still landless and another 9.84 percent rural families possess as low as 0.5 acre of land. It is clear that 12.5 percent of the rural families are thus practically landless and 19.21 percent possess land ranging between 0.5 acre and 2.5 acres. In sum, about 46.83 percent families in Rajasthan, on an average, possess 5 acres or less land whereas 47 percent of the families own less than 9 percent of the total land. Figures relating to the ownership of land by a privileged few reveal a grim picture. The top 3.33 percent of the families enjoy the ownership of 24.34 percent of the total land having more than 50 acres of land each. Another 15.23 percent own more than 20 acres of land; each thus possessing 56 percent of the total land of the state. These statistics show that 25 percent of the rural families possess only 2 percent of the land whereas top 25 percent own 35 times of the land possessed by the equal percentage of the cultivators at the lowest level.[39] Quite evidently, these studies prove that the erstwhile jagirdars have been able to avoid the full impact of the effort at democratization of landownership.

The surveys have also brought into focus the implementation of certain other clauses of the tenancy laws. It was revealed that the earlier practice of payment of premium on land leased in by the tenant, which had been declared illegal under the tenancy laws, continued to prevail. Numerous cases, especially in the jagir areas, have been reported wherein landholders take premium for subletting their holdings. Cases of forced labour were rare and to be found only among tenants with uneconomic holdings and landless agricultural workers. In most cases, the implementation and the spirit of the Act were negated by the lower level revenue officials, particularly the Tehsildars, Patwaris etc.[40] Either, they are themselves ignorant about the law or they intend to harass the tenants with some ulterior motives. The cumulative effect of the sluggish implementation has led to the consolidation and creation of a strong class of capitalist farmers out of old feudal landlords and well to do peasants.

Despite the fact that the land reform measures in post-independence India suffered from numerous weaknesses, both at the levels of drafting as well as implementation, there is certainly no doubt that the process signifies a bold and determined effort to overthrow the entrenched institutions that had hitherto controlled political, social and economic life in the erstwhile states of Rajputana. It is undeniable that the leadership at the top echelons was steadfast in its commitment to democratize agrarian relations. Whenever any shortcoming or hindrance in the implementation of laws became obvious, the government was prompt enough to remove the lacunae to render them progressive and tenant friendly. The numerous additions and amendments to the earlier laws, at times complete overhauling, testify to the continued persistence of the political will as far as land reforms were concerned. In this context, in addition to the progressive approach of the national leadership who were extremely keen to alter the feudalistic pattern of landownership, one needs to highlight the commitment, sincerity and initiative of the regional leadership as well. Leaders like Manikya Lal Verma, Baldev Ram Mirdha, Mohan Lal Sukhadia, Nathu Ram Mirdha and others had in fact built pressure on the central leadership to initiate and hasten the process of jagirdari abolition in the state.[41] Mohan Lal Sukhadia as the first Revenue Minister and later his successor Damodar Lal Vyas played a seminal role in expediting and implementing the land reform measures. Ram Prasad Ladhdha was another prominent leader whose contribution to the rehabilitation process was crucial. It was their determination in the face of threats of violence and bloodshed by the jagirdars that ultimately led to this rapid and peaceful transaction.

It is undeniable that abolition of jagirs and conferment of *khatedari* rights heralded comprehensive changes in the village community life. In the pre-independence era, the feudalism as represented by the jagirdar did not merely endow him with immense economic power or control over land but he influenced the total ethos of the rural life in his domain. For the powerless tenant the jagirdar was a larger than life figure exercising ultimate control over their lives - both at the individual and the social levels. Declaration of *aan* or oath of allegiance created social bonds between the peasants and the chiefs. These oaths did not carry the weight of law yet they were held to be sacred and inviolable. The new land laws liberated the peasant from this pervasive presence of the jagirdar. Mohan Lal Sukhadia, who as the first Revenue

Minister of Rajasthan had played a key role in pushing the agenda of land reforms, while touring some of the villages in the state had expressed deep satisfaction at the perceptible change in the social relationships and community life as a result of land reforms. He observed that the earlier rural hierarchy comprising the two groups of landlords and virtual serfs has been replaced by a relationship based on mutual respect. According to him, only those who have been familiar with the rural life 15 to 20 years back can appreciate and comprehend this positive shift in agrarian social structure.

Sukhadia was also pleasantly surprised by the economic prosperity that was noticeable after the implementation of the land reforms in the region. He felt that conferment of ownership rights on the tenants had induced capitalist development of agriculture leading to improvement in agricultural production and techniques. According to him, in the earlier exploitative system, the tillers of the soil had neither the incentive nor the capital to undertake improvement in agricultural yield or fertility of land. However, in the post-land reforms era, there was emergence of progressive cultivators making investments and improvement in productivity. The farmers initiated several improvements like using better techniques of farming, increase in irrigation facilities and investing in tractors and other machines. Thus, in the economic realm, the agrarian reforms proved productive and beneficial and fulfilled one of the major objectives of land reforms, i.e., to create a class of well-to-do cultivators.[42]

It is true that the Land Reform Acts provided a profitable deal to the jagirdars who were able to retain extensive tracts of land and also numerous other benefits. However, as Bipan Chandra has pointed out that one needs to distinguish between feudal lords and feudalism. Compensation and provision of *khudkasht* had ensured the existence of jagirdars as individuals who continued to be rich and powerful but they eventually disappeared as a social category with a hegemonic aura.[43] There was a fundamental change in their class orientation, as they could neither perpetuate feudalism or feudalistic relations. Consequently, there was beginning of change in the community life as well as inter-caste and inter-class relationships in the villages.

A brief perusal of the numerous measures of land reforms underscores certain aspects of the transaction in the region of Rajputana states. Undeniably, the central and the state leaderships earnestly took up the task of transforming the agrarian relations. The process was initiated in the immediate aftermath of independence. They lost no time or allowed the jagirdars to sabotage the endeavour. This was reflected in the immediate or the interim measures that were enacted pending the passing of permanent laws. These preliminary enactments were accompanied by a series of bold initiatives and pioneering measures that sought to revolutionize the pattern of landownership in the rural areas. The Acts of 1952, 1959 and 1964 exemplify the commitment of the government towards democratization of land relations. The government's sincerity was further reflected in the numerous measures that it took to plug the loopholes in the Acts. The entire process of land reforms indeed had a spectacular beginning. The subsequent developments, however, could not substantiate and carry forward the intrepid beginning. The fiery zeal and passion that had characterized the earlier generation of leaders, who had undergone the grind and suffering of the period of struggle, had started waning. There was a perceptible decline in the enthusiasm and dedication of the political and bureaucratic elite of the later period. The culture of compromise and the pressures for adjustments to enable formation of government overshadowed their commitment to the ideals that had inspired the freedom struggle. The conclusion of the reforms detracted from its glorious beginning. The state was deprived from demonstrating a trendsetting example in the realm of land reforms, which remained only a partial success story.

In spite of all limitations, the commendable feature of the entire transaction was the manner in which people in the state responded to the changes in the agrarian structure. It is true that there was some resistance from the jagirdars who had used recourse to courts and their contacts with the executive, judicial and the legislative authorities to extract a profitable package for themselves but in totality, the process of transition has been of far-reaching consequences. Till date, one can observe that some states which were directly governed by the British and wherein land settlements had been enacted long before they were introduced in Rajasthan, have not been able to free themselves from the oppressive social structure and deep-rooted psychological and social biases. Feudal shackles and relationships continue to characterize rural life in these states which is occasionally marked by bloodshed between the classes. Interestingly, Rajasthan, which is often projected, rather decried, as a stronghold of feudalism, has got over the feudal past in a much better way than some other states.

The critics of the Act are unanimous that given all evasions, leakages and loopholes, it involved a sea-change in the status of the tenants from their lowly position as weak tenants subjected to a life of abject submission and slavery under the jagirdars. By one single measure they acquired the status of virtual owners and superior tenants. While there may be some doubts regarding the actual economic or material benefits that accrued to the tenants, it was a psychological triumph for the peasants who had not even visualized *malikana* or *khatedari* rights for themselves. For millions of such tenants, it was a dream come true.

Notes

1. Dool Singh, *A Study of Land Reforms in Rajasthan* (Government of India, Research Programmes Committee, Planning Commission, 1964) p.31, 44.

2. J.N. Sarkar, *Fall of the Mughal Empire*, Vol. I, p.131, cited in A.C. Banerjee, *The Rajput States and British Paramountcy*, p.19.
3. James Tod, *Annals and Antiquities of Rajasthan* (henceforward *Annals*), Vol. I, p.394.
4. *Ibid.*, p.135.*Kala Patta* was an expression of disapproval as land endowments to non-clan chiefs was viewed as a deviation from old custom and violation of the prescriptive monopoly of the clan.
5. Out of these the Shaktavat, Chundavat and the Sarangdevot are Sisodiya septs.
6. *Annals*, p.139. According to Tod, three things in Mewar were the exclusive privileges of the rulers and the chiefs with which the subjects could not meddle with: (1) *Aan* or oath of allegiance, (2) *Dan* or transit duties on commerce, and (3) *Kan* or mines of precious metals. *Ibid.*, p.139.
7. *Ibid.*, p.127.
8. A.C. Banerjee, *op.cit.*, p.85.
9. Lloyd & Susanne Rudolphs, *Essays on Rajputana: Reflections on History, Culture and Administration*, p.9.
10. Dool Singh, *op.cit.*, Appendix B, p.32.
11. *Ibid.*, p.33.
12. Shankar Sahai Saxena, *Shri Manikyalal Verma*, pp.19-20; Dool Singh, *op.cit.*, pp.33-34.
13. Dool Singh, *op.cit.*, p.34. Heart-rending stories of such tortures were narrated by prominent leaders of the freedom struggle. Interviews with Shri Balwant Singh Mehta and Shri Rajendra Singh Chaudhary.
14. The cultivators and other lower social groups were deprived of numerous privileges: they were not allowed to ride a horse or a mare; they could not wear shoes in front of their social superiors; they were also debarred from wearing certain types of jewellery.
15. *Annals*, p.386.
16. Bipan Chandra & others, *India's Struggle for Independence*, pp.329-331.
17. Rudolphs, *op.cit.*, p.51.
18. Dool Singh, *op.cit.*, p.36.
19. Bipan Chandra & others, *India After Independence* (henceforward, *India After Independence*), pp.377-378. For a discussion on land reforms in post-independence period, refer *Ibid.*, pp.374-410.
20. *Ibid.*, p.375.
21. For a detailed discussion on the provisions and clauses of the numerous interim land reforms measures, refer *Government of Rajasthan Administrative Reforms Commission Report*, Vol.I.
22. For details regarding the Land Reform Acts, refer Dool Singh, *op.cit.*, pp.36-107.
23. Bipan Chandra, *Essays on Indian Nationalism*, p.200.

24. Dool Singh, *op.cit.*, pp.53-57.
25. Ram Pandey, 'Land Reforms: A Historical Perspective' in Ram Pandey (ed.), *Land Reforms and Social Change*, p.102.
26. Rudolphs, *op.cit.*, p.57.
27. For details on tenancy laws, refer, Dool Singh, *op.cit.*, pp.109-220.
28. Rudolphs, *op.cit.*, p.55.
29. *Ibid.*, pp.55-57.
30. K.L. Kochar, *Mohan Lal Sukhadia*, pp.19-20.
31. Dool Singh, *op.cit.*, p.43.
32. *India After Independence*, pp.376-377.
33. K.L. Kamal, 'Land Reforms in Rajasthan: Myth and Reality' in Ram Pandey (ed.), *op.cit.*, p.16.
34. *Ibid.*, p.17.
35. M.L. Shrimal, 'Last Phase of Land Reform in a Society Marching from Feudalistic Pattern to Socialistic Pattern' in Ram Pandey (ed.), *op. cit.*, pp.107-108.
36. K.L. Kamal, 'Land Reforms...' in Ram Pandey (ed.), *op.cit.*, p.17.
37. *India After Independence*, pp.376-377.
38. Dool Singh, *op.cit.*, pp.113-115.
39. K.L. Kamal, 'Land Reforms...' in Ram Pandey (ed.) *op.cit.*, pp.15-16.
40. For a reflection on the adverse image of the Patwari, refer *Government of Rajasthan Administrative Reforms Commission Report*, Vol. I, pp.114-115.
41. M.L. Sukhadia recounted the fearful scenario that had emerged in the wake of threats of violence and bloodshed by the erstwhile jagirdars and bhomias. On one occasion, when they had gone to distribute landownership deeds to the tenants the erstwhile landed elite had threatened with massacre. K.L. Kochar, *op.cit.*, p.82.
42. K.L. Kochar, *op.cit.*, p.82.
43. Bipan Chandra, *Adhunik Bharat Mein Vichardhara Aur Rajniti*, p.208.

9

Process of Transition: Change and Continuity

The people in the state of Rajasthan have a deep consciousness of their distinctive cultural roots. It has been observed by sociologists, anthropologists and eminent intellectuals that it is not easy for any group, region or nation to cast off its cultural heritage. Octavio Paz, an eminent poet and philosopher in Mexico, has tried to explain this phenomenon of inevitable connectedness with the past. According to him, "each civilization consists of certain complexes, pre-suppositions and mental structures; while they may not appear at the conscious level, they keep on stubbornly resisting the erosions of history and its changes."[1] In the context of Rajasthan, Irfan Habib has observed that glorious past of the region has impacted common people's attachment to state. Even today, there is a distinct glow in the eyes of the people when they talk about the heroic traditions of their region.

A distinctive feature of the state of Rajasthan, however, is that its venerated symbols, remembered histories and relics of royalty continue to generate nostalgia not only amongst the inhabitants of the region but even those living in other regions of India. The royalty of Rajasthan, its code of honour, splendour and romance have generated considerable interest among foreign scholars, creative writers, theatre groups, performance of folk arts etc., certainly much more than the ruling classes of any other state.[2] The continuity of the state's fascinating culture is reflected in religious rituals, literary styles, art forms, distinctive cuisine, marriage relationships, mannerism, sense of values and ideologies. The people also recall with great pride architectural monuments like the historic forts of Chittor, Ranthambhor and Amer, the *havelis* adorned with picturesque wall paintings and numerous magnificent palaces that reflect the aesthetic tastes of the erstwhile rulers and jagirdars.

The state is also often projected as a stronghold of feudal values, where the emphasis has been on conservation of traditional institutions and practices rather than on modernization and development. It is true that the past looms large, particularly over the state of Mewar. While passing through the streets of Udaipur, the outsider can feel the stirrings of a bygone era. In addition to the shops bearing the names of historical personages and the imposing statue of Pratap in the heart of the city, the demeanour of the people reflects a culture of commitment, values and propriety. The people, even the youth born and brought up in a modern democratic polity, are not only familiar with the descendants of the erstwhile Maharana but cherish a sense of respect for him. It appears ambivalent that on the one hand, they are active and enthusiastic participants in a democratic polity, and on the other hand, there is a culture of veneration for the royals.

I

Ever since its ascendancy, the monarchical polity of the erstwhile state of Mewar was confronted by numerous challenges to its survival and supremacy, the most notable being the Mughal imperialism, followed by Maratha onslaughts and British paramountcy. However, the Sisodiyas managed to tide over these political vicissitudes to maintain the continuity of their rule and sustenance of a political culture defined by medieval institutions, power structures, rituals and value system. Paradigm shift in the political culture of the state took place as a result of three momentous processes. Initially, the peasant struggle followed by Praja Mandal movement against the jagirdars and the British imperialists. And, then, the extinction of princely rule with the merger of the erstwhile states into the Indian Union signifying a transition from feudal rule to democratic polity. Finally, the series of land reform measures that deprived the jagirdars of their source of political authority and substantially reduced their economic power.

During the period of British paramountcy, an attempt was made to modernize old notions about what constituted a ruler's legitimacy. There was British pressure on rulers to justify their rule by performance. As Curzon put it, "a ruler's *gaddi* (throne) is not intended to be a *diwan* (couch) of indulgence but the seat of duty."[3] It is another matter that British did not tolerate those native rulers who tried to be assertive and independent. Even outside Rajputana states there are many instances when British authorities sought to ignore and even curb initiatives of the princes in the realm of administrative reforms.

The princely states of Bikaner, Jaipur and Jodhpur responded to some extent to the progressive standards of governance set by the British authorities. However, in Mewar, especially under Maharana Fateh Singh, there was a consistent attempt to maintain personal rule in the literal sense. Although, even the so-called progressive reforms in other states were more often formal rather than substantial, in Mewar, no real concessions were made to political participation of the larger community and there were no institutional restraints on the autocratic power of the ruler.[4]

The freedom movement signified a change in the value system that defined legitimacy and honour in political culture. The imperatives of the struggle demanded elimination of hierarchies founded on birth, wealth and education. Gandhi brought forth a style of protest, vocabulary and symbols that led to basic shifts in the monarchical political culture. The restricted political community witnessed a sudden broadening up. As Nehru rightly observed about the impact of Gandhian movements: "New standards and values were set up and the pomp and glamour of the viceregal court and the princes which used to impress so much suddenly appeared supremely ridiculous and vulgar and rather shameful... Rich men were not so anxious to flaunt their riches; outwardly at least many of them adopted simpler ways and in their dress became almost indistinguishable from the humbler folk... the popular respect for British given titles disappeared and they became symbols of degradation."[5]

Pertinently, in most of the Rajputana states, permeation of new values and ideas through the freedom movement which sought to denigrate autocratic regimes in the region never translated into disregard for the rulers. In Mewar, the Maharana continued to be a venerated figure not only amongst the commonfolk but even the regional leaders of the freedom struggle never cast aspersions on the Maharana. Their anger and protests were directed against the jagirdars for their excesses and atrocities on the tillers of the soil. The people in the Indian states did not show any perceptible inclination to rid themselves of their rulers. The post-independence political scenario further corroborates this fact wherein the termination of monarchical rule did not lead to dilution of respect for the erstwhile political elite - both the rulers as well as the much-maligned jagirdars.

During the freedom struggle, no attempt was made at the level of public symbolism to discredit monarchy. In fact, the new leadership sought to give symbolic expression to their own views and values through an extensive use of the classical symbols of the state of Mewar. Divinities, heroes, monuments and even battlefields of Mewar, which had become veritable symbols of resistance, sacrifice and pride in one's culture and independence, were extensively deployed by the leaders of the freedom struggle to mobilize people. 'Har Har Mahadev' - the chant venerating Eklingji - became a popular cry among the

Mewaris during the nationalist agitation. A similar attempt was made in the state of Marwar where the heroic figure of Durgadas was resurrected as a symbol of resistance against alien rule. Significantly, the rulers entertained paranoid fears regarding the widespread popularity of their own traditional symbology. Paradoxically, they felt threatened by those icons and emblems that had been jealously preserved, flaunted and proclaimed as the source of their honour and claim to pride. The traditional symbology underwent a transformation and emerged as symbols of freedom from autocratic rule. Some of the most venerated of these classical symbols were Rana Pratap, Haldighati, Kirti Stambh, etc.

Even after independence, there was no renaming of streets and cities that were named after the erstwhile political elite. Significantly, the former rulers continued to be sensitive to their own emblems of power. The controversy over the flag question raised by Sadul Singh, the ruler of Bikaner, demonstrated their urge to retain their symbolic sovereignty within their kingdom. In this contexts Nehru's attitude was reflected in his speech at the seventh session of the All India States' People's Conference wherein he remarked: "We respect the Udaipur flag but historically and otherwise the national flag represents the nation as a whole."[6] Thus, while upholding the supremacy of the symbology of the nation, Nehru showed deference to the symbolism of the erstwhile royalty. The new leadership did not make any deliberate effort to eradicate the adversary symbolically. In fact, the leadership of the Indian national movement and, later on, the new political elite did not consider local patriotism and loyalty to a region and its culture as disruptive of the nation. According to Bipan Chandra, "even the national movement functioned as an all India movement and not as a federation of regional national movements. It also did not counterpose the national identity to regional identities. It recognized both and did not see the two in conflict."[7]

After the merger of the erstwhile Rajputana states into the Indian Union, the central leadership, particularly Nehru and

Patel, strove to uphold the dignity and public honour of the scions of the former ruling houses. Maharana of Udaipur Bhupal Singh was appointed as Rajpramukh of the United State of Rajasthan for his lifetime with a privy purse of Rs. 10 lakhs. Significantly, the Rajpramukh continued to be a rubber stamp and his appointment was merely a symbolic gesture to accommodate the old aristocracy into the new political structure. In the numerous disputes between the Rajpramukh and the Prime Minister of United Rajasthan, Manikya Lal Verma, the decisions of the latter were upheld as final. In a subtle manner, the Home Minister Sardar Patel was able to impress upon the Rajpramukh, the supremacy of the democratic political set-up.[8]

II

The post-independence political scenario in the erstwhile Rajputana states clearly exemplifies the gradual modernization of the state's political culture. At one level, persistence of respect, in some ways amounting to a fetish, for royalty and its erstwhile glory continued to define the psyche of the people. The people respectfully address Maharana Arvind Singh, the present scion of the Sisodiya clan, as 'Shreeji' or 'Bapji'. Similarly, the Maharaja of Jodhpur returned to a tumultuous welcome to Jodhpur in 1970 after a long liberal education in England. In this context, he observed: "It was the ultimate statement of continuity, of expectation from that continuity. But I had nothing to offer in terms of power, so it was even more touching....people see... me as symbol of Jodhpur, of a past in which they have pride."[9]

Even today, within their esoteric confines, the rituals and ceremonies in the ruling families are conducted with the same grandeur. Code of protocol is strictly adhered to and seating places are arranged in accordance with the individual's ranking on the royal scale. The former rulers have kept up regal traditions and occasionally try to recreate the romance of royalty. They continue to hold formal *durbars* on important occasions – the most notable being their birthdays, *Dushehra*, *Gangaur*, coronation of the new scion, etc. In 2002, Maharaja of Jodhpur, Gaj Singh relived his glory days with a spectacular *durbar* to commemorate the golden jubilee of his coronation. The event received wide media coverage. Quite pertinently, the descendants of the former ruling Rajput clans are proud of their ancestry and their past contribution to the development of the region. In the words of Gaj Singh, "The privy purses, official perks and privileges went with the XXVI amendment to the constitution but centuries old *gaddi* of the Rathores will remain till such time as clan and brotherhood will and with it the social customs, our lifestyle and order of doing things"[10]

Some of the erstwhile ruling clans have sought to enhance their public image and mass appeal by instituting awards in the names of their iconic personages and symbols. In Udaipur, the Maharana Mewar Foundation constituted by Maharana Arvind Singh sponsors awards in the fields of art, music, history, protection of environment, promotion of national integration, journalism and social work in memory of its illustrious Maharanas and other historical icons. The Maharana Mewar Foundation awards are named after glorious figures and symbols from the saga of Mewar: Haldi Ghati Award for Journalism; Col. James Tod Award for Upholding the Values of Mewar Through Writings; Panna Dhai Award for Contribution to Society; Maharana Udai Singh Award for Environmental Protection; Maharana Mewar Award for Nation and Character Building.[11] In the erstwhile state of Marwar, the former royal family has instituted Marwar Ratna Award and Rao Siha Award which are conferred on people with distinguished achievements and for excellent services to society. The awards are given on Jodhpur Day on May 12 in a lavish ceremony. Gaj Singh, the former Maharaja of the state, leads the celebrations and performs traditional rituals and also pays obeisance at Rao Jodhaji ka Phalsa. In Jaipur too, the royal family just a few years back instituted awards in the name of Sawai Man Singh for excellence in numerous fields. Through such measures, they seek to perpetuate the memory and glory of their clan and to keep in touch with the people of the state.

Rajmata Gayatri Devi, the queen of the last ruling Kachchawa Maharaja Sawai Man Singh of erstwhile Jaipur state, remains a charismatic figure who is still a huge draw in public functions. She also runs two schools in Jaipur. There are many other rulers who showed keen interest in the establishment of educational institutions in their respective states.

Significantly, attachment to royalty, its icons, rituals and personages is a phenomenon that is not peculiar to the state of Rajasthan. There are many instances of countries, other than India, wherein constitutional monarchy and democracy co-exist. In fact, people have deeply felt emotions for the royal family in countries like England, Norway, Japan, etc. England has not only retained kingship, but there has been a deep-rooted and widespread culture of deference for the monarch. In the media age a culture of celebrity has grown around the royalty. For its entire vicissitudes, the monarchy remains shockingly popular: 70 percent prefer it to a republic – a percentage that has barely budged in 50 years. Very few Britons labour to figure out, why in the 21st century the Queen ought to exist. At the end of 50 years, despite changing times and attitudes, she is still on the throne and still admired.[12] The monarchy, above all, conveys a sense of continuity and stability. Everything else may change and falter but monarchy, it seems, goes on forever. However, when it comes to the region of Rajasthan, people's fixation for royal symbols is often interpreted as reflection of feudalistic attitudes and projection of medieval mindset.

III

After the integration of Rajasthan into the Indian Union, responsible form of government was established in the state. People started electing their representatives to the state and central legislatures, known as Vidhan Sabha and Lok Sabha respectively. The first elections to these representative bodies were held in 1952. The results of the first few elections to the Vidhan Sabha as well as Lok Sabha, the Lower House of the

Parliament, sought to prove the continued hold of the former royal families on the minds of the people.[13] The Indian National Congress, the premier political party which led and organized the mainstream freedom struggle in India, had to contend with the opposition of the feudal elements due to its declared policy of abolition of jagirs (landed estates assigned by the rulers) and introduction of land reforms. The jagirdars contested the first general election in 1952 on the symbol of Ram Rajya Parishad – a political party that had mobilized reactionary elements. The Congress lost 11 of the 20 seats in the Lok Sabha. Even stalwarts and highly respected leaders of the freedom struggle in Mewar, Manikya Lal Verma and Gokul Bhai Bhatt lost elections to the erstwhile feudal elite. The Ram Rajya Parishad captured as many as 24 seats emerging as the second largest party in the State Assembly. A number of jagirdars contested elections as independent candidates under the leadership of Maharaja Hanwant Singh, the former ruler of Jodhpur. Many veteran Congress leaders, including the highly respected leader of the freedom struggle Jai Narayan Vyas, had to suffer defeat. It was jocularly said that even a donkey could have won if Hanwant Singh put him up as a candidate. The election result of the Bijoliya assembly constituency in the erstwhile Mewar state was the most shocking instance of support to the former feudal elements where Vijay Singh Pathik, the hero and charismatic leader of the peasant agitation in Bijoliya, lost to the descendant of the former jagirdar.

In the second general elections Ram Rajya Parishad secured 17 seats retaining its position as the second largest party in the State Assembly. Later on, the former rulers, landowners and other conservative people had collaborated to form the Swatantra Party in 1962 under the leadership of C. Rajgopalachari. In Rajasthan, the party was led by the highly popular Rajmata Gayatri Devi. The party captured 36 seats in the State Assembly in the third general elections and was the second largest party in a 176-member house. Gayatri Devi herself achieved spectacular and record-breaking victories in two consecutive parliamentary elections. She secured a place in the Guinness Book of World Records for victory margins in both the elections. In 1967, the Swatantra Party captured 49 seats. The success of the party signified the persistent reverence for erstwhile political elite. However, despite the fact that the feudal forces represented by the rulers and nobility achieved remarkable success, it was the Congress party that remained in power, albeit very precariously.

With the Congress determination to carry out land reforms becoming clear and party's consistent victories in bye-elections, the jagirdars, especially the larger ones, realized the futility of their hostility to the Congress. Consequently, in January 1954, 18 of the prestigious jagirdars, who were members of State Assembly, crossed the aisle to join the Congress Legislature Party. By March, 25 MLAs (Members of Legislative Assembly), one MP (Member of Parliament) and 43 leading jagirdars announced their decision to join the Congress. They appealed to other jagirdars to do the same by arguing that the popularity of the Congress has been increasing since 1952 and it had secured victories in ten bye-elections. The traditional political elite too was succumbing to the inexorable forces of political change brought about by the republican revolution.

In the succeeding elections it became clear that respect for erstwhile rulers and fascination for their rituals and lifestyle has not undermined the democratic urges of the people which had permeated the mindset of the people. In the first few elections, they (erstwhile rulers and jagirdars) were able to win large number of seats but were gradually marginalized by the triumph of liberal democracy. As people gained experience in democratic polity, it became clear that distinguished genealogy and a glorious past could no longer guarantee them a cakewalk in the elections. The former royal elite did not win a single seat in the elections after 1971. The scion of the erstwhile ruling family of Mewar, Mahendra Singh had contested Lok Sabha election from Chittor – the most celebrated, exalted and remembered symbol of the Sisodiyas' saga of chivalry.

However, despite constant underscoring of the sacrifices and contribution of his predecessors in the electoral campaign, he failed to secure victory in the election. Similarly, Maharaja Bhawani Singh, the present scion of the Kachchawa clan of Jaipur, lost the parliamentary election. It has become clear that members of royalty cannot win an election merely by recalling their past glory and glamour. They have to respond to public aspirations and developmental needs to secure political legitimacy.

In the state of Rajasthan, popular sovereignty has effectively replaced the so-called divine theory of kingship commanding unquestioned loyalty and allegiance. The democratic set-up has redefined the notion of legitimacy and honour in political culture. The defeats, which many royal stalwarts had to suffer at the election hustings, are an unequivocal statement on the supremacy of popular sovereignty in the region. Nevertheless, despite the shifting of the electorates' emphasis from the royalty to the commoners in their voting process in a democratic polity, at the social level the values of bygone princely days have not eroded and, in some ways or other, there exist nostalgic memories of the past.

Notes

1. Octavio Paz, *The Other Mexico: Critique of the Pyramid*, quoted in S.P. Varma, 'Modernization: In the Perspective of History, Tradition and Culture' in P. Bannerjee and S.K. Gupta (eds.), *Man, Society and Nature*, p.79.
2. Even Lord Curzon, the champion of British paramountcy over Indian ruling houses, himself expressed admiration for the code of ethics of the Rajputana princes and its continued relevance for the Indian social system: "I realize more perhaps in Rajputana than anywhere else, that they constitute a school of manners valuable to Indians and not less valuable to the Europeans, showing in the person of their chiefs that illustrious lineage has not ceased to implant noble and chivalrous ideas and maintaining those old fashioned and punctilious standards of public spirit and private courtesy which have always been instinctive in the Indian

aristocracy, and with the loss of which, if ever they were allowed to disappear, Indian society will go to pieces like a dismantled vessel in a storm". See Charles Allen and Sharda Dwivedi, *Lives of Indian Princes*, pp.14-15.

3. Lloyd and Susanne Rudolphs, *Essays on Rajputana: Reflections on History, Culture and Administration*, p.7.
4. *Ibid.*, pp.5-8.
5. Jawahar Lal Nehru, *Discovery of India*, p.361.
6. M.S. Jain, *Concise History of Modern Rajasthan*, p.196.
7. Bipan Chandra and Others, *India After Independence*, p.119.
8. B.L. Panagariya and N.C. Pahariya, *Rajasthan: Polity, Economy & Society*, pp.22-24. After the completion of the process of integration and formation of greater Rajasthan in 1949, Maharana of Udaipur was conferred upon the position of Maharajpramukh and the Maharaja of Jaipur was made Rajpramukh for life.
9. Royina Grewal, *In Rajasthan*, p.202.
10. *India Today*, January 6, 2003, p.54.
11. The Maharana Mewar Charitable Foundation (MMCF) was set up by Maharana Bhagwat Singh in 1969 as a means of "protecting, honouring and preserving the duties of custodianship". The Foundation seeks to perform activities, which are harmonious with all the principles, responsibilities and duties of former times. Charity or philanthropy forms its major focus, as it has been an integral part of the concept of Mewar. The Foundation has also initiated a major project called 'A City within a City' which aims at preserving the heritage, particularly architectural heritage, environment and ecology management and promotion of local crafts and arts. The Foundation has undertaken extensive and admirable restoration and conservation work in City Palace complex, Jagmandir and royal cenotaphs. For details, refer pamphlets on Maharana of Mewar Charitable Foundation, Udaipur and *The City within a City: Impressions*.
12. In United Kingdom, if you want someone to inaugurate something, the Queen is indisputably top of the list. In 50 years as Queen, she has undertaken 25 official overseas visits to 128 different countries and conferred 3,80,630 honours and awards. Refer Tim Heald, 'Queen Elizabeth II: The Great Survivor', *Readers Digest*, August 2002, pp.134-150.
13. For more details on trends and events related to first few election in Rajasthan, refer Panagariya and Pahariya, *op. cit.*, pp.65-67; Rudolphs, *op. cit.*, pp.61-66: Allen & Dwivedi, *op. cit.*, pp. 253-278.

Appendix

I
Rules and Rituals of Bhindar Thikana

In the present document in a scroll we have the details of the list of prevalent rules, regulations and rituals of Bhindar estate. In the local dialect, it is called '*Mautad*'. As the upper part of the document is damaged, the first three points of the list are not available. This material is important for understanding the rules and regulations prescribed for each *Thikana*. The present document underscores the intricacies, formalities and unnecessary preoccupation with petty details regarding court life.

The jagirdar of Bhindar belonged to the highest category of nobles, i.e., first grade nobles in Mewar also known as '*Solah Sardars*' (the sixteen nobles) who were given the epithet of *Umraos*. They belonged to the Shaktawat *khamp* (sept) of the Sisodiyas, tracing their lineage from Shakti Singh, brother of the illustrious Maharana Pratap. Bhinder and Bansia were two first grade jagirs assigned to Shaktawats. Bhindar is situated 58 kms, noth-east of Udaipur in Vallabhnagar tehsil. Shaktavats were deliberately given special privileges and marks of honour to balance the increasing arrogance and assertiveness of the Chundavats. The noble of Bhindar was given the exalted title of Maharaja. Like other nobles, Bhindar Maharaja was entitled to rights, privileges, ceremonial and ritualistic honours and royal insignia which were meticulously documented and strictly adhered to till the last detail in all the ceremonies and functions. Most of these rules and rites were related to procedure of reception, departure and seating; dress, especially the decorations on the turban and jewellery; rules of etiquette to be observed by the Maharaja and Maharana during their meeting; royal insignia to be used by the nobles. These rules even specified the jewellery and decoration of the horses and elephants used during processions. Interestingly, there was a special protocol department headed by *Mosal* and lower officials called *chhadidars*, *gotawalas*, *jalebdars* and *nakeebs* who supervised these ritualistic details. Even a slight transgression invited punishment in the form of fines. The *chhadidar* could stop the noble from attending the court or the regal procession if he flouted even the smallest of the ceremonial details. On one occasion Maharana Swaroop Singh reprimanded the *Kunwar* of Bhindar for deviating from the prescribed shape of his turban. The present document also makes it clear that visits by chiefs of first grade jagirs to the capital were elaborately planned and executed. The details of the ceremonial procedure also reveal the fact that parity rather than abject subjection marked noble's relationship with the Maharana.

RĀH MARJĀD

List of Rules, Regulations and Rituals of Bhindar Estate (Thikana)

1. Correspondence No. 1 (available in the form of a scroll)
2. Measurement : 530 cms X 13.75 cms
   Total no. of lines : 317
   Document/Location & time : Bhindar/Beginning of the 19th century
   Language and script : Rajasthani/Devnagari
   Writer of the Document : Not Known
3. The choice of *naupati* (horse or elephant that led the procession) was left to the discretion of the Bhindar Maharaja. It was decorated by gold and silver jewellery.[1]
4. Bhindar Maharaja has the discretion to keep gold and silver to his liking.
5. Beating of drums, *shehnai* (wind-instrument) and other musical instruments preceded the procession. In the procession, there were elephants, horses and forces.

The original document is in local dialect. Dr. Menaria contributed towards Hindi translation of the document. The English translation is by the authors.

6. In the procession of Bhindar Maharaja, there used to be a special horse whose seat was covered with *banati jeen* (a special kind of cloth) and the horse rider wore red coloured uniform.
7. On the occasion of the main procession two people used to hold *mashaals* (oil torch).
8. Accompanied by Charans.
9. On Saturday, at the time of *chauki,* Bhindar Maharaja used to visit royal palace of Udaipur and there he had his meals and he used to wash his hands in the main courtyard. After this he used to go and meet Maharana, who offered him *pan ka beera* (roll of betel leave). He used to submit to the Maharana if there was any assignment or work for him. After this Maharaja with the *chhadidar* (herald or staff-bearer) used to go to Bhindar ki haveli located at Udaipur.
10. Sreeji (Maharana of Udaipur) with his *chhadidar* used to go to Bhindar ki haveli, (residential mansion in Udaipur), enquired about Maharaja's well-being and Bhindar Maharaja reciprocated; this was customary courtesy.
11. Every day there were messages and posts from royal palace of Udaipur as well as other thikanas.
12. On arrival in Udaipur, Bhindar Maharaja gave his turban, and Rs. 5 to the *Kapaddwara* (incharge of wardrobe).
13. *Amar Valena* (perpetual grant of a horse) remained with him.[2]
14. The special dress worn by the Maharana on the occasion of Dhinga Gangaur was presented to Bhindar Maharaja. At the same time, silver coin of Rs. 5 was given to *Kapaddwara.*[3]
15. Whenever Bhindar Maharaja visited Udaipur Maharana at palace, he was made to sit in the *durrikhana* (main reception room) on his arrival, the chief of the bodyguard and other officials offered two rolls of betel leaves. Out of which one Maharaja himself ate and the other he gave his accompanist. Later on, according to his wish he used to visit Bhindar Haveli, situated at Udaipur. On leaving the Maharana's palace, he was again offered *pan ka beera* (roll of betel leaves) by *Daroga* of *Tambolkhana* (storehouse for betel leaves) and other chief officials.
16. In his haveli, the man who brought towel was immediately given two silver coins.
17. On the festival of Akha Teej, the man who brought saffron colour and also offered Re 1 was tipped three silver coins.[4]

18-19. On the occasion of Maharana's procession in Udaipur, a *chhadidar* (herald) used to go to Bhindar haveli to inform the Maharaja about the procession. If he desired to join, he paid obeisance to the deity and joined the royal procession from Jagdish Temple. On the way back from the procession, Bhindar Maharaja took leave at Jagdish temple and paid his respects. He returned along with accompanists.

20. The rider on the elephant wore *kalangi* (ornament on turban, aigrette) of *honkara's* (a bird) feathers.
21. The palanquin was decorated with gold work.
22. The *dhoop shedi* (parasol for protection from sun) used to be of red *banat* (a special kind of cloth) with a new rod.
23. The drummers used to beat till Jagat Shiromani temple.[5]
24. While he was in the royal palace for *chowki* (duty assigned to each jagirdar for protecting the palace) he was given comfortable bedroll to sleep and gold and silver utensils for drinking water and eating meals.[6]
25. There was an elephant of his choice that had red coloured cover and decorated with silver and gold ornaments.
26. *Junjarba* (salute guns carried on camels) were carried on camels in the processions and were removed while mounting and dismounting of the Maharaja from his elephant.
27. *Jalebdars* (those who carried spears) and *Kamaandars* (archers) accompanied the Maharaja in the procession.
28. Four accompanists with silver rod and one gold polished rod also accompanied.
29. When Maharaja Saheb (Bhindar) visited Udaipur palace he used to arrive in the *palki* upto to the corner platform of the palace *durrikhana.*
30. The *chobdar* (mace-bearer) with a silver rod accompanied him upto Ganesh Deori.
31. Gold *hukka* (device to smoke tobacco) and silver *chilam* (device attached with *hukka* for inhaling tobacco) could be used by him at Ganesh Deorhi.
32. When Maharaja reached *durrikhana, chhadidar* announced *juhar* (respectful greetings) to the Maharana on his behalf. Sreeji used to stand and greet him (offered *Tazim*). Then Maharaja would humbly have conversation showing respect for the Maharana who gave him specific instructions.[7]

33. In the palace, Maharaja Saheb used to be given *Amarshahi Kamarband* (waistband) and *Shaktavati pag* (turban). This dress was presented to him as a mark of honour.
34. Whenever Maharaja Saheb arrived at the palace, his son, chief (pradhan), vakil (agent, advisor or ambassador) and others accompanied him. Some of them used to sit in the palace courtyard but his eldest son, the chief and the vakil seated in the main Audience Hall of the royal palace where several officials waited in their attendance.[8]
35. When Maharaja Saheb seated to take a meal there would be an attendant dressed in red who used to serve water and *kunja* (vessel containing water) used to be covered with red cloth.
36. On the occasion of special lunch, ten bodyguards accompanied Bhindar Maharaja.
37. In a procession, gunmen accompanied.
38. While Maharaja Saheb of Bhindar was in the royal palace, Maharana did not sit on the throne and the bed, did not use *hukkah* and did not look at the mirror.[9]
39. On the occasion when rulers of Jaipur, Jodhpur and other equivalent Maharajas arrived at royal palaces, Bhindar Maharaja used to be present in *durrikhana*. On the occasion of the visits of other nobles, the presence of Maharaja of Bhindar was not considered necessary.[10]
40. On the auspicious occasion of the wedding in Maharana's family, Bhindar Maharaja was accompanied by his wife, who would be received by the chief queen at the doors of the palace and a special ceremony of *Kalash Bandhai* was performed to welcome her. They sat together where they were attended with flywhisks and accompanied by bodyguards with gold mounted sticks.
41. When Bhindar Maharaja's wife Baiji Raj travelled in palanquin, it used to have gold engraved frill and there used to be a *kalash* and on the way was attended by flywhisks.
42. When Maharaja Saheb was invited to wedding in the royal palace in Udaipur, elder sons of the Pradhan used to go to invite him. As long as he stayed in Udaipur all his expenses were borne by the palace treasury. At the time of his departure, he was gifted a *siropav* of *seekh* and a decorated horse.[11]

43. On the occasion of marriages, gifts were presented to the barber, scavenger, drumbeater and personal attendant of Bhindar Maharaja. If there was more than one personal attendant each one was given a *siropav. Davri* (maid) was gifted Rs. 7 for dancing, Re. 1 as tip and a basket of sweets.
44. Drum beating took place in Bhindar Maharaja's haveli.
45. *Jadap* (a big ceremonial fan forming a part of the royal insignia, was used when Maharana or the noble sat on his throne) had silver stick.
46. Silver chair with legs covered with silver work and low stool with silver work was used for Bhindar Maharaja.
47. The person who informed the Maharaja of the birth of a son was given a tip for bringing the goods news.
48. In case of Kunwar's (Maharaja's son) marriage in Udaipur all the expenses were borne by the Maharana.
49. In the procession of Maharaja Saheb all his accompanists walked, except his brothers, son, chief and vakil who rode on horses.
50. Wherever the procession halted a *kanaat* (boundary of thick cloth) was raised all round along with a large tent in the front.
51. In the ceremony of *Talwar Bandhai* (accession of new Umrao) no tax was levied.
52. When the custom of *Talwar Bandhai* was performed, on this occasion, Maharana's eldest son used to go to Bhindar to invite the heir apparent of the deceased noble. If Kunwar could not go then any body from the three havelis (Bagore, Karjoli and Shivrati) visited Bhindar. In case Kunwar of the Maharana visited then Bhindar Kunwar used to come down from the horse and offer *nazrana* (ritual offering) and *nichhrawal* (offerings for long and prosperous life). If anybody from the three havelis went, then he gave Rs. 500 to Motdar, Rs. 500 to Pradhan and Rs. 1,000 were given in the name of Sreeji. After these offerings the prospective Bhindar Maharaja was brought to Udaipur where *Talwar Bandhai* of Maharaja was performed by the Maharana himself. As per the custom, during the ceremony Bhindar Maharaja received elephant, horse, *siropav*, pearl string, *paag*, etc. from Sreeji. In addition a sword with gold engraved sheath was also given. As per custom *aarti* (oil lamp moved around circularly as an act or homage and blessing) was performed. Priest was given a uniform and a horse, then after that, they would proceed to pay obeisance

to Banmata (*kuldevi* of Mewar) and Ganeshji. There he made an offering of Re.1. Then he took leave from Sreeji to proceed to his palace in Bhindar. As per custom, offered *nazrana* and departed with a roll of betel leaves.[12]

53. On the occasion of death of a jagirdar, Sreeji visited Bhindar haveli and after greeting would sit down with his head covered with a piece of cloth and expressed his concern, enquired about welfare. He used to remove the clothes of mourning, offered him (the new incumbent) a horse[13], brought him to the palace, gave him a roll of betel leaves as permission to depart for his haveli in Udaipur.
54. On the occasion of boat ride, Bhindar Maharaja did not accompany the Maharana.
55. On the occasion of pleasure or displeasure of Sreeji, Maharaja of Bhindar heard the aggrieved's appeal and could get Sreeji's pardon for the guilty.
56. Except for Sreeji and the British officials Bhindar Maharaja did not take initiative in greeting or entering into conversation with other Sardars. He responded only if the other nobles addressed him.
57. The Maharaja wore a pair of *toda* (gold ornaments worn in the feet) above the anklets.
58. On his turban he tied gold and silver *karan* (a decorative lace).
59. On his *paag*, another decoration called *nad* was tied.
60. On the day of Diwali (festival of lights to venerate Goddess Laxmi and Lord Rama) a high official used to bring roll of betel leaves and was given 20 silver coins.
61. Maharaja Saheb of Bhindar took off his shoes on mud coated courtyard.
62. On Maharaja Saheb's arrival at *durrikhana*, Sreeji used to embrace him (*wagalgiri*) and he offered Rs. 5 as *nazrana* and offered *nichhrawal* of Rs. 2 and then was seated on the right side (most honourable seating order) of the Maharaja. Earlier, Salumbar Rao Saheb sat on the floor near the Maharana but in the time of subsequent Maharanas, Maharaja was also seated next to the Maharana. Once on the demise of Bhindar Maharaja, his uncle Prithvi Singh sought accession but this was protested by Thakurani of Bhindar. Yet he did not give up his accession. At that time, one of the loyal officials of the deceased Bhindar Maharaja took his son Sagat Singh to Mewar Maharana Sreeji and pleaded for his rights. Sreeji called for Sagat Singh and ordered his *Talwar Bandhai* and gave

permission to him to sit in his presence. Then Sagat Singh reached Bhadsode (a *jagir* within Bhindar estate) where he died and over this issue there was controversy. Therefore, Sreeji called khawas named Deva and Jaitsinghji. Initially, they hesitated to go to Udaipur fearing they would be accused of Sagat Singh's murder. After some time, they were fearless and reached Udaipur where Sreeji ordered his *Talwar Bandhai* and assigned him the *patta* (land deed) of Bhadsode. He was given a lower seat in the court along with Kanora Raoji.

63. On the occasion of Bhindar Maharaja's daughter's wedding an elephant, a coconut, decorated horse, *siropav* and cash Rs. 5,000 were given by Sreeji.
64. Pearl studded decorative ornament was worn on *paag.*
65. Another pearl studded ornament was worn on *paag.*
66. On *paag* there used to be gold and silver *pachevadi* (band on the turban).
67. A special string prepared at Jagpura (a village in Bhindar) was worn in the neck.
68. In the procession, *hukka* and *chilam* were carried.
69. When Maharaja Saheb offered *nazrana*, Sreeji's hand remained below and Maharaj Saheb's hand remained on top.[14]
70. On the occasion of Dussehra, Maharana visited Bhindar haveli to perform *juhar* (customary greeting for nobles).
71. On the occasion of *phag* (the festival of colours) small cloth bags of *gulal* (coloured powder) were brought by Sreeji to the haveli.
72. On Sheetala Saptami, Sreeji visited the haveli.
73. Bhindar Maharaja used to be present on the occasion of Maharana's procession. On return from procession till he sat on the throne, Bhindar Maharaja did not depart.
74. During the festivals of Diwali and Holi, Bhindar Maharaja used to be with him in the *durrikhana.*
75. Whenever Sreeji went out of station and it was in the knowledge of Bhindar Maharaja, then Baiji used to send food in a plate for Sreeji.
76. Maharaja Saheb would take two steps forward, whenever Sreeji goes out.
77. On the occasion of special work, he would find out the auspicious time and work accordingly.

Rules and Rituals Regarding the Elder Kunwar (Son)

1. On the occasion of the birth of a son, pearl embedded *kara* (ornament worn in the hand) is gifted.
2. A decorated horse remains with the *Kunwar.*
3. In the procession, he walked in the front and was accompanied by *chhadidar,* bodyguard and other officials who preceded him.
4. He was offered roll of betel leaves in the *durrikhana*
5. His horse had silver and gold ornaments and there used to be gold and silver border on the *jerband* of the horse.
6. He wore pearl ornaments and in his feet gold ornaments.
7. When *Kunwar* visited royal palace at Udaipur, he got off and mounted on the horse from the same place where Bhindar Maharaja did.
8. He used to be present when Maharana appeared.
9. In the procession, he used to be seated on the *kathi* (saddle) of horse.
10. He wore *honkar kalangi.*[15]
11. When Sreeji wrote an official letter called *Rukka* he also communicated *juhar* (greeting) to *Kunwarji.*
12. Whenever he left Bhindar, he was given gifts (*seekh*) and turban as he desired.
13. On the occasion of mourning, there used to be a death feast and Sreeji used to distribute utensils to the jagirdars assembled there.
14. As expected, *Kunwarji* used to be present.
15. On the auspicious day of Anant Chaturdashi, Maharana's *angochha* (small piece of cloth) was gifted to *Kunwarji.*
16. On the festival of Diwali, Sreeji gifted sugarcanes to him.
17. On Holi, he was given coconuts.
18. He took foods in silver utensils and his water jug (*ramsagar*) was of silver.
19. On the festival of Sheetala Saptmi, he was given garlands.
20. Shreeji served double *prasad* (ritual food offerings) in his platter on the occasion of *Pantya Bhoj* (privilege of attending the meals hosted by the Maharana).
21. Gun used for hunting had red cover of *banat* (special kind of cloth).
22. On other occasions, customary gifts were given according to his desire.

Rules and Rituals for the Younger Son

1. Gold ornaments in the feet.
2. Silver waistband was given to him.
3. In a meeting of dignitaries and officials, he would also sit in the front.
4. Silver ornaments were used for his horse.
5. His ornaments were embedded with pearls.
6. A special kind of *pachevadi* was tied on his *paag*. He wore gold in his feet and rode horse and appeared in the service of Sreeji and used to get down from the horse at Tripoliya.[16]

Rules and Rituals for the Sons of Paswans (kepts)

1. *Chowkdi* embedded with pearls was given to them.
2. They were also assigned villages.
3. They were also seated in the front in a meeting at the royal palace.

Rules and Rituals for Dignitaries Living in Udaipur

1. If an honourable person makes a request, he was called and given hearing.
2. They did *mujra* (a form of customary greeting in which one bows down) everyday.
3. He could present himself in the main *durrikhana.*
4. On requirement, they could appear before Pradhan's office rather than go to the courts where common man used to go.
5. They did not have to give *aan* (guarantee) in the bazaar for exchanges.
6. An attendant called *Harkara* accompanied them.
7. They used to get down outside palace Tripoliya.
8. In big feasts, they were seated with the *Paswans* and served in platter of leaves.

Formalities Observed when Maharana Resided Outside Udaipur

1. He used to be accompanied by elephants, horses and other paraphernalia related with royal insignia.
2. Behind the main procession was army.

3. When Maharana Saheb moved out of Udaipur and accompanied by Bhindar Maharaja, all his expenses were borne by Maharana and was also given gifts.
4. Whenever he was required to go out of Mewar state, he moved with the paraphernalia of his thikana and Sreeji paid him as much as he requested for.

Rules and Rituals Regarding Bhindar Thikana's Court

1. *Adani* (a big fan used while one was mounted on a horse) had a silver rod.
2. *Avadagiri* (a part of the royal insignia) was of silver rod.
3. There used to be *kiraniya* (a part of royal insignia).
4. *Morchang* (a fan made of peacock's feathers) and *chanwar* (flywhisk) had gold rods.
5. There used to be royal paraphernalia.
6. There used to be a special palanquin.
7. Seat of the palanquin used to be of *shisham's* (a tree) wood covered with silver plate. The palanquin used to be covered with a red cloth.
8. Sheath was covered with red *banat.*
9. Boats used to be there.
10. Musical instrument called *dandi* used to be played.
11. Musical instrument called *chaugadia* used to be played.
12. Another musical instruments called *udardi* also played.
13. Security guards accompanied the procession.
14. Drums were played.
15. Archers also walked along in the procession.
16. In the reception room when court used to be in session mattresses used to be covered with white sheets
17. In the procession, guns were fired when the Maharaja mounted and dismounted.
18. A musical instrument called *satari* used to be played on camels.
19. Marseilles tune was played.
20. For riding on an elephant coloured cloth loops were there and the *howdah* (seat on elephant without a canopy) on the elephant had arched (*burjidar*) border.
21. Elephants that could run fast were also there.

22. *Gotha* (a rod mounted with the image of a lion either golden or silver) of gold and silver used to be there.
23. Beating of drums accompanied the processions.
24. The cover of the palanquins of dignitaries who accompanied the procession were made of *banat* cloth and had engraved silver border.
25. The fan (royal insignia) carried during procession had silver rod.
26. Bhindar thikana had its own local mint.[17]
27. Jewellery of the Queens of thikana was embedded with precious stones and they wore gold in the feet.[18]
28. Water basin (*hauj* or *chevcha)* was also there.
29. Royal palace maids wore gold ornaments and could wrap around a shawl.
30. Curtains used in the palace were tailored of special red cloth called *banat.*
31. On occasions of marriage and reception to welcome arrival of *Saheb Bahadur* (British officials) or other close relatives, gun salutes were given.
32. There were celebrations in the royal palace.
33. From time to time they went out for all kinds of hunting.

Notes

1. Only a few nobles had the privilege of decorating their horses with gold jewellery. Generally, they were allowed silver jewellery for their horses.
2. *Amar Valena* was a special privilege, which meant that if a horse gifted by the Maharana or any other dignitary fell sick, or died, it was replaced by a new horse. This privilege was conferred on Shahpura, Banera and Kothariya. Bhindar Maharaja received *Amar Valena* from the Rawat of Salumber.
3. It was a special honour to receive the dress worn by Maharana on festivals and other occasions. The dress worn during the procession of Dussehra was conferred on Rawat of Kothariya.
4. On the auspicious day of Akha Teej, the royal palace organized celebrations and a procession. The feudal lords who took part in the procession wore saffron coloured jackets. Later, a new ritual was devised wherein their jackets were sprinkled with saffron drops, which were sent by the Maharana in a silver bowl to the jagirdar's haveli.

5. The nobles were required to dismount at a fixed point from their *palkies* (palanquins), horses or elephants and then move on foot till the *durrikhana.* The drummers were also allowed till a fixed place. The drummers of most nobles in Mewar could beat till Debari Dwara but Banera jagirdar could bring his till Tripoliya gate. Sadri and Bhindar nobles' drummers could accompany them till Jagannath Temple.
6. The day for each jagirdar's *chowki* was fixed. Bhindar Maharaja's *chowki* used to be on Saturday. He reached the royal palace in the evening and had meals with Maharana. They were required to sleep overnight in the palace. Some jagirdars like those of Banera and Bedla, as a matter of special privilege, were exempted from the customary overnight stay.
7. When the noble holding the privilege of *Tazim* entered the court, the Maharana rose from his seat to receive him. The noble placed his sword in front of him, bowed down and touched the hem of the Maharana's coat. The Maharana placed his hand on the shoulder of the noble who then stood straight and the Maharana moved his hand on his own chest. After the *nazar* was offered the noble took his seat.
8. The privilege to bring accompanists was given only to a few *Umraos.*
9. The Maharana could not use the *hukka* in the presence of the *Umrao* (first grade noble) till he himself requested the Maharana to do so.
10. The *Solah Sardars* (first grade of nobles) of Mewar, whenever they visited other Rajput states, were given a place on the right side next to the ruling prince of the state concerned. This ranked them above the nobility of that state.
11. *Siropav* of *seekh* meant robes of honour indicating permission to depart.
12. When the incumbment of a jagir died, his estate was placed under *zabti* (escheat or sequesteration). There was an elaborate procedure called *Talwar Bandhai* for the investiture of the heir to the deceased jagirdar. On the demise of a chief, the Maharana immediately sent a party consisting of a civil officer and a few soldiers who took possession of the estate in the Maharana's name. On the request of the heir apparent for his installation, Maharana sent the Kunwar or the jagirdar of Shivrati, Bagore or Karjoli (three important jagirs assigned with a special status as they were descendants of Maharana Sanga) for *matampursi* (mourning) and who later brought him to Udaipur. They also settled the amount he would pay as *Talwar Bandhai*, which was a kind of succession fee. Thereafter, he was brought to Udaipur for the ritual of *Talwar Bandhai* which was performed by the Maharana in his court. It was an imposing ceremony. A sword was buckled to the side of the new incumbent and he received *siropav* and a steed. The *zabti* was then recalled. Some thikanas like Bhindar, Amet, Gogunda, Banera, Devgarh, Kanod and Shahpura were exempted from payment of *Talwar Bandhai.* They had to pay installation fees, which amounted to 8 percent of their total income. The thikana of

Salumbar was exempted from *zabti* and Maharana himself went to Salumbar for *Talwar Bandhai*.

13. It was known as *Mokhaniya* horse, which formed a ritual offering to close the period of mourning.
14. This style of receiving *nazar* (ritual offering) wherein the hand of the *Umrao* remained on top of that of Maharana's was considered as a sign of honour by the *Umraos*.
15. *Kalangi* was a decoration on the turban made of the feathers of a bird. *Honkar Kalangi* was made of the feathers of a bird called *Honkar* and was the privilege that was bestowed on individuals of high rank.
16. This was the place where first grade nobles dismounted from their horse.
17. Minting of coins was a royal prerogative of the Maharana but three Mewar chiefs started their own coinage for a certain period of time although they had not been given explicit permission to do so. They were Rawat of Salumbar (Salumbar Dhingla, 1804-1870), Maharaja of Bhindar (Bhindariya Paisa, 1799-1827 AD) and also the Shahpura chief who struck gold, silver and copper coins till 1870.
18. Specific instructions were there regarding the kind of jewellery (gold, silver or stone) to be worn by different social groups and classes according to their status in the social hierarchy.

II
Pan ka Beera
(Roll of Betel Leaves)

Pan or betel leaf is a heart-shaped leaf, which is commonly eaten in the Indian sub-continent. It is chewed after meals as a mouth-freshener and a digestive agent. It is usually folded in the shape of a triangle and filled with aromatic spices. The commonly used ingredients are pieces of areca nut *(supari)*, catechu, calcined shell lime, aniseed, and cardamom. At times, people also chew tobacco with pan. The roll is also garnished with *gulkand* (a type of jam made of the petals of roses), peppermint, and other fragrant substances according to the peculiar taste of the individual. On special occasions and for esteemed guests the roll is covered with silver flakes to give it a more ornate look. There are many instances of both, men and women getting addicted to the chewing of pan and are seen carrying them in specially crafted boxes.

In Rajputana court culture, roll of betel leaves or *pan ka beera,* as it was popularly known, emerged as a symbol and a revered ritual offering which assumed great importance on account of its multivocality, i.e., variety of different meanings attached to a single symbol. It was a mark of honour, confidence and friendship. *Doyam beera* (two rolls) which was a special privilege was offered to *Umraos* when they entered the main *durrikhana*. They showed respect to the ritual offering by touching the same with their eyes. He consumed one and returned the other to the *Purohit* who had brought it. Only after this did he proceed to the other *durrikhana* to have an audience with the Maharana. Special *beeras* (rolls) known as *durrikhana ka beera* were distributed on behalf of the Maharana after the rituals and proceedings of the court were over. These were offered only to those *Umraos,* chiefs, relatives and *Rajpurohit* who were entitled to it. This particular beera was round in shape and was held together by 11 sticks.

It was used to symbolically convey messages. It was said that through *pan ka beera* the Maharana could communicate messages and express his feelings without writing or uttering a single word. It emerged as a silent and symbolic communicating device. Number of sticks inserted in the roll and its shape signified different meanings. For example, *seekh ka beera* was offered to announce dispersal of the court or given to a noble who took permission to depart when the stipulated period of his *chakri* (service) got over. No one could leave without accepting the same. It had a elongated shape with 13 sticks inserted to make a roll. In Rajput political culture, when warriors took the final leave to sacrifice their lives in the fatal encounters called *sakas* they ate the last *beera.* On such occasions thousands of Rajputs consumed the *beera* together and put on saffron robes to attain *virgati.* When Maharana was offended with a jagirdar he expressed his displeasure by taking out three sticks from the *beera.* This was a cause of serious anxiety for the jagirdar. Those who were exiled were given *beera* with only three sticks. Therefore, on receiving the *beera,* the recipients immediately counted the number of sticks to know about the message from the Maharana. When jagirdar desired to take leave before the expiry of the stipulated period and Maharana would be away on a hunting expedition, he would send the *beera* attached to the point of a *vallam* (spear) implying urgency and sheer necessity of sudden departure. *Pan ka beera* was also sent to that particular queen with whom the Maharana wished to spend the night.

In the native states, there were specific and pre-determined ritualistic gestures to express courtesy to esteemed individuals and guests. For example, special *beeras* were prepared on different occasions and offered as a mark of honour and courtesy. Festival *beeras*, which had different number of sticks specified for each festival were sent on behalf of the Maharana to the jagirdars. Even horses and elephants received *beeras* on festivals. *Reshmi beera*, which was filled with dry fruits and covered with gold flakes, was offered to highly revered guests or to the Maharana when he undertook *padravni* (visit) to the haveli of a distinguished personage, noble or official. *Kapuri beera,* which was sprinkled with camphor, was also prepared. Maharana Pratap had sent 100 rolls of such perfumed betel leaves to Raja Mansingh to show courtesy, despite the fact that both were opposed to each other.

Beera was at times poisoned and offered to rivals with the intention to murder them. At times, individuals accepted such *beeras* despite knowing the truth since it was considered cowardly to refuse a *beera*. Maharana Ari Singh had offered poisoned betel roll to Rawat of Salumber, Jodh Singh.

Since *pan ka beera* had acquired centrality as a ritual offering in a variety of situations, particularly because it came to be attached to the sensitive issues of honour, dishonour, prestige and hierarchy, a special department called the *Tambolkhana* was set up headed by *Khawasji.* Trusted and reliable employees were appointed as *Tambolis* (those who prepared *beeras*). This department received daily orders from different sections of the royal palace for particular kind of *beeras.*

The present discourse underscores the multifarious uses of *pan ka beera* in the court life of the erstwhile native states. On the one hand it was a ceremonial offering which was given at the time of arrival and departure. It also emerged as a potent indicator of an individual's status and rank in the court. More significantly, in court practices it was used to indicate pleasure and displeasure, recognition and derecognition. It is indeed interesting to note how certain food items, animals and clothing acquired a key place in the rituals of the court and became integral to the dynamics of hierarchy and sustenance of the distinctive court culture of the Rajput polity.

III
Ruling Period of Important Maharanas

1. Bappa Rawal 734 AD, 753 AD*
2. Ratan Singh - ruled till 1303 AD*
3. Laxman Singh 1303 AD*
4. Rana Ari Singh 1303 AD*
5. Maharana Hammir 1326 AD - 1364 AD
6. Maharana Lakha 1382 AD - 1421 AD
7. Maharana Mokal 1421 AD - 1433 AD
8. Maharana Kumbha 1433 AD - 1468 AD
9. Maharana Sanga 1509 AD - 1528 AD
10. Maharana Vikramaditya 1531 AD - 1536 AD
11. Maharana Udai Singh II 1536 AD - 1572 AD
12. Maharana Pratap 1572 AD - 1597 AD
13. Maharana Jagat Singh 1628 AD - 1652 AD
14. Maharana Raj Singh I 1652 AD - 1680 AD
15. Maharana Jai Singh 1680 AD - 1698 AD
16. Maharana Amar Singh II 1698 AD - 1710 AD
17. Maharana Raj Singh II 1754 AD - 1761 AD
18. Maharana Ari Singh II 1761 AD - 1773 AD
19. Maharana Bhim Singh 1778 AD - 1828 AD
20. Maharana Jawan Singh 1828 AD - 1838 AD
21. Maharana Sardar Singh 1838 AD - 1842 AD
22. Maharana Swaroop Singh 1842 AD - 1861 AD
23. Maharana Shambhu Singh 1861 AD - 1874 AD
24. Maharana Sajjan Singh 1874 AD - 1884 AD
25. Maharana Fateh Singh 1884 AD - 1929 AD
26. Maharana Bhupal Singh 1930 AD -

* There is ambiguity about the exact dates regarding regimes of some of the rulers. For further genealogical details, refer G.H. Ojha, *Udaipur Rajya ka Itihas*, Vol. I and II; Shyamaldas, *Vir Vinod*, Vol. I and II.

Bibliography

Books

Allen, Charles and Sharda Dwivedi, *Lives of the Indian Princes*, Eeshwar, 1998, Mumbai.

Altekar, A.S. *Position of Women in the Hindu Civilization*, The Culture Publication House, Benaras Hindu University, Benaras, 1938.

Asopa, Jai Narayan, *Origin of the Rajputs*, Bhartiya Publishing House, Delhi, Varanasi, Calcutta, 1976.

Bahadur, P. Krishna(tr.), *Mira Bai and Her Padas*, Munshiram Manoharlal Publishers Pvt. Ltd., New Delhi, 1998.

Banerjee, A.C., *The Rajput States and British Paramountcy*, Rajesh Publications, New Delhi, Allahabad, 1980.

—, *Lectures on Rajput History*, (R.P. Nopany Lecture Series, Calcutta University, 1960), Firma K.L. Mukhopadhyaya, Calcutta, 1962.

Banerjee, P. and S.K. Gupta *Man, Society and Nature*, IIAS Occasional Papers I, General Ed. Margaret Chatterjee, Motilal Banarassidas, Delhi, 1988.

Bhanavat, Mahendra, *Sanskriti ke Rang*, Bhartiya Lok Kala Mandal, Udaipur, 1971.

Bhati, Hukam Singh (ed.), *Chundavat Vansh Prakash*, Pratap Shodh Pratishthan, Udaipur, 1994

—, (ed.), *Itihaskar James Tod: Vyaktitva evam Krititva*, Pratap Shodh Pratishthan, Udaipur, 1992.

—, (ed.), *Mewar Itihas ke Katipay Pehlu*, Pratap Shodh Pratishthan, Udaipur, 1995-96.

—, (ed.), *Mewar Jagirdaran ri Vigat*, Pratap Shodh Pratishthan, Udaipur, 1993.

—, (ed.), *Mewar ke Atihasik Patte-Parwane*, Pratap Shodh Pratishthan, Udaipur, 1993.

—, *Mewar ke Atehasik Granthon ka Sarvekshan*, Rajasthani Granthagar, Jodhpur, 1998.

—, (ed.), *Mewar Thikanon ke Abhilekh*, Pratap Shodh Pratishthan, Udaipur, 1994.

—, *Maharana Pratap ka Pariwar aur Samantgan*, Pratap Shodh Pratishthan, Udaipur, 1991.

—(ed.), *Rajsthan ke Itihaskar*, Pratap Shodh Pratishthan, Udaipur, 1988.

—, *Yug Purush Maharana Pratap*, Pratap Shodh Pratishthan, Udaipur, 1991.

Bhati, Hukam Singh and Narain Singh Bhati, *Gora Hat Ja: Swatantrata Andolan ki Rajasthani Prerak Rachnain,* Rajasthani Shodh Sansthan, Chaupasani, Jodhpur (first published 1956), 1997.

Bhatt, Rajendra Shankar, *Mewar ke Maharana aur Shahenshah Akbar*, Panchsheel Prakashan, Jaipur, 1997.

Bhattacharya, Sukumar, *The Rajput States and the East India Company*, Munshiram Manoharlal, New Delhi, 1972.

Bhutodiya, Mangilal, *Itihas ki Amar Bel: Oswal* (2 Vols.), Priyadarshini Prakashan, Calcutta, 1988.

Bipan Chandra, *Adhunik Bharat mein Vichardhara aur Rajniti*, Anamika Publishers, Delhi, 1997.

—, *Essays on Indian Nationalism*, Har-Anand Publications, Delhi (1993), Reprint 1999.

Bipan Chandra, Mridula Mukherjee and Aditya Mukherjee, *India After Independence*, Viking Penguin India, New Delhi, 1999.

Bipan Chandra, Mridula, Mukherji, Aditya Mukherjee, K.N. Pannikar and Sucheta Mahajan, *India's Struggle for Independence*, Penguin Books, New Delhi, England, 1991.

Brookes, J.C., *History of Meywar*, Office of Baptist Mission Press, 1859.

Burnett, Whit (ed.), *The Human Spirit*, George Allen & Unwin Ltd., London, 1960.

Chakravarti, Amiya (ed.), *A Tagore Reader*, the Macmillan Co., New York, 1931.

Chundavat Laxmi Kumari *Sanskritik Rajasthan*, Rajasthan Peoples's Publishing House, Jaipur, 1994.

Deliege, Robert, *The Bhils of Western India*, National Publishing House, New Delhi, 1985.

Dharmpal, *Bharat ka Svadharma*, Vagdevi Prakashan, Bikaner, 1994.

Elizabeth I: *Red Rose of the House of Tudor* (ed. Kathryn Lasky), The Royal Diaries Series, Scholastic Inc, New York, 1999.

Fox Richard G., *Kin, Clan, Raja and Rule: State Hinterland Relations in Preindustrial India*, Oxford University Press, Bombay, 1971.

Friese, Kai and Mukul Keswani (eds.), *Civil Lines 5*, India Ink, New Delhi, 2001.

Gayatri Devi, *A Princess Remembers*, (Memoirs of the Maharani of Jaipur), Rupa & Co., Calcutta, Allahabad, Bombay, New Delhi, 1997.

Gehlot, Sukhvir Singh, *Rajasthan: Swatantrata Purva evam Pashchat (1857-1997)*, Jain Brothers, Jodhpur, 1998.

Ghosh, Shri Aurobindo, *Speeches*, Calcutta, 1922.

Ghurye, G.S., *Caste and Race in India*, Kegan Paul, Trench, Trubner & Co. Ltd., London.

Gordan, Stewart (ed.), *Robes of Honour: Khil'at in Pre-Colonial and Colonial India*, Oxford University Press, New Delhi, 2003.

Grewal, Royina, *In Rajasthan*, Lonely Planet Publications, Melbourne, Oakland, London, Paris, 1998.

Gupta, L.C., *Land Ceiling and After*, Institute of Development Studies, Rawat Publications, Jaipur, New Delhi, 1994

Harlan, Lindsey, *Religion and Rajput Women: The Ethic of Protection in Contemporary Narratives*, Munshiram Manoharlal Publishers Pvt. Ltd., New Delhi, 1994.

Jain, Jawahirlal, *Sidharaj Dhaddha: Jiwaṇ, Vyaktitva aur Vichar*, Shri Sidharaj Dhaddha Abhinandan Samiti, Jaipur, 1984.

Jain, M.S., *Concise History of Modern Rajasthan*, Vishva Prakashan, New Delhi, 1993.

Jain, Pratibha, *Gandhian Ideas, Social Movements and Creativity*, Rawat Publications, Jaipur, 1985.

—, *Gandhi Chintan: Atihasik Pariprekshya*, Hindi Grantha Academy, Jaipur, 1983.

Jain Pratibha and Rajan Mahan, *Women Images*, Rawat Publishers, Jaipur, New Delhi, 1996.

Jain Pratibha and Sangeeta Sharma, *Bhartiya Stree: Sanskritik Sandarbh*, Rawat Publications, Jaipur, New Delhi, 1998.

Joshi, Sumnesh, *Rajasthan Mein Swatantrata Sangram ke Senani*, Granthagar, Jaipur, 1973.

Joshi, Varsha, *Polygamy & Purdah: Women and Society among Rajputs*, Rawat Publications, Jaipur and New Delhi, 1995.

Kathuria, R.P., *Life in the Courts of Rajasthan*, S.Chand & Company Pvt. Ltd., New Delhi, 1987.

Kaushik, Asha (ed.), *Gandhi: Nayi Sadi ke Liye*, Rawat Publication, Jaipur, New Delhi, 2000.

Kaushik, Neelam, *Rajasthan ke Chundavaton ka Itihas (1710-1818)*, Publication Scheme, Jaipur, Indore, 1988.

Khan, Shah Alam, *Meera: Loktatvik Adhayayan*, Sanghi Prakashan, Jaipur, Udaipur, 1989.

Khouri, Norma, *Forbidden Lore*, Bantam Books, Sydney, 2003.

Koertzer, *Ritual, Politics and Power*, Yale University Press, New Haven & London, 1988.

Kohn, Hans, *The Idea of Nationalism*, Macmillan, New York, 1956.

Kothari, Dev and Lalit Pandey (eds.), *Swatantrata Andolan mein Mewar ka Yogdan*, Sahitya Sansthan, Rajasthan Vidyapeeth, Udaipur, 1991.

Kulshreshtha, Shyam Swaroop, *Mewar ka Rajya Prabhandh*, Saraswati Book Depot, Udaipur, 1941.

Kumar, Radha, *History of Doing*, Kali for Women, New Delhi, 1993.

Laird, M.A. (ed.), *Bishop Heber in Northern India* (Selections from Heber's Journal), Cambridge University Press, Cambridge, 1971.

Manav, Fateh Singh and Bhanwar Singh Samor, *Charan Badi Amolak Cheez*, Charan Sahitya Shodh Prakashan, Ajmer, 1989.

Mankekar, D.R., *Mewar Saga: The Sisodiya's Role in Indian History*, Vikas Publishing House, New Delhi, Bombay, Calcutta, Bangalore, Kanpur.

Manohar, Raghavendra Singh, *Rajasthan ke Rajgharanon ka Sanskritik Adhyayan*, Panchsheel Prakashan, Jaipur, 1991.

Mathur, L.P., *Protest Movements of Bhils under the British Raj*, Publication Scheme, Jaipur, 2000.

—, *Role of Press in the Growth of Representative Institutions in Rajputana*, Books Treasure, Jodhpur, 1998.

Mathur, R.M., *Rajput States and East India Company*, Sundeep Prakashan, Delhi, 1979.

Mathur, Tej Kumar, *Feudal Polity in Mewar (1750-1850)*, Publication Scheme, Jaipur, Indore, 1987.

Mathur, Vishnu Dayal, *States' Peoples' Conference: Origin and Role in Rajasthan,* Publication Scheme, Jaipur, Indore, 1984.

Mehta, Lalit, *Caste Clan and Ethnicity*, Rawat Publishers, Jaipur & New Delhi, 1999.

Mehta, M.S., *Lord Hastings and the Indian States*, Bombay, 1930.

Mehta, Rama, *Inside the Haveli*, Arnold-Heinemann, New Delhi.

Menaria, Shivcharan, *Rajasthan ke Nari Ratna*, University Book House, Jaipur [n.d.].

Mishra, Ratan Lal, *Rajasthan ka Swatantrata Sangram: Durlabh Dastavej*, Surabhi Publication, Jaipur, 1997.

Mishra, R.L., *The Forts of Rajasthan*, Kutir Prakashan, Mandawa, 1985.

Nagar, Mahendra Singh, *Rajasthan ki Paag Pagriyan*, Mehrangarh Museum Trust, Jodhpur, 1994.

Nagarkar, Kiran, *Cuckold*, Harper Collins Publishers, New Delhi, 1997.

Nanda, B.R., *Mahatma Gandhi: A Biography,* Oxford University Press, Delhi, Calcutta, Chennai, Mumbai, 1958.

—, *Gokhle: The Indian Moderates and the British Raj*, Oxford University Press, Delhi (first published 1977), Reprint 1979.

—, (ed.), *Indian Women: From Purdah to Modernity*, Nehru Memorial Museum & Library, Radiant Publishers (first published 1976), 1990.

Nehru, Jawaharlal, *The Discovery of India*, Jawaharlal Nehru Memorial Fund, Oxford University Press (first Published 1946), 1982.

Nensi, *Khyat* (ed. Acharya Jinvijay Muni), 2 Vols., Rajasthan Oriental Research Institute, Jodhpur, 1982.

Ojha, Gaurishankar Hirachand, *Rajputane ka Prachin Itihas*, Rajasthani Granthagar, Jodhpur, (Reprint), 1997.

—, *Udaipur Rajya ka Itihas* (2 Vols.), Rajasthani Granthagar, Jodhpur (first published 1928), 1994.

Oommen, T.K., *Charisma, Stability and Change*, Thompson Press (India) Ltd., New Delhi, 1972.

Panagariya, B.L. and N.C. Pahariya, *Political, Socio-Economic and Cultural History of Rajasthan (Earliest Times to 1947)*, Panchsheel Prakashan, Jaipur, 1997.

—, *Rajasthan: Polity, Economy & Society*, Rawat Publications, Jaipur & New Delhi, 1996.

Paliwal, D.L., *Mewar and the British (1857-1921)*, Bafna Prakashan, Jaipur, 1971.

—, (ed.), *Mewar Through the Ages*, Sahitya Sansthan, Rajasthan Vidyapeeth, Jaipur, 1970.

Pannikar, K.M., *Relations of Indian States with the Government of India*, Martin Hopkinson & Company Ltd., London, 1927.

Pandey, Ram, *Land Reforms and Social Change*,

Qanungo, K.R., *Studies in Rajput History*, R. P. Nopany Lecture Series, Calcutta University, S.Chand & Company, Delhi, 1969.

Rajasthan State Gazetteer, Volumes I & II, Directorate District Gazetteers, Government of Rajasthan, Jaipur, 1995.

Rajasthan Swatantrata Sangram ke Sakshi: Kuchch Sansmaran (Udaipur, Dungarpur, Banswara), Rajasthan State Archives, Bikaner, 1995.

Rathore, Vikramsingh, *Rajasthan ki Sanskriti mein Nari*, Rajasthani Granthagar, Jodhpur, 1995.

Richards, J.F. (ed.), *Kingship and Authority in South Asia*, Oxford University Press, Delhi, Calcutta, Chennai, Mumbai, 1998.

Rizvi, S.H.M., *Mina: The Ruling Tribe of Rajasthan*, B. R. Publishing Corporation, Delhi, 1987.

Rousellet, Louis, *India and its Native Princes* (Travels in Central India and in the Presidencies of Bombay and Bengal), revised and edited by Lt.Col. Buckle, J.S.Virtue & Co. Ltd. London, 1875.

Rudolph, Lloyd and Susanne Hoeber Rudolph, *Essays on Rajputana: Reflections on History, Culture and Administration*, Concept Publishing Company, New Delhi, 1984.

Said, Edward, *Culture and Imperialism*, Vintage, London, 1993.

—, *Orientalism*, Pantheon, New York, 1978.

Sangari, Kumkum and Sudesh Vaid, *Recasting Women: Essays in Colonial History*, Kali For Women, New Delhi, 1989.

Sarda, Har Bilas, *Maharana Kumbha*, Vedic Yantralaya, Ajmer, 1932.

—, *Maharana Sanga*, Vedic Yantralaya, Ajmer, 1924.

Saxena, Shankar Sahai, *Jo Desh ke Liye Jiye: Yashogatha Loknayaka Shri Manikyalal Verma*, Muktavani Prakashan, Bikaner, First Edition, 1972.

Schomer, Karine, John L.Erdman, Deryck O. Lodrick, Lloyd I. Rudolph (eds.), *The Idea of Rajasthan: Explorations in Regional Identity*, Volumes I & II, American Institute of Indian Studies, Manohar, New Delhi, 1994.

Sharma, C.L., *Ruling Elites of Rajasthan,* M.D. Publications Pvt. Ltd., New Delhi, 1993.

Sharma, Dashratha, *Rajasthan Through The Ages*, Vol.I (from the earliest times to 1316 AD), Rajasthan State Archives, Bikaner, 1966.

—, *Lectures on Rajput History and Culture* (Raghunath Prasad Nopany Lectures, 1966), Motilal Banarasidas, Delhi, Patna, Varanasi, 1970.

Sharma, Dharampal, *Mewar: Sanskriti evam Parampara*, Pratap Shodh Pratishthan, Udaipur, 1999.

Sharma, G.N., *Glories of Mewar,* Shivalal Agrawal & Company, Agra.

—, *Mewar and Mughal Emperors*, Agra, 1951, 1962.

—, *Mewar-Mughal Sambandh*, Rajasthan Hindi Granth Academy, Jaipur, 1976.

—, *Social Life in Medieval Rajasthan (1500-1800 A.D.),* Agra, Laxmi Narain Agarwal, 1968.

Sharma, G.N. and V.S. Bhatnagar, (eds.), *The Historians and Sources of the History of Rajasthan*, Centre for Rajasthan Studies, University of Rajasthan, Jaipur, 1992.

Sharma, K.L. (ed.), *Social Stratification in India*, Manohar Publications, New Delhi, 1986.

—, *Social Stratification in India: Issues and Themes*, Sage Publications, New Delhi, 1997.

Shastri, Hiralal, *Pratyaksh Jiwan Shastra*, Anupam Prakashan Mandir Pvt. Ltd., Jaipur, 1970.

Shastri, S.R. *Women in the Vedic Age*, Bhartiya Vidya Bhavan, Bombay, 1960.

Shekhawat, Bhoor Singh, *Maharana Yash Prakash*, Shree Venkateshwar Press, Bombay, 1909.

Shukla, Dinesh Chandra, *Rajasthan ke Pramukh Sant evam Lokdevta*, Rajasthani Sahitya Sansthan, Jodhpur, 1996.

Shyamaldas, *Vir Vinod: Mewar ka Itihas* (4 parts), Motilal Banarasidas, Delhi, Varanasi, Patna, Madras, (First published 1886), 1986.

Singh, Dool, *A Study of Land Reforms in Rajasthan,* Government of India, Research Programmes Committee, Planning Commission, Pilani, Rajasthan, 1964.

Singh, K. Suresh, *Tribal Society in India*, Manohar, New Delhi, 1985.

Singh, Kesri, *The Hero of Haldighati*, Books Treasure, Jodhpur, 1996.

Singh, Kunwar Pal (ed.), *Bhakti Andolan: Itihas aur Sanskriti,* Vani Prakashan, New Delhi, 1995.

Singhi, N.K. and Rajendra Joshi (eds.), *Religion, Ritual and Royalty*, Institute of Rajasthan Studies, Rawat Publishers, Jaipur & New Delhi, 1999.

Spellman, John W., *Political Theory of Ancient India*, Clarendon Press, Oxford, 1964.

Srinivas, M.N., *Social Change in Modern India*, Orient Longman, New Delhi, 1966, (Reprint 1988).

—, (ed.), *Caste: Its Twentieth Century Avatar*, Viking, Penguin Books India Ltd., New Delhi, 1996.

Suda, Jyoti Prasad, *Main Currents of Social and Political Thought in Modern India*, Vol.I, Meerut, 1963.

Swamy, K.R.N., *Mughals, Maharaja and the Mahatma*, Harper Collins Publishers, New Delhi, 1997.

Tagore, Ravindranath, *Nationalism*, Macmillan & Co. Ltd., London, 1918.

—, *Crisis in Civilization*, Vishwabharti, Calcutta, 1941.

Tanwar, Dhabhai Tulsinath, *Sansmaran: Maharana Fateh Singhji, Maharana Bhupal Singhji, Maharana Bhagvat Singhji*, Udaipur, 1982.

Tharu, Susie and K. Lalita, (eds.), *Women Writing in India: 600B.C. to the Present*, Vol.I, Oxford University Press, Delhi, 1993.

Tod, Col. James, *Annals and Antiquities of Rajasthan* or *The Central and Western Rajpoot States of India* (2 vols.), M.N.Publishers & Distributors, New Delhi, (First published 1829), 1995.

—, *Travels in Western India*, V.H. Allen & Company, London, 1839.

Leaflets/Pamphlets/Booklets

Bhanavat, Mahendra, *Devnarayan ro Bharat*, Bhartiya Lok Kala Mandal, Udaipur, 1972.

—, *Kavad*, Bhartiya Lok Kala Mandal, Udaipur, 1975.

—, *Lokdevta Tejaji*, Bhartiya Lok Kala Mandal, Udaipur, 1970.

—, *Lok Kala: Mulya aur Sandarbh*, Bhartiya Lok Kala Mandal, Udaipur, 1974.

—, *Mewar ke Rasdhari*, Bhartiya Lok Kala Mandal, Udaipur, 1970.

—, *Rajasthan ki Gangaur*, Bhartiya Lok Kala Mandal, Udaipur, 1977.

Maharana of Mewar Charitable Foundation, Udaipur, Information Brochure.

Paliwal, D.L. and Girish Nath Mathur (eds.), *Mewar ke Rajaon ki Raniyon, Kunwaron aur Kunwarion ka Hal*, Sahitya Sansthan, Rajasthan Vidyapeeth, Udaipur, 1985.

Panchamsingh, *Rajput Maratha ek hain: Kuchch Praman*, Rajput Maratha Sangh, Alijah Durbar Press, Gwalior, 1931.

Sambhavami, Shri Bhai Bhagwan Abhinandan Granth, Udaipur, 1997.

Smarika, Rajasthan Swatantrata Senani Prantiya Sammelan, Rajasthan Swatantrata Senani Samiti, Jaipur, 1995.

The City within a City: Impressions, Media Coverage on the City within a City Project of the Maharana of Mewar Charitable Foundation (MMCF).

Vyas, Jai Narayan, *Marwari Rashtriya Geet*, Rashtriya Pustak Bhandar, Jodhpur, 1941.

Series

A series entitled *Rajasthan mein Swatantrata Sangram ke Amar Purodha* published by Rajasthan Swarn Jayanti Samaroh Samiti, Jaipur, 2000:

1. Chaturvedi, Satyendra, *Rajasthan mein Swatantrata Sangram ke Amar Purodha: Yugal Kishore Chaturvedi*, Rajasthan Swarn Jayanti Samaroh Samiti, Jaipur, 2000.
2. Kochar, K.L., *Rajasthan mein Swatantrata Sangram ke Amar Purodha: Mohanlal Sukhadia*, Rajasthan Swarn Jayanti Samaroh Samiti, Jaipur, 2000.
3. Ojha, Dushyant, *Rajasthan mein Swatantrata Sangram ke Amar Purodha: Vijay Singh Pathik*, Rajasthan Swarn Jayanti Samaroh Samiti, Jaipur, 2000.
4. Sharma'Kusum', Narendra *Rajasthan mein Swatantrata Sangram ke Amar Purodha: Manikyalal Verma*, Rajasthan Swarn Jayanti Samaroh Samiti, Jaipur, 2000.
5. Tripathi, Natwar, *Rajasthan mein Swatantrata Sangram ke Amar Purodha: Bhogilal Pandya*, Rajasthan Swarn Jayanti Samaroh Samiti, Jaipur, 2000.
6. Trivedi, Bhagwan Sahai, *Rajasthan mein Swatantrata Sangram ke Amar Purodha: Hiralal Shastri*, Rajasthan Swarn Jayanti Samaroh Samiti, Jaipur, 2000.

Reports

Government of Rajasthan Administrative Reforms Commission Report, (2 volumes), 2000 & 2001.

Reports of Akhil Bhartiya Charan Sammelan, 1911, 1927, Jodhpur Press.

Seminar Papers

Papers presented in the seminar on Bhartiya Svadhinta Sangram evam Rajasthan ki Sahbhagita, Department of Political Science, University of Rajasthan 22-23, March, 1986.

Ujjwal, K.S., 'Charans: Their Origin, Status and Importance', paper presented at the Second International Seminar on Rajasthan, Udaipur, 17-21, December 1991.

Journals and Magazines

Asian Profile, Asia's International Journal, Asian Research Service, Hongkong.

Charan, newspaper of Akhil Bhartiya Charan Sammelan, Kalol.

Chaumasa Pustaka, Madhya Pradesh Adivasi Lok Parishad, Bhopal.

Gandhi Marg, September 2002, New Delhi.

Harijan

India Today, Living Media India Ltd., New Delhi
Jijnasa, A Journal of History of Ideas and Culture, Department of History and Indian Culture, University of Rajasthan, Jaipur.
Manushi, Centre for the Study of Developing Societies, Delhi.
Mewar Prajamandal, Kendriya Daftar, Udaipur.
Moolprashna, Udaipur.
Outlook, New Delhi.
Paraṃpara, Rajasthani Shodh Sansthan, Chaupasani, Jodhpur.
Rangayan, Bhartiya Lok Kala Mandal, Udaipur.
Reader's Digest, Reader's Digest Association, Inc., U.S.A.
Sujas, Directorate of Information and Public Relations, Government of Rajasthan, Jaipur.
Tribe, Manikyalal Verma Tribal Research and Training Institute, Udaipur.
Time, Time Inc. International, New York, U.S.A.
Young India.

Interviews

Mahamandaleshwar Mahant Murli Manohar Sharan Shastri, Udaipur.
Prof. G.N. Sharma, Udaipur.
Rani Laxmi Kumari Chundavat, Jaipur.
Shri Balkrishna M. Thanvi, Jodhpur.
Shri Balwant Singh Mehta Udaipur.
Shri Rajendra Singh Chaudhary Udaipur.
Shri Ranchchoddas Gattani, Jodhpur.
Smt. Geeta Bajaj, Jaipur.
Smt. Ratan Devi Shastri, Vanasthali.
Smt. Shanta Trivedi, Udaipur.

Index